Windhorse Warrior

R C Friedericks

NIYOGI
BOOKS

Published by
NIYOGI BOOKS
Block D, Building No. 77,
Okhla Industrial Area, Phase-I,
New Delhi-110 020, INDIA
Tel: 91-11-26816301, 26818960
Email: niyogibooks@gmail.com
Website: www.niyogibooksindia.com

Back cover image: Eric Pema Kunsang
Front cover images (source): www.commons.wikipedia.com

Editor: Vibha Chakravarty Kumar
Design: Shraboni Roy

ISBN: 978-93-86906-51-9
Publication: 2018

Printed at: Niyogi Offset Pvt. Ltd., New Delhi, India

Ride on, Warriors!

*To all who dream of a more just and
beautiful world.*

Richard Friederich

Contents

Love is the felt experience of connection to another being. An economist says 'more for you is less for me'. But the lover knows that more for you is more for me, too. If you love somebody, their happiness is your happiness. Their pain is your pain. Your sense of self expands to include other beings.

Charles Eisenstein

The Long Trek to Exile for Tibet's Apostle

It was only when I went to China in 1954–55 that I actually studied Marxist ideology and learned the history of the Chinese revolution. Once I understood Marxism, my attitude changed completely. I was so attracted to Marxism, I even expressed my wish to become a Communist Party member.

Tibet, at that time, was very, very backward. The ruling class did not seem to care, and there was much inequality. Marxism talked about an equal and just distribution of wealth. I was very much in favour of this. Then there was the concept of self-creation. Marxism talked about self-reliance, without depending on a creator or a God. That was very attractive. I had tried to do some things for my people, but I did not have enough time. I still think that if a genuine communist movement had come to Tibet, there would have been much benefit to the people.

Instead, the Chinese communists brought Tibet a so-called 'liberation'. These people were not implementing true Marxist policy. If they had been, national boundaries would not be important to them. They would have worried about helping humanity. Instead, the Chinese communists carried out aggression and suppression in Tibet. Whenever there was opposition, it was simply crushed.

…That is why I still have hope. The Chinese people, too, have a rich culture and a long history. For thousands of years the Tibetans and the Chinese have lived side by side. Sometimes there were very happy moments. Sometimes there were very difficult moments. But one day, they will see that my middle approach will bring us all genuine stability and unity. I am sure that a day of good things, full of friendship, mutual respect and helping each other, will come.

Contributed by **The Dalai Lama**
TIME Asia, 27 September 1999, Vol. 154, No. 12
http://www.cnn.com/ASIANOW/time/magazine/99/0927/lhasa.html

Introduction

This story is based on the events leading up to the general uprising against Chinese occupation in Lithang in 1954, which spread across Tibet and culminated with the Dalai Lama going into exile in 1959. This novel is fiction in the context of these events.

The idea for this story came when I lived in Nepal, where I had several Tibetan friends and acquaintances. Since then I have visited Kham several times—including Lithang, and the beautiful stretch of the Lithang River where Gyawa and Mola are situated. These are real places but the events of the story, including the creation of a cooperative, are entirely fictitious.

The Dalai Lama's interest in communism, as expressed in the quote in the previous page, inspired me to present the possibility of an alternative, truly Tibetan brand of communism. What would Tibet have become if the Chinese Communist Party had encouraged a home-grown revolution rather than forcing their brand of communist on Tibetan people?

I do not wish to give the impression that I am promoting communism; I am neither pro-communist nor pro-capitalist. Both systems have failed to provide the means and the freedom for us to achieve our full potential as individuals or as a civilization. As indicated by the 'Golden Way' in this story, we need a new system that goes far beyond the promises of current systems.

The idea of telling the story from the point of view of an idealistic Chinese communist came from the story of Baba Phuntso Wangle, a Tibetan revolutionary who wanted to start an authentic, independent Tibetan version of the Revolution but was caught up in the political machine of the Chinese Communist Party, and was misled by its leadership. My fictional protagonist, Chuang Wei Ming, tries to accomplish what Phuntso could not.

None of the characters in the story, with the exception of Phuntso, are actual people. Many are inspired by, or are sometimes composites of, people I have read about or people I have met. For example, Palden Rinpoche is based, in part, on Loten Namling—a popular Tibetan singer living in Switzerland who promotes the cause of freedom for the Tibetan people through his songs. The character of Dechen is based on Dolma, a vivacious singer with a beautiful voice, who owns and manages a roadside hotel, the Golden Sun, where I often stayed while visiting Kham.

Acknowledgements

Information about the situation in Eastern Tibet in the 1950s came from several books written by people with first-hand experience of the situation and people who were in close contact with participants in the struggle, as well as men, women, and children who had to flee over the Himalayan mountains to Nepal and India. Some of these are listed here:

> *Cavaliers of Kham*, Michel Peissel
>
> *Buddha's Warriors*, Mikel Dunham
>
> *Orphans of the Cold War*, John Kenneth Knaus
>
> *The CIA's Secret War in Tibet*, Kenneth Conboy and James Morrison
>
> *Warriors of Tibet*, Jamyang Norbu
>
> *Four Rivers, Six Ranges*, Gompo Tashi Andrugstang
>
> *Adventures of a Tibetan Fighting Monk*, Hugh Richardson
>
> *A Tibetan Revolutionary: The Political Life and Times of Bapa Phuntso Wangle*, as told to Melvyn C Goldstein, Dawei Sherap, and William R Siebenschuh

Inspiration and insights for the story came from many sources. Central to the story is the legend of King Gesar of Ling, which I learned about through Chogyam Trungpa Rinpoche and, more specifically, through one of Trungpa's students, Douglas J Penick. I am most grateful to him for allowing me to paraphrase parts of his *The Warrior Song of King Gesar*.

My insight into Buddha dharma comes from extensive reading and attending the teachings of His Holiness the Dalai Lama, Chogyam Trungpa Rinpoche and Dzongsar Khyentse Norbu Rinpoche. I do not pretend to be an expert in this area but hope I have not been unfaithful to their teachings. My intent is to give expression to a universal spiritual yearning that is the common thread through all religions, and in this I must mention three Christian teachers—Richard Rohr, Cynthia Bourgeault and Wayne Teasdale—who have opened my eyes to the possibility of a true inter-spirituality.

Among these teachers, I am truly grateful to Khyentse Rinpoche who read earlier versions of the story, offered suggestions, and encouraged me to pursue the telling of this tale.

I want to express my hearty thanks to several friends who listened patiently to my ideas, who offered suggestions and read various versions of this story, whether in its incarnation as a screenplay—yes, it started as a screenplay—or as a novel. They include friends I am lucky enough to have in Nepal who helped me initially: Wangyel Lama, Nawa Dorje, Kiran Shrestha, and Tashi Tsering; my colleagues in Hong Kong: Janet Tan, George Coombs, Marty Schmidt, Marianne Lyon and Susan Kuyper; friends from my school days in India: Philip DeVol, Mark Wagner, Iris Hunter, Peter Petersen, and Rajan Kose; and friends here in Port Townsend, who read and helped edit later versions, including: Marga Kapka, Hendrick Taatgen, and Richard and Susan Watson.

My editor in India, Vibha Chakravarty Kumar, had the tedious task of cleaning up my manuscript, but throughout, has tirelessly championed this story and continues to do so. And Nirmal Kanti Bhattacharjee, my publisher at Niyogi Books,

India, has turned my manuscript into a beautiful, real-life book. To both of them, I am indebted for their belief in me, and for their encouragement.

Several friends, students and tour guides who ventured into Kham with me, and my three children—David, Ethan, and Elizabeth—who have been enthusiastic about Tibet and the telling of this story. I am tremendously grateful for this, but most of all I continue to be grateful for the wisdom, insights, guidance, and devotion of my own *Dakini*, Suzanne.

Part One

Shanghai
1947

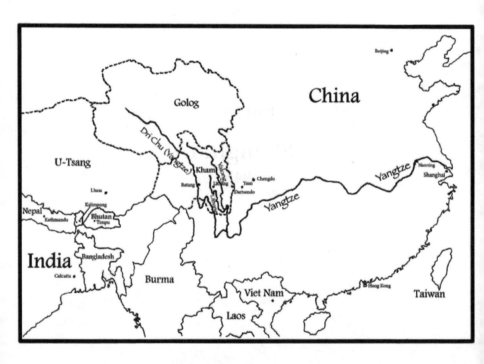

The Yangtze and tributaries in Kham.

Protest

The swaying streetcar didn't go fast enough for any reprieve from the swelter of the Shanghai summer but I leaned out the window to escape the press of sticky bodies and keep track of the cross streets. Two more stops and I'd get out to start looking for her.

A mutual friend said she was on a protest march.

What was she thinking? I had to find her.

I admit I wasn't completely surprised. She had talked about marching but I never thought she'd actually do it.

Looking down the next cross street, I saw armed nationalist soldiers marching in even rows parallel to the trolley line. One group was a block away. There were other groups even further down at other cross streets, the barrels of their guns glinting in the fierce blaze of the sun. It didn't register as being out of the ordinary; nationalist troops were a common enough sight around the city.

At the next street crossing, I heard voices shouting a communist slogan.

'Out capitalist pigs.'

There they were. I stood up and pushed my way to the rear door.

'Down with capitalist greed.'

That was Jiachen's voice. She was not just one of the marchers, she was the one shouting through the bullhorn.

I surprised myself. I was proud and awe-struck by her daring, by the strength she portrayed, by her beauty. Her luxuriant black hair spilled out of her red bandana as her fist punched the air with each slogan. Like the goddess of justice, I thought. With righteous intention, she was leading 30 or 40 enthusiastic young cadres dressed in Party uniforms. They followed her as one body, responding in one voice to her call for justice. My frustration with her melted away instantly.

'Out capitalist pigs' came the rehearsed response. Clenched fists punctured the air above the big red star on their caps.

Suddenly, I remembered the nationalist soldiers on the parallel street. It was a trap.

My beloved Jiachen was in danger.

Fixing my eyes on her, I stepped off the moving streetcar. The pavement moved under me but I managed to stumble into a run.

I had to warn her.

'Jiachen,' I shouted, 'they're coming. Get away.'

'Liberate the people,' she shouted into the megaphone. She did not hear me.

'Long live the Revolution,' came the refrain.

Behind me, I heard the cadence of marching boots as soldiers emerged from several side streets.

The trap was set.

Seeing what was happening, Jiachen's followers came to a confused, frightened stop.

But Jiachen remained fearless.

'Keep moving,' she shouted.

'Forward. Our cause is just. We will not be stopped. Forward. Our cause is just. We will not be stopped.'

The protesters regained confidence from Jiachen's courage and moved forward.

'Our cause is just. We will not be stopped.'

An officer raised a megaphone to address the marchers.

'Stop. I order you to disperse. If you obey, you will not be arrested. If you continue to march, you will be forced to stop.'

'Keep moving', was Jiachen's cool response. The marchers had not hesitated while the officer announced his intention to stop them.

The march continued.

'Raise rifles,' the officer ordered. I watched in horror as soldiers immediately in front of the defiant revolutionaries formed two rows; one row dropped to their knees while a second row stood behind them in classic firing squad formation. Rifles, in two rows, above and below, took aim at the marchers.

Meanwhile, the soldiers behind the protesters moved the pedestrians and vehicles out of the line of fire. It was clear the officer meant to open fire if the marchers did not stop.

'I order you to stop,' the officer warned once again.

In spite of the wall of guns, Jiachen moved forward. Her left hand held the megaphone to her mouth, while she clenched her right fist and raised it to the sky in defiance.

'Jiachen,' I shouted, hoping to stop her. Realizing she was willing to die for this cause, I ran toward her but soldiers on the sidewalk stopped and held me.

While I helplessly watched, I suddenly remembered our conversation the previous night. I told her I had no feelings one way or the other about the Revolution but my feelings for her were unshakable. She just looked at me with love and gently said that my exclusive attachment to her made me blind. She said, 'You don't see the oppression, the poverty forced on workers by the elite class and the corrupt system they propped up. You are living the dream-life of the privileged class. You need to wake up and see that life is not just about you and your feelings. We are all connected. Your passions should be more expansive...they must include more than just the two of us.'

'Liberate the people. We will not be...' Jiachen's shout was cut short by the volley.

'No!' I screamed in disbelief. I pushed my way free. One moment, I was running to her, and next, I was cradling her fallen body in my arms. The blood...it wouldn't stop flowing. It bubbled in her mouth as she struggled to shout her slogans. Her wounds were fatal; as a medical student I immediately understood that.

Then she saw me. Her hand reached up to touch my cheek in loving recognition. Her touch conveyed our shared grief.

It was the same hand that had, moments ago, declared 'revolution' and I recalled what she often said to me: 'There are powerful forces determined to keep us ignorant. The truth is we are one; each of us part of the whole—when one suffers, we all suffer.'

My grief was all the more poignant as Jiachen's eyes remained on mine. They shone with radiance not of hope but of something else. My jujitsu and archery master, a wise old man, spoke of death as a transition. Those who are close to death see things we can't. It is, he said, like waking from a dream and seeing things as they are.

Jiachen's hand dropped from my cheek but a triumphant smile lit her face while her body relaxed in peaceful acceptance.

She was departing.

I didn't want to let her go. But as I tried clinging to her, something quite extraordinary, something I can only call mystical, happened to me—or more accurately, to us. I began seeing our bodies—me holding Jiachen in my arms—from several meters overhead. I was aware it was Jiachen's point of view; that she was deliberately including me so that we now saw the entire street, the injured marchers, the confused soldiers, and the gathering crowd of onlookers. To my surprise, I was awash in a flood of love. A golden torrent of love coursed through her to me, connecting us to everyone in the street. It was an all-embracing maternal love that united everything at its core.

Even while this was happening, I maintained my own awareness that this was an incredibly unusual event. Could Jiachen deliberately be sharing her transformation with me? Was she allowing me to witness what happens when a mortal expands into a new, limitless multi-perspective of compassionate knowing?

Together, we were seeing, hearing, and feeling what each person was going through around us. And together, our love now extended to the injured and suffering comrades as well as to the conflicted or remorseful or self-righteous assailants.

Through Jiachen, I was experiencing life from the inside; from that place where we all share a longing for unity with the colossal love that transcends and includes all beings and all things.

That briefest of insights ended just as suddenly as it arose. When it passed, I was aware of Jiachen's lifeless eyes staring up at me. Though I was back on the ground holding her corpse, I continued to feel embraced, accepted, and cherished. Participation in her ascendance gave me an assurance more real than words can describe and, because of this, I let her go knowing her transition was joyful. And despite the confusion and noise of the city around me, I thought I heard the cry of an eagle, high overhead. I smiled; Jiachen was letting me know she still was near.

The humid air, suddenly heavy with gun smoke and the metallic taste of blood, cloaked me and brought an acute awareness of the chaos around me.

People gathered from the surrounding streets. When they saw and understood what had transpired, they reacted in collective outrage.

'Liberate the people,' someone deliberately echoed Jiachen's slogan.

This became a catalyst for the rest of the crowd.

'Our cause is just. We will not be stopped' echoed up and down the street once again. The people in the streets of Shanghai turned on the nationalists soldiers and took up the call for revolution.

'Liberate the people.'

'Our cause is just. We will not be stopped.'

The chanting of the slogan grew louder, more confident and defiant with each repetition.

This is what Jiachen wanted.

Hundreds of ordinary people began putting themselves between the soldiers and the wounded communist protesters to prevent arrests.

Shouting desperate orders, the officer in charge gyrated in confusion. His soldiers ignored him and stood gaping at the massacre they had committed and the collective surge of outrage filling the street around them.

Jiachen's lifeless body began to feel heavy in my arms. One of Jiachen's comrades urged me to my feet. Two others took Jiachen's body from me. With shock setting in, I followed them to a waiting vehicle on a side street.

I cradled Jiachen's precious body against mine in the back seat. I remember streets filled with people as we inched forward until, suddenly free, the car sped on. I was asked where to take Jiachen's body. I must have provided the right information because we were soon at the doorstep of her family's apartment building.

Jiachen

We carried Jiachen's body up the two flights of stairs to her family's apartment. Jiachen's grandmother, Yangchen, answered the door. Nearly sobbing, I couldn't tell her what had happened. One of Jiachen's comrades told the story. After we carried Jiachen into her bedroom, Yangchen put her arms around me and I felt her hot tears on my neck. But her tears were brief and with the help of the family servant, Huizhong, Yangchen lovingly began attending to Jiachen's body on the bed.

Jiachen's comrades, having delivered Jiachen's body, disappeared. Still in shock, I stayed.

'Her life had great power, Wei Ming,' Yangchen said tenderly, adding, 'she has returned to her rightful place.'

Her words were powerful. I thought I understood what she meant by 'rightful place' in light of my participation in Jiachen's departure. I was about to tell Yangchen about it but Jiachen's parents arrived from their shop.

Seeing Jiachen, Mr Fang burst into tears. I tried to describe what had happened but Mr Fang looked at me shaking his head.

'I, I know,' he sobbed, 'I know what happened. And I know you warned her as much as I did, but she wouldn't listen!'

Mr Fang knelt beside the bed. Stroking Jiachen's face, he held her hand and whispered, 'Oh, my precious girl. So determined to fix the world.'

In sharp contrast, Nuying, Jiachen's mother, remained dry-eyed and cool. Standing behind her husband, she watched dispassionately. I had frequently noted this aloofness in Nuying on visits to Jiachen's home. I caught Yangchen giving Nuying a stern glare, which Nuying seemed to shrug off.

Mr Fang and Nuying had a clothing shop and hired tailors to create hand-made suits and gowns for the wealthier families of Shanghai, families like mine who lived in bungalows within the International Enclave. Like any Chinese family, they had high hopes for their daughter. When Jiachen started spouting communist slogans and questioning their decidedly capitalist business practices, Mr Fang looked to me to help sort her out. I was, after all, a member of the elite who was supposed to know the way things work in the 'real' world.

We Chinese, the argument goes, are naturally capitalistic; we know how to work and make money. In this 'real' world, we spend every waking minute accumulating wealth, too often by exploiting the services of less fortunate people. But though we are focused entirely on the material world, there is a streak of superstition in our nature. We harbour an irrational, on-going relationship with the departed that we hope to use for our practical benefit. We figure if the departed continue to exist in some fashion after death, why not put them to work to help us accumulate wealth, too.

I never subscribed to the practice of petitioning our ancestors to change our luck by burning incense and offering food at an altar. And I never seriously considered the possibility of life after death because my upbringing inevitably steered me toward a more rational, atheistic Western mindset in which the 'other' world of the spirits and ancestors was considered nonsense, a fantasy. This physical world, what we can see and use, is the only reality according to the world's dominant civilization. True, the Catholic nuns and, later on, the Jesuit priests who taught me in secondary school preached the existence of God, the Holy Spirit and Heaven, but I soon understood they regarded the 'spirit' world to be a completely separate reality. They professed a dualistic system; created beings live in this physical world while God and His angels live in another unattainable realm that, if examined rationally and scientifically, is non-existent. Somehow, after death, we are transferred to this non-existent realm of the spirit to either suffer eternally for our sins in Hell or to glorify God forever in Heaven; apparently dependent on the strength of your beliefs.

Watching the others react to Jiachen's death, I reflected that my own understanding of death had just been drastically changed. I could no longer justify my scepticism since I'd just experienced a 'soul' continuing after death. I felt connected to Jiachen and was sure she still existed somewhere.

I stayed to keep vigil with Jiachen's family. Jiachen's father was inconsolable. She was the joy of his life! I was puzzled that Nuying was not behaving like a distraught mother would. It was Yangchen who had connected with Jiachen, and therefore with me, more than her mother. Yangchen had always been happy to see me; to see us together.

Eventually, unable to control himself, Mr Fang got up and left the room in tears, followed by Nuying.

Yangchen noticed my sigh of relief. She smiled at me, as if inviting me to speak my mind.

I remembered her words of comfort: 'She returns to her rightful place'. I wanted to know if she believed Jiachen was in heaven. Yangchen was a Buddhist, I knew, and Buddhists don't believe in heaven the way Christians do. Buddhists believe in reincarnation; in the idea that beings return in an embodied form of one kind or another countless times until they are finally able to 'extinguish' any sense of an individual selfhood and dissolve into nothingness—or so I was told by my Christian teachers.

'Will Jiachen be reincarnated?' I asked suddenly.

'Yes,' Yangchen said with a kind smile, 'when she wants to be. She is good and will do good. This time was complicated. With you, I mean.'

I found myself accepting her belief in reincarnation.

'Is that what you meant by "returning to her rightful place"?' I asked.

'Ah,' she replied with a twinkle in her eye. 'You come to the heart of things quickly. As I said, she is a powerful spiritual presence. I think you know that. That's why you two were attracted to each other. Now she is free of physical limitations. That's what I meant.'

In a flash of insight, I realized Jiachen had taken me across the divide between life and death where I'd glimpsed a larger, more connected reality overflowing with love. I'd seen that life is, after all, a continuous unity; the idea that life ceases at death is wrong. It no longer mattered whether Jiachen continued as a unique personality in heaven or as the spark of life that would incarnate in a new physical body. What mattered was that our shared love had proven large enough to bridge the chasm between life and death. We remained inseparable because the idea of separation is an illusion within the larger context of our ultimate unity in love.

Like any young couple, Jiachen and I had imagined a future together. I grew up expecting life to be a natural progression from university to a career in medicine. We would get married and live a lifestyle similar to my own, in a comfortable bungalow with servants and a nice car. Jiachen scoffed at my bourgeois ideas but marriage was always in our plan. She had a much more romantic idea; it would have been the two of us, side by side, creating a New China after the Revolution.

We met at Tongji Medical University in 1945, after the war and the departure of the Japanese. We both wanted to be doctors. Jiachen started out well but, as an outspoken feminist, gradually became more and more radical in her political outlook. It seemed to me the more I pleaded with her to stay away from the communist movement on campus, the more she went to their meetings. Soon, she was one of their strongest leaders.

An intellectual communist, she was enthused about implementing an economic and social model described by Karl Marx. She believed it was the solution to China's problems. The nationalist government, the Chinese elite class and, of course, the huge community of foreigners in Shanghai were immersed in capitalism, and were corrupt to the core. Their system needed to be overthrown because it tolerated and fostered every form of oppression on the working class and peasants. Jiachen wanted revolution. She wanted to follow the Communist Party and its chairman, Mao Tse Tung.

And now, laid out on the bed was her beautiful body, radiant even in death, reminding me how we shared our bodies in secret. With a lump in my throat, I suddenly struggled to hold back tears. But they were not tears for her; they were tears for me, for what I would be missing. I would be deprived of her touch, the scent of her hair, her body; the thrill of our embrace, our kisses, and the physicality of our bursting joy in one another. All those hopes and dreams, our plans—both hers and mine—were gone. What would ever fill this void in my life?

'I know why she loved you so much,' Yangchen suddenly spoke from the other side of the bed, adding, 'you are not only tall, good-looking and well-built but you are a thoughtful, aware human being. She chose well.'

I looked at her shyly and replied. 'I, we, loved each other very much.'

It was good to be here with Yangchen. She knew her granddaughter well and it appeared she understood and appreciated me, too.

'You know,' I found myself saying to her, 'as Jiachen lay in my arms and life was fading from her body, we were lost in each other's eyes. For a moment it was as if I ascended with her; out of my body, above the street. From there we shared an expansive, liberating experience of love so powerful it included everyone in the street below. We felt a deep compassion for everyone on both sides of the conflict. There was no blame, no hatred, no fear, and no anger. Only love, a love that united us all; a never ending love.'

Yangchen's face glowed, 'What a gift she gave you. Treasure that experience, never let it slip away as you go through the rest of your life.'

Yangchen reached out and gently touched Jiachen's face again. I noticed a tear in her eye as she looked up at me. I moved my stool closer to the bed to be nearer to Jiachen's body, and to Yangchen, when a recollection took me by surprise. Like a puzzle burning to be solved, I needed to know who the people she called 'my people' were. Were they her communist friends? The larger group of people in the street following the massacre? The nation? The world?

'Jiachen couldn't speak to me because of her wounds,' I said, 'but I heard her clearly tell me to "awaken my people". What did she mean?'

Smiling, Yangchen evaded the question. 'Hearing unspoken words is also a gift. I have no doubt one day you will understand what she said and you will do what she asks.'

In the morning I accompanied the family to the funeral chapel and the crematorium, where we watched Jiachen's body go up in flames.

In a daze, I continued attending classes at the university. What else could I do? It was easier to live an automatic, mechanical existence. Get up, get dressed, grab a bite to eat in the cafeteria, go to class, lose myself in vigorous physical activity in the afternoon, exchange politeness with some of Jiachen's comrades (who were genuinely concerned about me), and study in the evenings. I kept myself so busy I didn't have time to brood.

No one around me understood the idea of my continuing union with Jiachen, and because I couldn't share it with anyone, she seemed more and more distant day by day. Jiachen's comrades called her a martyr, a great hero of the Revolution. Her courage inspired them to continue, they said. Soon, I began to see her through their eyes rather than my own. After all, she was absent as I went about my daily business.

My interest in studies began to falter. I admit it; I developed an interest in Marxism. It was through discussions with Jiachen's comrades that my eyes finally opened to the plight of the working class. As a member of the elite class in Shanghai, I had never really given serious thought to social justice.

The stories of Mao's Long March and the Red Army's commitment to liberating the people from oppression intrigued me. Even though most of us at university were from families who could afford to educate us, we began to see the current system in China as an endless treadmill designed to make the rich more powerful at the expense of the poor. I, too, wanted a society in which everyone enjoyed equal benefit, shared responsibility, and had an equal say about their own lives and a happy future for their children. I was soon an active communist leader—not only on-campus but in the community of factory workers, too. It was risky, as Jiachen's death demonstrated, to be a communist in nationalist-held Shanghai but I felt I had little to lose...that there was so much to gain for the working class, for China.

Jiachen's gift to me, the experience that love is our eternal foundation, was replaced by communist idealism. Like Jiachen's comrades, I began to believe that Jiachen lived on in our memory; she was an inspiration, a hero of the Revolution... and I felt I could be close to her by following her example. I told

33

myself that Jiachen had wanted to fix the world and I needed to carry on for her. This, after all, was the way any self-aware individual ought to live in the 'real' world.

And so, I fell into this way of seeing this tangible, physical world as the only reality, broken as it is. Anything else, including my special connection with Jiachen, was fantasy, illusion, hallucination, wishful thinking. It became easier and easier to think this way since there is always so much to do to fix things in this world.

Student

The defeat of the Japanese in 1945 left a vacuum in Shanghai and the rest of China. The nationalist government of President Chiang Kai-shek eagerly filled this vacuum while fighting off Mao's forces—which were gaining territory and more influence in the countryside. Shanghai became one of the nationalists' primary economic and strategic bases in their determination to hold out against Mao. As their position in most of China deteriorated, they withdrew to the cities where they hoped to hold out until World War III when, they fantasized, America would intervene to defeat communism.

Of course, in the midst of all this, we students in the communist movement criticized the nationalists for misusing the city's resources. Instead of helping the country recover economically from decades of Japanese occupation, the nationalists were bleeding Shanghai dry to support their military campaign against the Red Army. Emboldened by Mao's continuing victories, we students grew more outspoken and active. We began to contact factory workers and common labourers to help them form cells and unions. Enthusiastically, I helped organize meetings and teaching sessions with the workers and felt that I was doing my country a great service by sharing the dream of a social and economic system in which all would be equal, and all could live a peaceful, happy life.

Though I lived at the university, attended classes and remained committed to the Party, I continued spending every Sunday with my family. It was much the same each time; early in the morning I met mother and my little sister at the park to do tai chi. I enjoyed this quiet time with them. Afterwards, I went home with them for breakfast. Then I'd hurry off to the martial arts hall at the club where Master Tashi, my martial arts instructor, put me through tough challenges. At noon, father, mother and my sister came to the Foreigner's Club where I joined them for a leisurely lunch. Afterwards, father golfed. He often asked me to join him but I would excuse myself. I hated the tedium of the game and the chatter of old men that was always focused on money and politics; especially as capitalism revolted me more and more. Instead, I went to the stables where Master Tashi was ready to ride on horseback with me over the web of pathways across the marshes of the Yangtze estuary, where we hunted fowl with bow and arrows. Besides being my martial arts teacher, Master Tashi had also been my riding and archery instructor since I was a young boy. Over the years, he taught me to shoot with ease. I was able, like Master Tashi, to shoot arrows and hit my targets from a running horse.

These afternoon outings in the wild marshes were exhilarating. Riding, hunting, shooting arrows involved my total being; mind, body, and spirit.

'Arrows find their target,' Master Tashi often said to me, 'when your whole being flows together.'

He spoke a little about his background. As a boy in Mongolia, he'd been singled out and apprenticed to a shaman who passed on to him ancient skills and wisdom. Later, he began to teach people the ancient warrior skills he had learned.

He came to Shanghai when the Russians turned his homeland into a communist state. Here, he continued developing his personal skills when he met a Japanese jujutsu master and learned to defeat armed opponents bare handed. These skills and the inner discipline necessary to use them were passed on to me, though I was mostly unaware of their true value at the time.

One day stands out most in my memory; a day of warm spring breeze filled with promise. In mid-afternoon, Master Tashi and I quickly rode away from the city in search of migrating wild geese. It was the height of migration season and the wetlands were filled with fowl. At sunset we made our way slowly back to the club, our bags overflowing with ducks for our respective dinner tables. I couldn't shake the feeling that this would be the last time we'd be doing this. Changes, great changes were on the way and I was concerned about Master Tashi's future. His livelihood depended on the likes of me in my role as 'spoiled rich kid' who frequented the Foreigner's Club.

'Where will you go?' I asked Master Tashi, 'and what will you do when Mao's Red Army defeats the nationalists?'

'Will that really happen?' Master Tashi seemed surprised by the suggestion. I remember noticing, too, that the setting sun, a fiery ball over the city, cast a red glow across the fields and marshes.

'Oh yes, soon now, I think. It is a matter of a few weeks.'

'What about you? What about your family? Surely, the communists will...' he didn't complete the sentence but we both understood that privileged families like those who frequented our club stood to lose everything, as that had been the case in other parts of China.

37

'Yes, I'm sure father is worried. I don't know what he'll do. He hasn't said yet.'

'Well, if things get bad here I can't go back to Mongolia. So perhaps I'll go to Taiwan, or maybe to Tibet.'

'Tibet?' I was taken by surprise. Tibet, or Xizang, the 'wild western treasure house', had always stirred my imagination. 'Why there?'

'Well, I'm Tibetan but I grew up in Mongolia. My father was a Tibetan government official posted there.'

'Really?'

'Yes, but I have no idea what Tibet is like,' Master Tashi confessed, 'only stories about it.'

'It's a very religious place, I understand. But I've also heard it is a dangerous place filled with wicked, violent people.'

Master Tashi laughed. 'That's a convenient rumour to keep outsiders away. But what about you, Wei Ming? What will you do?'

We generally kept our conversations to our shared activities so we'd never discussed my private or political life.

'Oh,' I began with hesitation, 'I'll stay here.'

Master Tashi didn't look surprised.

'Of course,' he said calmly. 'You're a communist. Just like your girlfriend.'

I was surprised that he seemed to know more about me than I'd revealed. 'How did you know?'

'Oh, I have my ways of knowing things,' he said with a big smile but didn't divulge his source of information.

At the club I bade him goodbye before he led my horse to the stables and added, 'Please take what I say seriously, Master Tashi. Within a couple months, the nationalists will be defeated. The communists will not take kindly to this club nor to those working here. I suspect most of the members will be gone soon and if they don't go, they will certainly wish they had. Your source of livelihood will disappear. I advise you to make plans to leave soon. I don't want anything to happen to you and your family.'

Father was just finishing a round of drinks with his golfing friends when I walked into the club house. Some of the gentlemen were shocked that I was carrying a bag of freshly killed fowl, but thankfully, father made an effort to look pleased.

'Well done, son. Let's go home and have those birds cooked, shall we?'

Father's siblings and their families usually gathered at our bungalow for dinner as they did on that early April evening in 1949.

After all the relatives left that night, Father unexpectedly asked me into his study for a chat. He poured himself a whiskey and offered to pour one for me. I declined. He shrugged his shoulders, walked over to his big easy chair and sat down. I remained standing stiffly, anticipating an uncomfortable conversation. As you can imagine, my father was not happy about my extracurricular activities. I expected another lecture about loyalty to the family, taking my studies seriously, or the problems with communism. But when he sat silently, swirling the whiskey in his glass, I knew something else was on his mind.

'We're leaving Shanghai,' my father announced without preamble. It was his abruptness that startled me rather than what he said. I was actually relieved that he was aware of the imminent takeover of Shanghai by Mao's forces.

39

'Oh?' I hoped to sound disinterested.

'There's no future for the likes of us here, son. I've arranged a place for you in medical school at Hong Kong University.'

I remember staring at a nail hole in the wall where a picture used to hang; a presumptuous picture of London Bridge. A faint outline of the frame remained.

'I'd rather finish here, sir,' I replied without emotion.

'I understand that but we want you to come with us I'll pay for your education in Hong Kong but not if you stay here.'

'Fine. I will manage.' I was quite angry but hid it with a flat response.

He stared at me. He did not want to believe me. Perhaps he thought I'd change my mind if he let the reality of the situation sink in. When he didn't speak for a long time, I knew he was waiting for the right answer.

'There's another matter,' he broke the silence with the other topic that strained our relationship; another fantasy he had about my future.

I pre-empted the inevitably thorny argument by blurting, 'If you want me to marry your banker partner's daughter, there is nothing to discuss.'

Father's reaction was quick.

'You're right. There will be no discussion. The arrangements are made. You and your bride will accompany us to Hong Kong—within a month.'

'No Father, I'm not marrying—,' I could not even say her name. 'And I will not go to Hong Kong.'

At this point father could not contain his anger. He leapt from his chair spilling whiskey over his trousers and stepped closer to me. We stood eye-to-eye.

'You'll do as I say.'

As if for the first time, I think, he realized I stood taller; he unconsciously stepped back which gave me the courage to be direct, to speak from my heart.

'Since they murdered my Jiachen two years ago, I have been married to the Communist Party.'

My words turned father's rage into dejection. His shoulders sagged but he kept his eyes fixed on mine. The barrier between us broke. I suddenly realized that my father had also suffered from my loss. He had liked my intelligent and vivacious Jiachen despite her family's 'lower' social position. I believe he would have welcomed our marriage. I glimpsed true concern and compassion in his heart, but at the same time his anger remained; I'd betrayed the family because I chose to bury my sorrow in communism.

'Wei Ming, my only son,' he said sorrowfully.

I was breaking his heart.

'You have chosen a terrible partner. Communism is an ugly ideology copied from Europe. It is not suitable for China.'

We'd had this discussion before. He insisted China needed capitalism because it fit our traditional social order better than an imported socialist ideology. 'Wealth generates wealth'. That was his motto. China needed the upper class to build the factories and employ workers to make the economy strong.

'No,' I replied, standing firm.

My argument was that the capitalist approach made the wealthy richer at the expense of the poor whom they enslaved. Centralizing wealth in the hands of a few ensured that the poor would get less and less. Marxism offered a revolutionary way

41

of reorganizing resources to guarantee the equitable spread of the country's wealth.

'We have made communism our own,' I said, standing up to him. 'The nation is strong when all its people are strong. We will rebuild our great civilization and shine for the whole world to see.'

That was that. I knew neither of us would change our way of seeing the world. I felt sorry for him. He was trapped in a system that used him as much as he thought he was managing it. There would be no mutual understanding; we would hang on to our own views and go our separate ways. I left the house sad, and feeling there was more I needed to say, but it would fall on deaf ears.

The family left a month later for Hong Kong. Mother and my sister wept most of that month, I think. They were sad about leaving their lovely home in Shanghai, about the uncertainty ahead and, of course, that I would not be with them. I continued to do tai chi with them on the remaining Sundays and tried to console them by saying they would continue to enjoy the lifestyle they'd grown accustomed to. I was relieved they would be out of harm's way when the Red Army arrived to take Shanghai.

On the last Sunday morning together, I went to see Master Tashi at the club's stables to discover he had already left Shanghai. Other staff said that he'd gone to Taiwan; he had a connection at a club in Taipei.

Showing up at the pier in my Party uniform would have been risky, and father would have been livid. Instead, to please mother, I wore my suit. I bade my dear grandparents farewell with embraces, gave my sister a big hug, kissed my mother goodbye, and formally shook my father's hand. We did not speak. Neither they nor I knew when or if we'd meet again.

I caught a glimpse of my 'intended' boarding the same boat. She saw me, too, and turned away with her nose in the air. I don't know how father dealt with the cancellation of the wedding, but that was not my problem; it had been his doing, not mine.

By the middle of May 1949, the Red Army had surrounded the city. It was rumoured, and later corroborated, that the nationalists planned to burn the city down as they escaped by air and sea. When the time came, they were unable to do so because communist students like myself, who, due to our extensive community involvement, were able to rally the local population into Factory and Property Protection Squads. We organized the people to surround the factories, the markets and as many businesses as possible in those final hours to successfully prevent the nationalists' scorched-city program.

The nationalists did manage, however, to rob Shanghai's banks of its gold, and its factories of some of its production equipment and resources. By the time Mao's Red Army marched into Shanghai, everything had already been sent by plane and shipload to Taiwan or Hong Kong; businessmen and factory owners absconded with their wealth.

On June 2, the Red Army walked into Shanghai and took control without much of a fight. Thankfully, due to our efforts in preventing the nationalists from ravaging the city and the low level of Nationalist Army resistance, damage to streets and buildings was minimal. I was proud that we, the people of Shanghai, had saved our city from destruction. There was great elation throughout the city. Most of the people were delighted with the communist victory. Party members like myself were regarded as heroes wherever we went. It was an exhilarating time.

Many nationalist foot soldiers were left behind when the upper levels of the army fled with the capitalists. These soldiers willingly put down their weapons and helped us in our People's Work Groups to round up those in need of food, shelter, and clothing.

With the elite gone, factories and public utilities were, for the most part, without upper level management. It was encouraging to see the workers rise up and keep public services going, and to see factories resume production again. I was involved with one factory; the workers, with my encouragement, gathered to discuss their situation and make decisions, with every worker participating. This was my first experience of the power of participatory democracy. Worker cooperatives were formed; instead of the elite owning the factory, the workers now made all decision and shared the benefits. This was the fruit of the Revolution!

Life in the city continued more or less as usual. The university reopened even though many professors had fled to Taiwan or Hong Kong. For leftist professors and students alike, the political change was a great relief. We were able, at last, to openly express our views and collaborate with the Party.

We felt liberated.

Volunteer

One evening several months later, I was in a large lecture hall at my university, listening to a well-known Party leader. He called for volunteers to take the revolution to minority groups living in areas oppressed by feudal lords and powerful chieftains. He wanted volunteers to dedicate themselves to learning the local language and culture; to join communities, to adopt the ways of the people and to encourage them to create their own cooperatives. By this approach, volunteers would win the people's hearts and minds to help the people rise up against their oppressors to demand a better way of life. The volunteers would help stir up revolutionary fervour among these groups and encourage them to join the greater brotherhood of communist nations.

This struck a chord. The idea of living among peasants in a remote area and helping them voluntarily embrace communism resonated with me. This was a unique and necessary approach to initiate social change. I felt committed to the idea that the revolution should come from the hearts of the people themselves.

As I listened, I remembered what Master Tashi had said about Tibet; that the Tibetan people were not the barbarians we Chinese made them out to be.

'We are in need of revolutionaries willing to go to Tibet,' the speaker was saying. 'If you volunteer, you must be smart and brave enough to find ways to encourage the people to rise up and create their own revolution. Are there any volunteers among you?'

I stood up.

What followed were four months of training in communist philosophy and community organizing in Nanjing for a small group of us going to Tibet. We had a Tibetan language tutor who was not very helpful. He was of the elite class and had spent most of his life outside Tibet, in the large cities of Chengdu, Shanghai, and Beijing. His knowledge of Tibetan culture and current events was less than thorough, and he could teach us only very basic language skills. I was frustrated but endured him as best as I could. In the end, I was thankful to have learned just enough to be able to begin communicating once I got to Tibet.

Back in Shanghai before being posted to Chengdu, I had the thought that I should visit Yangchen, Jiachen's grandmother. I knew she had family ties with Chengdu. I might be able to take a message to her relatives for her. I got to Jiachen's family apartment to discover that the Fang family, like my own, had left. The apartment was now in the care of their servants.

Huizhong, Jiachen's maid, was delighted to see me. She began to weep as she led me upstairs. She and her husband lived in Jiachen's small room; the rest of the apartment was occupied by the families of Fang's other servants. The Fang family had provided for their servants in a way that many other departed business people had not. She was grateful to them for this, she explained. I recognized Jiachen's bed, dresser, carpet and other furnishings; Huizhong's few possessions were added to make the room less familiar though quite homey.

Being in the bedroom brought back memories of innocent hours filled with talking, laughing, and getting to know each other. Huizhong began to pour her heart out about Jiachen's death until I stopped her by asking about Yangchen. She regained her composure and her face lit up.

'She lived for Jiachen. We both did, Wei Ming sir,' Huizhong said at once. 'It was "Jiachen", "Jiachen", "Jiachen" with her. How she had devoted herself to that child; such a bright and beautiful girl. There was nothing else for her in Shanghai. Yangchen madam loved her daughter, Nuying— I mean Madam Fang—but they were not close. She criticized Madam Fang for spending money on parties, clothing, and going out all the time.'

'I was never at ease talking with Madam Fang,' I offered, 'I was much more at ease with Grandmother Yangchen.'

'Of course, Wei Ming sir. She really liked you. We loved teasing Jiachen about you.'

'I'm sure you did,' I chuckled. 'Yangchen's from Chengdu, if I remember right?'

'That's right. She's such a wise and beautiful woman. Her wisdom and strength came from her Tibetan heritage.'

'Tibetan?'

'Yes, Grandmother Yangchen and her daughter, Madam Fang, are Tibetan. They have family in Tibet and in Chengdu. A few days after the funeral, Grandmother packed up and went back to Chengdu by train.'

Huizhong dreamily began telling the story of how Master Fang met Nuying in Chengdu and fell madly in love. I'd heard it before, of course, but I indulged Huizhong.

'Jiachen loved to hear Grandmother tell how Master Fang was in Chengdu for a cousin's wedding and it just so happened that Nuying was also invited. Their courtship was like a whirlwind that turned everything upside down! In the end, Yangchen's family agreed to the marriage. Grandmother Yangchen boasted that Master Fang's fortune greatly improved from the moment he saw her daughter.'

Huizhong stopped as if suddenly remembering something. She got up and went to open a dresser drawer. She returned with a note.

'Here, I nearly forgot. Grandmother Yangchen gave this to me just before she left. It is for you. She said I must give it to you if I ever saw you again.'

I accepted the note and read it eagerly. It was written in Chinese characters in Yangchen's own hand. 'If your life's journey ever takes you to Chengdu, please go to this address and ask for me.'

The address was a description of a street in the Tibetan quarter, the second street parallel to the road outside the ancient palace grounds and the cloth store on one of the corners that also sells sacred Tibetan texts and images. A vague address to be sure, but perhaps I would find it.

'It so happens I'll be going to Chengdu in a few days,' I responded aloud with excitement.

'You're going to Chengdu? Whatever for?'

'I've volunteered to go to Tibet to help liberate the people. I'll spend a short time in Chengdu and find a way into the mountains.'

Huizhong's eyebrows furrowed. I think she didn't understand what I was saying or if she did, she thought it an odd thing for anyone to do. But I was mistaken. What she said surprised me.

'Well,' she began thoughtfully, 'it must be fate. You going to help Jiachen's people in Tibet, I mean.'

Until that moment, I hadn't made this connection. Were the Tibetans the 'my people' she wanted me to liberate?

I sensed Jiachen, like a fragrance, suddenly near me. I attributed the fragrance to being in her old room and I shook the sensation of her presence off. I had conditioned myself, by this time, that it was unthinkable to fall victim to superstition. I'd long since decided that our connection beyond death was an illusion but, nevertheless, I was intrigued by Huizhong's reference to Jiachen's people.

Huizhong was speaking.

'I went to Chengdu with them once,' she continued. 'Jiachen was about 10- or 11-years-old. Grandmother Yangchen wanted Jiachen to know some Tibetan people. Madam Fang would have nothing to do with her family in Chengdu but she let us take Jiachen. We had a wonderful time. They are lovely people, so different from us. Grandmother Yangchen's family adored little Jiachen, of course.'

'What is her family name?'

'I don't remember exactly. I heard two names that sounded similar. Perhaps it was one of them. One was... well, they both ended with 'tsang'. I know that for sure. One was... oh, yes, one was Andru, Andrutsang. The other, I think was Gya, Gyato, that's it, Gyatotsang. But never mind if you don't know which of those two names is the right one, you'll find the right place. It's near to the old palace gardens, go to the main gate. It's two streets from there. You can't miss it. There are only three or four streets of Tibetan shops. Go to any one of them and ask for Yangchen, the grandmother who lived in

Shanghai. Everyone will know who you are asking for. They'll show you where to go.'

In the spring of 1951, I reported to the Chengdu office of the Southwest Bureau's Tibet Work Committee. The officer in charge of volunteers, Comrade Li, wanted to know what my true intentions and expectations might be. We had a long and frank discussion. It was my hope, I told him, to transform a village into a model cooperative guided by communist principles. If the cooperative was successful, it would be a model for other villages to emulate; a way to inspire a grassroots revolution.

'You are certainly full of great ideas,' Li said after listening to me carefully. 'But I must warn you, it will not be easy. The Tibetan people are not like us. Their way of life is completely different. I would not say they are backward, but compared to us, they are very far behind in regard to modern amenities, ideas, and technology. They are an intelligent people, but very fixed in their ideas. Their culture is surprisingly sophisticated, an ancient civilization that parallels our own but it is based on religion. A large section of the population is made up of monks and nuns. The religious system actually supersedes the secular structure. Their social structure is definitely feudal; both the monasteries and the wealthy aristocracy own most of the land and herds of domesticated animals. Most of the people are serfs of either the aristocracy or the monasteries—sometimes both.'

'I am over-simplifying, perhaps, but take what I say as an overview to keep in mind. Introducing new ideas is always possible, but you must be sure you understand their system first. Your first responsibility, to begin with, is to know the people and their situation.'

I listened carefully and took all that he said to heart. He'd been to Tibet and knew what I was going to encounter.

'I want to assure you,' I said to Comrade Li, 'that I will not let you down. I plan to spend up to a year learning the language and getting familiar with the culture before I make any proposals.'

'Good. I want to hear good things about you, Comrade Chuang,' Li said approvingly before changing the subject.

'Tell me,' he began, 'why are you choosing Tibet rather than one of the minority groups in Yunnan or the mountains of Sichuan? Why Tibet?'

'There were two people in my life who were very close to me with connections to Tibet. When I heard about this program of taking the Revolution to minority groups, I immediately thought of them and their homeland.'

'That's interesting,' Li observed thoughtfully. 'Who were those people, if I may ask?'

'Well, one was my riding and martial arts master. You see,' my face flushed with embarrassment, 'I was raised in a very privileged family and I had access to activities considered exotic by most people. Anyway, Master Tashi was Tibetan but never lived there. His family were Tibetan government officials in Mongolia. When the Russians took over Mongolia, he was forced to leave. He ended up in Shanghai as master of the stables at the Foreigner's Club. The martial arts were private lessons arranged through the club.'

Comrade Li nodded and waited for me to continue.

'The other connection was actually through my girlfriend whose mother and grandmother were Tibetan. Her father, a wealthy Shanghai cloth merchant, was visiting Chengdu to attend a wedding. At the wedding he met a Tibetan woman who became his wife after a brief courtship. So, of course, my girlfriend was actually half Tibetan. We met at university where she became a leader of the Communist Youth. She was martyred for the Revolution.'

'Oh really? How terrible for you,' he said with genuine sympathy, but he was also intrigued. 'What was her name?'

'Fang Jiachen.'

'Oh? I remember reading about her in one of the Party's newspapers,' his expression revealed he was impressed. 'There was even a photo as I recall. The photo of her; megaphone to her mouth, fist raised high and her long hair tied back with a red bandana. It was turned into a poster.'

'Yes, that was my Jiachen,' I said quietly, sadly, 'my revolutionary hero.'

'She was half Tibetan?' Li repeated as he got up from his desk. 'Come with me. I want you to meet someone. He will be most interested to hear the story of your girlfriend, I'm sure.'

Comrade Li took me down the hall to an office where he introduced me to Phuntso Wangyal, a tall, good-looking and articulate man who might have been 10 years older than me. At first I thought he was Chinese because of his Party uniform and short hair, but he introduced himself as a Tibetan from Batang, on the western edge of Kham. Comrade Li explained that Phuntso was a highly respected Tibetan communist.

'Gyatotsang? Andrutsang?' Phuntso repeated when I told him the names I'd heard in connection to Jiachen's family.

'They are both very well-known families from Lithang, an area east of Batang.'

'What a coincidence!' Comrade Li exclaimed. 'I am assigning our comrade to Lithang.'

'That would be a perfect assignment,' Phuntso agreed. 'We need a stronger base there. Come along with me. I'm going soon and I'll introduce you to some fellow revolutionaries up there.'

I liked Phuntso immediately. He was enthusiastic, intelligent, and determined to bring social change and economic improvement to his people. I was most impressed with Phuntso's vision for the peaceful liberation of Tibet. He hoped to persuade Tibetan officials and thought it would be in the best interest of Tibet to join the brotherhood of communist nations. As one of the first Tibetan communists, he'd made a name for himself among the elite members of the Communist Party and had, in fact, engaged in long talks with Deng Xiaoping about the liberation of Tibet. I felt proud to be taking part in his mission.

'It is too little, too late,' Phuntso commented, sounding regretful. 'I have done my best over the past decade, but it has not been enough. I'm excited that you are willing to help. Your presence, your guidance and efforts will, no doubt, be effective, but I just wish there were more of you, and that you could have started when I did nearly a decade ago.'

'But you have already sown seeds of change,' I said as encouragement, adding, 'that will make it easier for me.'

'We shall see.'

He smiled briefly but remained silent as if pondering the future of his people. With a frown, he informed me that the 52nd, 53rd, and 54th Divisions of the 18th Army were being deployed to Kham, the easternmost part of the Tibetan plateau.

'Since all of the plateau east of the Yangtze River was annexed to Sichuan Province by the nationalist government,' Phuntso said with a shrug of his shoulders, 'it now belongs to Communist China. The 18th Army is going in to begin road building and other works to improve the infrastructure. Party officials are going with them to establish our presence.'

'How will the people respond to the presence of the People's Liberation Army?' I asked.

'They will not like it much,' he admitted, 'but I've been assured the PLA will be a positive force for the progress of my people.'

I could see that he had faith in Deng Xiaoping and Chairman Mao. Deng had assured him that Tibet's cultural and religious freedom would be honoured. Revolutionary cells of local people would be created under the guidance of the Party for the peaceful transformation of Tibet's feudal system into a truly egalitarian society. It would be necessary, Phuntso was told, for the PLA to build up a modern infrastructure and help with an orderly transition of power from the aristocracy to the working class. Soldiers, instructed not to disrupt the lives and culture, would maintain strict discipline and not steal anything. Plans were being made for all food and supplies to be provided from Chengdu so that the PLA would not have to impose their needs on the local economy.

'I will be accompanying the 54th Division to Batang,' Phuntso announced. 'From there, I will join the other divisions and officials in Chamdo to help facilitate negotiations between the Party and Tibetan authorities in Lhasa. You must come with me as far as Lithang.'

'Of course,' I said enthusiastically, 'I'd be proud to be introduced to people in Lithang by a Tibetan comrade.'

There was much to do before the convoy of trucks was ready to depart. Over the next couple of months, Phuntso and I became good friends. He was a great help, teaching me more of the Tibetan language and answering many questions about Tibetan culture.

For example, he explained the importance of using gifts to smooth his relationship with various officials in Kham. And he wanted silver coins to take with us because paper money was worthless among merchants.

Our activities often took us into the Tibetan quarters of Chengdu. One time I visited the area on my own and decided to have lunch at a popular shop serving Tibetan food. Phuntso had introduced me to *tsampa*, barley flour, and yak butter tea which, I discovered, I liked. Many meals consisted of butter tea to which *tsampa* is added to create a paste thick enough to roll into balls and pop into your mouth.

The shop owner looked surprised, but with a wide grin brought me a bowl of smooth, golden tea along with a bowl of the *tsampa* to mix with my tea.

'I'm looking for a cloth shop that also sells sacred texts,' I said to her as she served me, 'I was told I might find Yangchen, a grandmother who lived in Shanghai, there.'

'Yangchen-la from Shanghai?' she asked, adding the personal honorific 'la' to Yangchen's name. 'Yes, of course, the shop is just down at the end of this block on the right,' she informed me.

She turned to walk away, stopped, and faced me again.

'She's not here anymore. She went back to Kham but her family is still here.'

After my tea, I went around to the cloth shop knowing Yangchen would not be there, but hoping to meet her family anyway. When I told the charming older couple in the store my name and connection with Yangchen, they immediately said they knew all about me. Yangchen had told them Jiachen's story which, I was pleased to hear, included me.

'Yangchen is my younger sister,' the woman said, 'she went back to our family village.'

'Oh, I was hoping to meet her again.' I did not tell them I was planning to go to Kham, nor did I try to use my limited Tibetan language.

'She was heartbroken, I think,' Yangchen's sister said in accented Chinese. 'Jiachen meant so much to her. She even had hopes that you and Jiachen would marry, Wei Ming. She thought highly of you and said you were studying to be a doctor.'

'I didn't continue with medical school.'

'Oh, you poor thing,' she said.

I could see she thought it was because I was devastated by my loss.

'What brings you to Chengdu?' her husband asked.

'Party assignment.'

'Oh, so you followed Jiachen's path and became a Communist Party member instead of becoming a doctor,' the old man observed shrewdly. He was immediately much colder toward me. 'We don't like the communists much around here.'

I realized he was openly unsympathetic to communism and very likely reflected the attitude of his compatriots. It shocked me, though I should have known better, that all Tibetans would not eagerly embrace communism.

'While Jiachen was still alive, I did my best to keep her from participating in protest marches against the nationalists but she wouldn't listen to me. Once she was gone, I decided to find out what she was so passionate about. When I understood, I became a communist myself.'

'There's nothing good in it to understand,' the old man blurted out caustically.

After a moment's pause he looked me directly in the eyes, adding, 'I saw you the other day with that communist Phuntso Wangyal, didn't I? I suspect you are working with him to convert Tibetans.'

'That's true, I'm with Comrade Phuntso.'

'I knew it.' The old man had fire in his eyes. 'Communism is wrong for us. It is concerned with external matters and ignores anything related to inner spiritual reality. I would say this to young Jiachen if she were alive. I don't know why Yangchen allowed her granddaughter to get involved. Perhaps it is good she didn't live to try forcing these illusions on her people in Kham.'

There it was again. That phrase jumped at me from a new source: 'her people'. Was this what Jiachen meant? Was I to 'awaken her people' in Kham? Were the people of Kham the ones she meant?

'Awaken'.

An interesting way of saying 'liberate'. Surely, I told myself, she meant 'liberate'!

❦

Curious about Tibetan history, I visited an excellent library in Chengdu with a good collection of books, maps, and letters written by travellers who had visited Tibet throughout the previous centuries. I began to frame a picture of events that had shaped the lives of the people I was hoping to understand.

Thirteen hundred years earlier, the Tibetan empire had extended over all of Central Asia. Its western borders included Afghanistan and Turkmenistan. To the south it held territory from Burma (present-day Myanmar) to the plains of northern India as far as the Punjab. In the north it included Tuva, Mongolia, Buryatia and parts of Siberia. And, of course, to the east, Tibetan warriors had swept across the plains of China, terrifying the Tang dynasty. The Tibetan Empire had been larger and perhaps more influential than any Chinese Empire. It was second only to the Mongolian Empire in the area conquered, but its influence on subsequent cultures was much more important than the Mongolian and, arguably, even the Chinese outside of central China. Tibet's influence can still be seen in the sophisticated art, architecture, religious practices, and Buddhist philosophy in large areas of Central Asia.

Tibet's encounter with China had resulted in an alliance with the Tang Dynasty. King Songtsen Gampo's warriors had so terrified Xian that Emperor Tang Gaozong agreed to give the Tibetan king his daughter in marriage. Thereafter, China paid tribute to the kings of Tibet to keep warriors from raiding the Chinese lowlands. The Chinese perception of Tibetans, like a nightmare lodged in their collective psyche, comes from these raiding parties.

The Khampas—the people of Kham, the area where I was headed—had long regarded themselves as 'a race of kings'. They had never been conquered by outsiders. Even when the Mongols swept across Tibet, they never subdued Kham.

Arrival in Tibet

I'd never been in mountains like these before. The road, as far as Dartsendo, was under construction and dusty. It was terrifying at times. In places, the road was just wide enough for one vehicle and cut into the side of cliffs hundreds, perhaps a thousand feet above tumbling rivers. It climbed over a high mountain only to descend to the Danba River Valley and then up the other side to Dartsendo, the centre of trade between the Tibetan highlands and the lower tea growing areas: the frontier between the Tibetan and Chinese civilizations.

The main road through the narrow mountain valley town was crowded with people and pack animals, lined with taverns and warehouses filled with tea, rice, and cloth from the lowlands or with wool, lumber, minerals, and herbal medicines from the highlands. Goods exchanged hands here.

Dartsendo was the frontier because above this altitude, lowland-bred horses and people did not adjust easily to the thinner air of Tibet. This was also the lower limit for yak and highland-bred horses; they needed the cool, clear atmosphere of the mountains.

I arrived with Phuntso and a vanguard of soldiers tasked with arranging thousands of pack animals for the journey into the interior. Our arrival by truck underscored a new reality; the existence and use of trucks was already eliminating the need for Chinese porters and horses on the China side of the tea-trade route. Trucks were quick and could carry as much as an entire caravan. Soon, the road would go over the pass to the West and onto the Tibetan plateau. But merchants in Dartsendo were adapting quickly and flourishing.

Phuntso and I visited local officials to ask for their help in organizing a huge number of pack animals for the 52nd and 53rd Divisions travelling north from here, and for the 54th travelling due west to Batang via Lithang. The Tibetan feudal *corvée* system required merchants and farmers alike, to provide animals and free labour to any government official or aristocrat on demand. The PLA, however, would pay cash, which made it much easier to arrange enough pack animals and handlers. The gifts we brought went a long way to encourage officials to agree to our co-opting their system.

Dartsendo was the place to buy a horse. It offered an excellent selection of animals bred to cope with high altitude. These hybrids were not full sized like I was used to riding at the club in Shanghai, but I was able to find a mare strong enough to carry me. She was chestnut brown, sleek and good-natured. To try her out I rode up to the local 'horse racing ground', a small plateau above the town. I was pleased with my choice and called her 'Chestnut'.

Soon after 52nd and 53rd Divisions arrived in Dartsendo, we had enough pack animals arranged for them to continue along a trail heading north out of Dartsendo. The 54th was last to arrive but quickest to leave on a trail that continued through the town going west. We would follow the way to Lithang, Batang along the 'southern route' to Lhasa. The new motor road was already under construction up and over the pass.

I felt sorry for the foot soldiers carrying their own packs. The altitude was taking a toll on all of us. Our lowland lungs could not handle the thinning air. Even walking uphill without a pack took my breath away and drained my energy. I felt fortunate to have my horse, though I dared not ride her up the steepest parts; glancing down the precipices from her back terrified me.

Workers busy digging the motor road took a break as we passed. They were mostly hired Tibetans who seemed happy enough with the work they were doing. I cheered them on in Tibetan as I passed, and they were pleased to hear their own language spoken to them by a Chinese man.

The second day, we climbed up and over the pass.

What an exhilarating day! My first glimpse of Tibet, the land of snow.

Colourful prayer flags framed the seemingly endless ranges of forest-covered hills and snow-peaked mountains. Pasture lands on the verge of turning summer-green lay below the pass. We were about to cross them.

'*Lha Gyalo!*' shouted the Tibetan animal handlers as they reached the pass. They sounded as exhilarated with the view as I was.

'*Lha Gyalo!*' shouted others as they tossed handfuls of coloured papers into the wind at the edge of the cliff. The papers rose so high they looked like twinkling stars in the deep blueness of the sky at this altitude. They continued rising until they disappeared altogether into the void.

I was curious about the papers and found one on the ground. It was covered with Tibetan script except for an image of a prancing horse at the centre. The horse carried three flaming objects of some kind on its back.

'*Lungta,*' one of the Tibetans said pointing to the paper.

I held the paper closer to him and pointed as best as I could to the objects on the horse's back.

'Three Treasures,' he said with a smile, 'Buddha, dharma, and sangha.'

'Why do you toss them into the sky?' I asked.

'The horse is *lungta,* the windhorse who takes our prayers into the void, to Buddha.'

'Ah, very beautiful,' I found myself saying again.

'Yes, blessings for our journey!'

Phuntso had been watching me with an amused expression. As if to divert me to more practical observations, he began pointing out features of the landscape we would be traversing.

He, too, was excited.

'Ah, home!' he exclaimed. 'All of us *tsampa*-eaters love our land. It is hard to leave, and always a joy to return.'

The *lungta*-throwers' plea for blessings worked; we journeyed onward without serious mishap. We crossed several streams and one major river, the Yalung.

It was a rare day that Phuntso and I had time for serious conversation. He was continuously engaged by the officers for translation and negotiations with the Tibetan caravan leaders. I helped with negotiations in the opposite direction, between Phuntso and the Chinese officers that is, when he was misunderstood or too frustrated to keep his cool. Between the two of us, we were able to keep things operating smoothly enough. When my interpretation skills and intervention was not needed, I found it pleasant to ride in silence and let the scenery and fresh mountain breeze penetrate my being.

One day as we neared Lithang, Phuntso and I had been riding together for most of the morning when I remembered and mentioned my exchange with the old Tibetan gentleman in Chengdu. I was curious to have Phuntso's perspective on religion and the old man's attitude toward communism.

'As Tibetan culture is so focused on religion,' I began, 'how do you respond to someone who attacks you with the observation that communism is deficient because it does not address the spiritual dimension?'

'Such deep thoughts, comrade,' Phuntso was surprised, I think. 'I'm not a religious person. Not all Tibetans are, you know. Some of us actually live in the real world and want a world in which people are not impoverished by an oppressive theocracy. The monastic system is just as oppressive as the aristocracy in our country. I see nothing good in maintaining either system.'

'I'm not talking about systems,' I clarified, 'I'm talking about spirit.'

'I don't believe in that stuff. When you die, that's it; it's the end of you.'

'Of course,' I agreed, 'but there are other points of view. I was educated in Western style schools by nuns and Jesuit fathers. They talked about God and going to heaven when you die, but I wondered how much they actually believed it themselves. They didn't live as if it were true. What they were teaching us focused entirely on this tangible, material world. Science, the cornerstone of modern Western civilization, is reliant on the senses and rational thought. Modern tools enhance the senses so we can measure, quantify and name the physical universe. Since God and spirit are unmeasurable, the existence of the spiritual dimension cannot be proven by science. Westerners, including the religiously-oriented, live as if science alone dictates what is real. The existence of God is merely something you choose to believe or not believe.'

'I choose not to believe.'

'Back to my initial question,' I continued, 'how would you respond to a Buddhist leader who might be curious about communism but is concerned that we do not recognize Buddha, his teachings, or the spiritual dimension?'

'Haven't given it much thought. I've never been approached by one of them. And, Wei Ming,' he added, using my first name so I knew he was deliberately trying to coach me, 'it's not wise to engage in dialogue with religious figures. There is no way to come to an understanding with them. Like your Jesuit fathers, they teach the existence of the spiritual dimension but my own observations indicate otherwise. It's obvious to me they are more in the material world. Their monasteries are full of treasures and they extract wealth from the people as much or maybe even more than the aristocracy! They are a contradiction. They do not practice what they preach.'

I recognized that Phuntso's advice about keeping my distance from religious figures was emotion-charged, so I decided to remain open-minded. In my desire to understand just how religious teachings fit into the larger picture, I suddenly realized I'd turned away from the 'gift', as Yangchen called it, that Jiachen had given me. My involvement with the Party had made me forget that I knew the importance of the spiritual dimension already.

As I rode in on silence, I wondered why, suddenly, I'd begun to entertain the possibility of a spiritual dimension? I decided it must be the beauty of the landscape and the presence of Buddhist monks, temples, monasteries and stupas, or chorten as they are called in Tibetan, in every settlement along our way. These constant reminders of the spiritual dimension were making an impression on me. Unlike Phuntso, I understood that this aspect of Tibetan culture could not be so easily dismissed. It was deeply rooted in the people's cultural identity. Despite Deng Xiaoping's assurance that cultural and religious traditions of Tibet should be honoured, I sensed, through Phuntso's attitude, they had no real appreciation of this rich heritage. I did not have a clear enough understanding of the monastic segment of Tibetan society to make a judgement myself yet, but I began to suspect that the Party would regard religion as useless unless religious communities fully supported the revolution.

'Comrade Phuntso,' I began on another occasion, 'I understand that despite historical evidence, we Chinese have always regarded Tibet to be within our sphere of influence. What is the real position of the Party, as you understand it?'

'As you say, they intend to extend the enlightened leadership of the Party to every corner of its sphere of influence. This includes all of Tibet, not just the portion of Kham annexed by Sichuan Province. But like all Tibetans, I have a different perspective and I have voiced it to the leadership. Tibetans will only accept a home-grown communist revolution; we will take our place as an independent and equal nation in the Worldwide Brotherhood of Communist Nations.'

'So what you are saying is that the Party is sending me to Kham expecting me to extend the Chinese brand of communism rather than to help germinate a truly Tibetan communist revolution.'

'I'm sure that is the intention of men like Comrade Li in Chengdu, but it is not my intention. You must decide for yourself which Revolution you are working for. I know what I want and will continue pressing the Chinese Communist Party to allow Tibet its independence.'

The deeper I travelled into the heart of this impressive landscape, the more I had flickers, reminders of the experience Jiachen had given me as she died. I would suddenly feel her presence in the sound of a gurgling stream of clear water, in the fragrance of evergreen boughs swaying in the breeze, or as, in awe, I beheld a vastness of range after range of forested mountains capped with snowy peaks. Here, I found a landscape sublime and delicate, full of heights and depths; a splendour moved by the primordial power of love once shared with my beloved, Jiachen. My heart burst in joyful response to the unity and perfection of it all; she was still with me. My very first view of the immense, verdant vale of Lithang, lush with new grass and sprinkled with wildflowers, took my breath away. I hadn't expected the Lithang grassland to be so extensive. As I hurried down the trail toward Lithang, my new home base, I passed the large Lithang monastery belonging to the Gelugpa sect. Scores of red and white buildings surrounded a large temple. The collection of monastic buildings seemed larger than the town spread below and was, in fact, the reason for the town's existence. I later likened the buildings of the town clustered below the monastery to pilgrims clamouring for the blessings of a revered teacher.

Our long caravan made its way through the town to an area on the grassland southwest of the town. A few days' rest was promised to the foot soldiers while fresh caravan animals were hired from the surrounding area.

We arrived a few days too late to enjoy the annual horse racing festival. Several festival tents remained to the west of our encampment and the town was crowded with nomads and villagers of every description. Women, especially younger women, strolled through town in groups dressed in bright silk *chuba*s, massive necklaces and jewellery, and elaborate hairdos under extraordinary headpieces or hats. The men, too, were brightly attired and swaggered with swords tucked into their colourful waistbands. *Chuba*s and boots, both multi-coloured, were proudly worn. I was impressed by the look of bold pride in these tall, handsome people. On the faces of the women, especially, I saw the self-assured grace that I had seen in Yangchen and in Tibetan women in Chengdu. I began to see that women held their own among the men. Like Jiachen and Yangchen, the women were strong and dignified. I liked that immediately about Tibetan society.

Phuntso introduced me to several officials and a few friends he knew to be sympathetic to communism. It was through Phuntso that I met Thupten, who was in town for the festival. Thupten invited us for a drink at a local tavern.

'How do you know each other?' I asked as Thupten ordered a round of *chang*. I did my best to ask the question in Tibetan for Thupten's sake.

'Phuntso is quite famous, you know,' Thupten said as he slapped Phuntso on his back, 'I helped him smuggle guns into Batang several years ago.'

Thupten spoke quickly. And he spoke in a dialect I was not familiar with.

'He wanted to take on the nationalist army,' Thupten continued, 'and then start a communist revolution in Tibet. He had plans to liberate Batang and form a new government that would gradually spread all over Kham. He's the Tibetan Mao.'

'No,' Phuntso objected. For my benefit, he switched to Chinese. 'I'm no Mao. Just a humble worker striving to liberate the people of Tibet. At first, I was working to overthrow the oppressive Kuomintang government and, yes, I hoped afterwards to set up a communist system to address the problems of oppression in Tibet. I saw the need for a strong, just form of government in Tibet. My aim was, and still is, to maintain our autonomy but maintain a close association with the Chinese Communist Party.'

'Tibetan Mao,' Thupten insisted in Tibetan, 'he's a hero.'

'Yes,' I agreed, speaking in Tibetan, 'he's an inspiration to me, certainly.'

'Let me tell you about Thupten,' Phuntso said to divert attention from himself. He, too, switched to Tibetan and spoke slowly and carefully for my sake. 'I was in Batang a few years ago at a friend's house when this young Lithang-pa appeared. Recognizing a progressive thinker after a short conversation, I challenged Thupten about the situation of ordinary people in Kham.'

'You helped me see that another system is possible,' Thupten acknowledged. He, too, spoke slowly.

'Now let me tell you about Chuang Wei Ming, my remarkable comrade from Shanghai,' Phuntso said to Thupten. 'Here is the real hero. He's come here, away from the comforts of city life, to start a model cooperative in one of our villages. I think what he plans to do is probably much more realistic and more important than anything I've tried to do. While I try to convince officials of the Tibetan government to consider change along communist principles, he will be doing the real work of implementing social and economic reform among the people.'

'Really?' Thupten's interest was genuine. 'This is a dream come true.'

'Indeed, it is, Thupten,' Phuntso said. 'What about your village? Is there any possibility you could influence your people to let Comrade Chuang implement socialist reforms?'

Thupten frowned while considering the question. I was afraid he would say no, but I was mistaken.

'I think the time is right,' he finally said. 'It's interesting how things work out. Our Lithang district governor, Lord Thampa Andrutsang, is from my village. We have been loyal friends since childhood.'

When Thupten said 'Andrutsang', I was immediately curious to know if this man, the district governor, was related to Yangchen and Jiachen but, for the moment, I kept my excitement to myself.

'I think Thampa-la, as I call him,' Thupten said using the governor's given name and the personal honorific, 'would be in favour. He became governor during the time of the nationalist government when Kham was annexed to Sichuan Province. Now that the communists have taken over, his days as governor are over. A communist-trained administrator named Nawang Tsering will arrive from Chengdu in a couple months to set up a new administration.'

'How does the governor, Lord Andrutsang, feel about communism?' I asked.

'He's of the aristocracy and owns a large estate, of course, but he's receptive to new ideas and has not objected to my involvement with Phuntso-la. When I explain the basic principles of communism, he is surprisingly receptive and enthusiastic. On many occasions, he has confided that he hates the injustice of our system but feels bound to it.'

'That's important,' I commented with interest.

'Do you think,' Phuntso asked, 'that once he returns to the village, you can encourage him to turn over his lands to a Cooperative Management Committee?'

Phuntso looked to me as he said 'Cooperative Management Committee' as if suggesting a name for the new entity but, to me, the idea hinted of authoritarian control. I nodded but not with enthusiasm. Taking note of my own reaction to this suggestion, I got to thinking how decisions effecting a cooperative should be made.

'I think, if it were only up to Thampa-la,' Thupten said immediately, 'he would do it. He's extremely sensitive to the

71

situation of the villagers and has, for an aristocrat, a unique sense of justice. There are other family members who might object, of course.'

'It sounds to me,' I said with rising enthusiasm, 'like your village may be the place to start. I'm excited.'

A few days later, the 54th Division of the People's Liberation Army left Lithang. The streets of Lithang seemed empty with both the soldiers and the out-of-town festival visitors gone. Only the common folk remained, and they were not dressed in fine chubas; they were the servants who kept the markets, the taverns, and the houses of the wealthy going. It was these people who yearned for the revolution, I mused, whether they knew it just yet or not.

I was grateful that Phuntso had introduced me to Thupten; I had at least one friend who understood my mission. Thupten introduced me to his friend Rabten, the owner of the tavern we had spent so much time in with Phuntso. Rabten, he told me, was also sympathetic to our desire for change. I decided to stay at Rabten's tavern.

Thupten took me to see Lord Andrutsang the day after Phuntso left. Thampa-la was a huge man; he had the archetypal stature of the Tibetan aristocratic patriarch, both tall and heavy. Thupten was his equal in height but looked slight next to his childhood friend. I imagined them as quite a pair in their youth.

The governor and his wife, Dawa, invited us into their stately home. Dawa was attractive and charmingly friendly while she served us *chang* in beautiful porcelain bowls. I liked both Thampa and Dawa immediately, and I was bursting with curiosity about their surname, Andrutsang. While Dawa refilled my bowl, I posed my question.

'Do you have relatives in Chengdu?'

'Yes, we do. Why do you ask?' She set the jug of *chang* on the floor and kneeled in front of me.

'I visited a store in Chengdu to ask about Yangchen, an elderly woman I knew in Shanghai.'

'Yangchen? My mother's name is Yangchen!'

'She was the grandmother of Jiachen, the woman I had hoped to marry.'

Dawa startled me by suddenly throwing her arms around me and weeping on my shoulder. Bewildered, I looked at Thampa. He, too, was overcome with emotion.

'We know your story, Wei Ming,' Dawa said through her tears. She knew my given name even though I had not mentioned it. 'We were so upset to hear Jiachen had been killed like that. But you must have been devastated!'

'Nuying and Dawa are sisters,' Thampa began to explain.

'If you and Jiachen had married...' Dawa interrupted but couldn't finish her own sentence. Shaking her head, she gave me another tearful hug. I knew what they were thinking: we would have been related by marriage.

'Mother will be pleased you've come,' Dawa said, wiping away her tears.

'Yangchen is here?'

'No, she's away but I'll send her a message.'

Thupten was impressed with this sudden change of circumstance.

'When were you assigned to Lithang?' Thupten asked, hoping to resolve the mystery of our connections. 'Was it your choice or was it a coincidence that you came here to Lithang?'

'I did not know Lithang was Yangchen's home when I was assigned here.'

Dawa was still looking at me with tears in her eyes. I wasn't sure if they were tears of joy, sorrow or possibly both, because she continued to smile.

'Yangchen likes you so much,' Dawa said quietly.

Dawa's mannerisms reminded me of Yangchen, Jiachen, and even Nuying. It was no surprise, I supposed, that both Jiachen and Dawa would have adopted Yangchen's mannerisms.

'Now, young man,' Thampa said with a chuckle, clearly amused by Dawa's fascination with me, 'why has Thupten-la brought you to see me?'

Thupten answered Thampa's question before I could collect my thoughts. 'I wanted you to meet Comrade Chuang because he has an interesting proposal. Hear what he has to say. I'm excited about it and I thought you might be, too.'

'Yes, of course I'll listen,' Thampa said. 'What we know about him changes everything.'

I noticed Dawa nodding. She continued looking at me with a smile on her face that would not go away. I hardly knew how to behave. Why would meeting the young Chinese man who almost married her niece create such an infatuation?

'Now, what is your proposal?' Thampa asked, giving me permission to proceed.

I thought the challenge of language would be my main hurdle so I started slowly in my limited Tibetan.

'Communism is about the equality of all people.'

'You may speak Chinese,' Thampa interrupted with a strong Chengdu accent, 'because we have lived in Chengdu long enough to learn your language.'

'Oh,' I replied in Chinese, a little surprised. 'Equality means that no person is more powerful or wealthy than another. It means that one person does not put another into debt or force anyone to work for them to pay off the debt. No one should be owned by another. No one should own another. Is it right for a man to work hard all day and not earn enough to feed his family? This is what we call oppression.'

'I understand,' Thampa said, 'but in one way or another everyone depends on others for livelihood, don't you think?'

'Yes, of course,' I said, 'but there is a difference between exploiting others and treating them fairly.'

'That's true,' Thampa agreed.

'Who,' I ventured to ask, 'are the owners in your home village?'

Thampa and Dawa were silent awhile; they looked at each other and then at Thupten.

'We are,' Thampa soon offered. 'We own the land and the herds. Most of the villagers work our land and care for our herds. We give them a share, of course. This is the custom here. We do as others do. But Dawa and I have been thinking about this already. When Thupten became a communist and explained to us how our system oppresses the people, we began to compare ourselves with other landowners and how we treat people in our villages. Compared to many others, we have not been cruel or too demanding.'

Thampa was defensive and Dawa put her hand on his arm to calm him.

'We follow Buddha dharma,' Dawa said to Thampa as much as to me. 'We try not to cause suffering for other people. We do our best to see that everyone in our village is well-fed, that their houses are in good repair and they have what they need. I think they are generally happy with us.'

'That's true, they are,' Thupten replied in Tibetan. He apparently understood Chinese well enough to follow our entire conversation.

'Even so,' Thampa added, 'Thupten has shown us that we are part of a system that keeps people in their place. We want to be good to people because we follow Buddha dharma, but we are inescapably part of the larger social structure.'

'We are in this position by birth,' Dawa added, 'we believe in reincarnation. If you are good in one life, you are born into a favourable position in your next.'

'Yes, I'm sure you are good people,' I affirmed, 'if all were like you, the system would be good for everyone. But I noticed in Shanghai that the wealthy get wealthier while the poor suffer; our traditional systems favour the wealthy, not the poor. I think you understand how hard it is to change a system when the rich do not want to change the way things are. Yet the poor need and want things to change. In China, the necessary changes have come through a violent revolutionary struggle. In my opinion, violence would not be necessary if there are more landowners like yourselves who want to make changes.'

Dawa and Thampa nodded; they seemed sobered by the thought of violent revolution.

'My family grew rich long ago,' Thampa offered, 'our village is in a fertile valley where three rivers come together and two caravan trails merge from the south. We were able to trade, raise crops and keep large herds of yak, sheep, and horses. To manage all of this, we had to have many people help us.'

I thought Thampa was getting defensive again but I was mistaken.

'When Thupten pointed out the truth of our situation to us,' Thampa continued, 'I had a glimmer of hope. You see, we have a daughter who could inherit our property but she's not interested. Neither are our relatives who live in Chengdu, Lhasa, and Kalimpong. We have wondered what to do with our property.'

Thampa silently looked at Dawa, who nodded for him to continue.

'When Yangchen was here, she told us about Jiachen and her commitment to communism. She has inspired us to consider our situation carefully. Yangchen encouraged us to think about giving our land to the villagers, but how can we do it so that it is fair to everyone?'

'You've asked a very good question,' I said, trying to hide my excitement. 'I think I can help you with that. I experienced a few things about forming cooperatives since Jiachen died. What I want to propose is that you give your land and herds to a cooperative.'

'A cooperative?' Thampa asked with interest.

'Yes, a cooperative belongs to all its members, and everyone in the village can belong to it. It's a way of organizing things so the land and herds belong collectively to all the people in the village. You see, all the property will belong to the whole village rather than to individual families.'

'I see,' Thampa seemed genuinely intrigued.

77

'An important place to start,' I suggested, 'would be by gathering all the villagers and asking them how they might organize themselves. You might be surprised what they suggest.'

The look on Thampa's face suggested I was projecting a little too far into the future.

'We will consider this proposal,' Thampa said. 'Even though the rest of the family shows no interest in the property itself, we must ask their permission to donate it to the village. I'm hopeful they will grant our request,' he added.

'Good!' I said with enthusiasm, 'this excites me!'

Thampa looked at Dawa to make sure she was in agreement with him. Her reaction was encouraging.

Thampa had more questions about the details of a cooperative.

'What about return for effort?' Thampa asked. 'What happens if someone doesn't do their share of the work?'

Thampa then proceeded to tell the story of Muni Tsempo, an ancient Tibetan king who, as a devout Buddhist, was horrified by the indifference of the rich toward the poor. His solution to alleviating everyone's suffering was to divide land, animals, and wealth equally among all the people. Unfortunately, his solution did not work. When the poor suddenly got land, animals and money, they started behaving like the rich people and didn't do any work. They got lazy, spent their money, or lost it all in gambling; they were tricked out of their money one way or another by the previously wealthy. Three times, the king tried this redistribution policy but each time the situation got worse; the wealthy got wealthier and the poor got poorer.

'There was so much resistance and objection to the king's program,' Thampa concluded with a look that pleaded for a more feasible plan, 'that the powerful and wealthy finally ended his life by poisoning him.'

'That's a remarkable story,' I said, and took a moment to think about a response. 'The king was very well-intentioned but lacked understanding. I think we will have a better outcome because there has been progress in social science.'

I began to assure him it would be possible to redistribute wealth without the results experienced during Muni Tsempo's time because cooperatives were based on mutual understanding from the beginning. Since everyone would benefit, they would want to participate but, I explained, telling him that it was up to each cooperative to make decisions about issues of non-participation. The infirm and the elderly can participate in their own way, but an able-bodied man or woman who does no work would be hard to tolerate. A sense of shared community responsibility is to be created through education so that antisocial behaviours are prevented. 'So, you're saying I'd better get out in the fields too if I'm to eat!' Thampa laughed heartily. He slapped his rotund belly and said, 'Perhaps, I'll get my youthful shape back again!'

Dawa laughed and patted his belly, too, 'This might finally go!'

'Let me just say this proposal is intriguing,' Thampa said in a jovial mood.

Turning suddenly to Thupten, he said, 'Thupten, I must ask a big favour of you. You are the best person I can think of to visit our relatives in Lhasa and Kalimpong. I know I can trust you to help them understand Wei Ming's proposal.'

'Of course, I'll go,' Thupten replied with enthusiasm. 'I'll tell them this is the best way forward, given the expectation that communism will come to Tibet one way or another.'

'What about your relatives in Chengdu?' I asked.

'I already know how they'll decide,' Thampa stated with a grin. 'Yangchen told me they're no longer interested in the village. The old couple will not return here and the young ones are now more Chinese than Tibetan. Meanwhile, Wei Ming, we will give thought to what you have said.'

Cultural Adjustment

Dawa wanted to adopt me in spite of the fact that Jiachen had not lived long enough to make me her relative. I was tempted to settle into the comfort and seclusion of the governor's compound but, as I told Dawa, I would learn more if I put myself in the midst of the townspeople. I elected to remain at Rabten's tavern, and even made the conscious decision not to look in on Thampa and Dawa unless absolutely necessary.

Once Thupten left a few days later, it really hit me that I was on my own among strangers in a strange culture. As long as I was with either Phuntso or Thupten, I didn't have to think much about how I should conduct myself as far as local customs were concerned. I just followed their lead. Now, I needed to watch for cultural cues and fit in as best as I could.

Daily walks through the streets helped me get a better sense of the town. Several large buildings clustered along the two main streets gave the place an urban feel. Most of the streets were paved with cobblestone or flagstone in an effort to control the ever-present clouds of dust. Behind high walls that lined the streets were grand houses belonging to wealthy merchants and aristocratic officials. On the outskirts were more modest houses, but even these had walls surrounding them.

Each day, I made a point of stopping to talk with the shopkeepers to build my vocabulary and make friends. They were pleased when I told them they were a great help to me. As these relationships developed, I was able to ask more questions and get more detail about their culture, their customs, their families, the kinds of goods available, and where the goods came from. I saw Chinese silks, cottons from India, and luxury goods from Europe.

The town existed in the shadow of the monastery and continued to draw my attention. I wondered what I might find inside the courtyards and temples. My curiosity about the religious side of Tibetan culture grew stronger than my inclination to heed Phuntso's warning about engaging with religious people.

One day, I found myself walking up the hill through the clusters of monks' houses toward the main gate of the temple courtyard. Several young monks appeared as I approached. They greeted me cheerfully and with considerable curiosity. I returned their greetings with a smile and hands placed together in front of me, making a slight bow.

'*Tashi delek,*' I said, 'may I go in to see the temple?'

'Yes, yes, of course,' one of them replied.

'I'm Chuang,' I said, 'I'm living in Lithang now, and wanted to see this place.'

'We've heard about you,' he replied. 'You've come here to teach people about communism, right?'

'That's right!' I said cheerfully and a bit surprised.

Monks were chanting in the main hall of the central temple. I was impressed by the depth and volume of their voices. The guides insisted I take off my shoes before stepping over the high threshold into the temple. Once inside, they immediately prostrated and indicated I should do the same. I felt rather foolish but, not wanting to separate myself too much, went along with it. I got down on my knees and stretched out flat on the ground and lay there for a moment. When I stood up, they smiled approvingly.

I had no idea, of course, what a prostration was all about. Buddhism, I was told by my Christian teachers at school in Shanghai, was a primitive and heathen religion. The extraordinary nature of what I was experiencing here—the incense, the butter lamps, the chanting of men in red robes, the drums and bells, the dark and cold interior dominated by immense statues—seemed to underscore that opinion.

The chanting monks were arranged in several rows to the left and right of a central aisle leading to a throne placed below the main Buddha image. On this throne sat an impressive, elderly monk leading the chant. He held a drum in one hand and a bell in the other. Occasionally, he rang the bell but he kept a steady rhythm going by turning the drum one way, then the other, so the two attached weights struck each side alternatively.

I stood completely transfixed, mesmerized in my effort to comprehend what was going on.

'A special ceremony is underway,' the young monk at my elbow leaned close to whisper, 'Rinpoche is performing the Kalachakra initiation. He's visiting from Dzongsar. It is a rare opportunity for us.'

Not having a clue what he was talking about, my expression betrayed my total ignorance and brought a chuckle from my young tour guide.

'I realize how strange this is for you,' he said kindly. 'Please, stay and listen as long as you like. Even if you do not understand, it is good for you to experience.'

Captivated, every sense inundated, I almost gave in to the hypnotic chanting of men in red robes surrounded by a rainbow of colours flowing from Buddha images, wall paintings, and decorated wooden pillars. I could not identify nor even categorize the feelings I was experiencing. They did not fit with anything I'd ever known.

If this was Buddhism, I found I was not only more in agreement with Phuntso's admonition to stay clear but also with my childhood teachers' opinion that it was darkness and evil. I could understood why Mao called religion 'the opium of the people' and how it was unnecessary in new China. The opulence of the place, an obvious testament to the power of the monastic system over the people, suddenly repulsed me. How hard did the peasantry have to work to support this monastery? How many people felt obligated to make frequent food and cash offerings?

Lest my fascination get the better of me, I decided to leave. I stepped over the threshold, quickly put on my shoes and hurried down the stairs to cross the courtyard. The young monks followed me but I didn't feel like being engaged.

'Excuse me, comrade,' the same young monk called out, 'has anything upset you?'

I ignored him and kept going.

'Comrade Chuang!' he persisted as I reached the massive doorway in the courtyard wall.

I hesitated; I was being rude.

'Please, comrade,' he begged, and I realized he was speaking Chinese. 'Let me answer any questions or concerns you might have,' he added.

'You speak Chinese well,' I said as a compliment when he caught up with me. 'Where did you learn?'

'I'm from Chengdu. My family sent me here to become a monk.'

'From Chengdu? But you're Tibetan?'

'Yes, I'm originally from Batang. My name is Nima.'

'Nima,' I said with a polite nod.

'You left in such a hurry, I was worried something had displeased you.'

'I guess I'm overwhelmed. I've never been inside a temple like this before. Perhaps I don't know enough to find it helpful.'

'It would be my pleasure to answer your questions, if I may.'

'No,' I responded with determination, 'I'll need to think about this experience before I can formulate questions. Another time, perhaps.'

'I understand,' Nima replied, 'Please do come again.'

I turned and hurried through the streets of monks' houses, and out onto the hillside above the town. I noticed the group of young boys who had followed me at a distance when I left town. They had waited for me on the hillside and were eager to talk to me.

'Where are you from?' the boldest among them called out as I approached.

'Shanghai,' I replied, 'have you heard of it?'

'No,' the boy replied.

I kept walking toward town and they jumped up to accompany me.

'It's in China, of course,' another retorted.

'That's right. On the east coast of China where the Yangtze flows into the ocean,' I pointed to the river meandering across the grassland. 'Did you know that your river, the Lithang, joins the Yangtze?'

The boys looked toward the river, then back to me, disbelieving.

'I come from the other end of the same river,' I said, to develop the idea that we shared something in common.

The ice broken, they asked many questions. I think I was able to help them understand how big China was, and that our standard of life was changing for the better in most of China. I don't know if they really comprehended but I hoped it would introduce them to new ideas and give them something to imagine for themselves.

I saw the young boys several times over the next few days. They encouraged me to go with them to the hillside below the monastery several times. It was their favourite thing to do in the late afternoons and I understood why; we could see the entire town, the vast grasslands beyond. It was a great place to think expansively. I took the opportunity to sing them a few inspirational communist songs, which they seemed to enjoy even though they didn't understand Chinese.

I decided I would translate these songs into Tibetan as soon as my command of the language improved. These young boys, most of them under 14, became my language teachers, too, and I think, from the way they doted on me, they hero-worshipped me.

One evening after I'd been out walking with 'my boys', I sat in my usual seat in the tavern drinking a bowl of *chang*. After a few minutes, a group of men moved from their table to mine. They were all very tall, muscular, and scruffy. Their presence, and their smell, at my table was overpowering. Each of them had a short sword handily stuffed into the bands of cloth used as a waist belt. At any moment, I imagined, one of them could slide out his sword to gut me if they found me disagreeable. It would be in my best interest to remain agreeable!

The tallest and most imposing, clearly their leader, introduced himself as Lobsang. He proudly informed me that he and his friends were from Chengtreng, the high wilderness to the south. I had heard of the area; it was notorious for bandits and outlaws. I tried not to show concern for my well-being nor to be too curious about their interest in me.

At first Lobsang was friendly, but gradually, the tone of his observations and questions focused more and more on the fact that I was Chinese.

'Why are you here, Chinaman?' Lobsang finally blurted out, his right hand resting on the hilt of his sword.

'I'm here to help you,' I replied, knowing this response would bewilder rather than satisfy him.

'What help can you give us,' he leaned further toward me and spat out, '*Gyame*?'—a term I was to hear often thereafter. Phuntso had warned me to expect to be called derogatory terms such as this. '*Gyame*' meant 'outsider' or, more to the point, 'enemy of Dharma', someone unfamiliar with their way of life and ignorant of their religion; more specifically 'Chinese'.

'Yes, I'm an outsider who knows nothing about your Dharma,' I agreed calmly, 'but that does not make me your enemy nor an evil person.'

'You're a communist,' another man volunteered when it was clear I wasn't getting rattled by this approach.

'That's right, too, but perhaps I can help you understand what a communist is before you leap to conclusions. You might appreciate what communism is all about.' I surprised myself with the range of my vocabulary and level of fluency. I felt energized.

87

'You came with those Red soldiers and I saw you with that Batang-pa, Phuntso. He's one of them Reds, too,' the same man, probably Lobsang's right-hand man, volunteered.

'That's right, I was with Phuntso-la.'

'Humph,' Lobsang grunted. In the warmth of the tavern, Lobsang's chest and right arm were bare. His body odour, his breath, his wild, long hair braided with red tassels and tied round his head—he was a Chinese child's worst nightmare: the barbarian highlander!

'Listen,' Lobsang said menacingly, his hand gripping the sword hilt tighter, 'we don't like you being here and we will be watching you.'

'Why don't you let me explain why I'm here?' I gambled that this was as good a time as any to make an inroad.

'I don't think that's necessary,' came a response in perfect Chinese from a well-dressed young Tibetan at another table. 'Most people already know you're here to introduce communist ideas and help the new Chinese government establish authority here so reforms can be implemented. I've explained this to them and they don't like the idea much,' he added.

The man got up, bowl of *chang* in hand, and came to my table. The others, reluctantly but deferentially, made room so he could sit down on the cushion-covered bench next to me.

'I'm Tsering Tenzin,' he continued in Chinese, ignoring the Tibetans around us. 'I live in Chengdu but I come back here occasionally. You may have heard of Nawang, my father. He will replace Lord Andrutsang as district administrator. Father is a Party member. I've been trying to tell these backward nomads that things are changing, but they don't want to hear of it.'

My impression of Tenzin was immediately mixed. I felt relieved that he'd come to my rescue, so to speak, but his haughty attitude toward the nomads didn't sit well. If he was a comrade, as he implied, he should dispense with his decidedly arrogant attitude.

'Yes, I've heard of your father,' I said in Chinese, trying not to make my smile seem false, 'I'm intrigued to hear how your father became a Party member at a time when it is clearly unpopular among your fellow countrymen. What about you? Are you a Party member?'

'Not yet,' he replied, 'but hopefully I will be soon. At school in Chengdu, several of my Tibetan classmates and I became enthusiastic supporters of communism. You may have heard of Phuntso Wangyal?'

'Yes, I came here with him.'

'Really, he was here?' Tenzin was genuinely surprised to realize he'd missed meeting him, 'when?'

'He came through with the PLA. They left several days ago.'

'Oh, bad timing. After the horse racing, I went with friends to their village. I'm sorry I missed him.'

'How do you know Phuntso?' I asked, making an effort to carry on a conversation.

'He came to our school years ago, and encouraged us to bring communism to our people.'

'That's interesting,' I said. I wanted to know why Phuntso and Thupten had not mentioned this young man. 'Do you know Thupten? He's also a comrade and very well-acquainted with Phuntso.'

'Yes, I know the man. He's the governor's lackey,' he informed me matter-of-factly.

Growing disgusted with Tenzin's attitude, I switched to Tibetan and glanced at the other men around the table. They were clearly put off by our private conversation.

'What is your plan?' I asked, looking at Tenzin. I think the question came across as I intended; I wanted to know how committed he really was to positive social change.

'My plan?' he responded in Tibetan. I'd tricked him into doing so. 'Like my father, I will take my orders from the Party.'

'I see,' I replied without emotion. I was disappointed. By his response, I knew immediately that he was without vision of his own; a follower without personal revolutionary initiative.

I looked around the group and decided to lay my cards on the table. 'I am here to demonstrate what the communist way of life can be. If I am successful, it will be the beginning of a purely Tibetan kind of revolution.'

No one volunteered a response or shut me up so I continued. 'I will begin by forming a cooperative as a model. Ownership of all the fields of a village and all the herds out on the grasslands will transfer from individual families to a cooperative. Every member of the cooperative benefits and everyone works to make life good for all. Do you understand this idea?'

They all, including Tenzin, stared at me in silence.

'What I'd like,' I summarized, 'is the opportunity to turn a village or a few nomadic clans into a cooperative.'

I explained that members of the cooperative would decide what is produced and how goods are equitably distributed among all the families of the cooperative; that members would decide how to trade excess produce and how to use that income to make improvements to their way of life. For example, hiring someone to teach the children to read and write or to buy a truck to take produce to the market.

'We don't need your ideas,' Lobsang replied confidently, 'we have survived in these mountains for thousands of years and we have what we need. We prosper in our own way. There are no landowners telling us what to do. Your cooperative might be fine for farmers but not for us. We own our herds and manage everything ourselves.'

'Yes, I'm sure you do,' I had to agree, 'however, the world is changing. Your way of life will be hard to maintain.'

'No, what is changing is people like you coming here. First a few, then more and more of you will crowd into our valleys, eat up our food and steal our resources.'

'Very true,' I agreed, 'the outside world will arrive sooner than you think.'

'We like our mountains and valleys. We like our way of life and,' he sat up straighter and continued proudly, 'we will defend it!'

That being said, he stood up. His companions also rose and, with a lot of noise, they left the tavern.

Tenzin and I sat uneasily beside each other at the table covered with emptied drinking bowls. I did not look at him and did not feel like pursuing a conversation. I wanted to think about what had just happened; I'd survived an interrogation by a group of nomads who distrusted Tenzin as much as they distrusted me!

'Pay no attention to them,' Tenzin said dismissively, 'they can be bought.'

I must have looked shocked because, realizing what he'd said, Tenzin blurted, 'I mean they are not as tough as they think. You saw how they deferred to me once I joined your table. They know their place.'

That sounded worse!

I gave Tenzin a cold, hard stare as I tried to fathom how this young man could become a genuine Party member.

Go Home, Gyame

My language skills kept improving. Rabten took particular interest in extending my vocabulary and fluency. I could carry on conversations in the tavern, on the streets, and frequently in people's homes as their guest. My awareness of the culture broadened and the more I grew to appreciate it, the more I also saw its underside.

Women, especially the younger ones, openly flirted with me. Standing together in colourful, graceful groups, they would watch me when I walked past. Sometimes they tried to detain me in a narrow street. It was clear they found me intriguing as an outsider. I must admit that I found several of them physically attractive, but their crude directness put me off.

'Hi there, Chinaman,' a bold one would say, 'I hear you can't get it up in our thin air!'

The girls would double over with laughter.

Used to replying honestly when people spoke to me, I lost my presence of mind when these young women crossed the boundary of decency. I couldn't think of humorous, light-hearted responses to that sort of teasing. So I did my best to ignore it and walk away. They soon gave up trying to evoke a response.

When I encountered any of these young women on their own, they were just as flirtatious and open about their desire to spend private time with me. This, of course, was flattering, especially if I found the young woman attractive. It was a challenge to excuse myself and maintain my dignity. Thankfully, none of them thrust themselves on me nor disturbed me in my room at the tavern. I didn't need an encounter of this sort to jeopardize my mission.

I came across instances where a merchant or an aristocrat was administering corporal punishment to a man and woman in his employ. The usual method was a whipping, using the same whip they used on caravan animals. It seemed a horribly cruel culture with penalties far out of proportion to the crimes. Punishments included cutting off a hand or a foot, putting out one or both eyes, disfiguring the face by cutting off the nose, pouring hot oil over the head, or locking both hands and head in a heavy wooden yoke across the shoulders. Most of these crimes were theft against the wealthy. But being Buddhists, they did not have capital punishment.

What disturbed me most was the way people accepted their lot. Why did they play the role of victim? What was it in their worldview that prompted them to surrender their right to fair treatment? Surely the underclass wanted to escape this oppression.

As a month turned to two and three, attitudes toward me became less friendly. I thought I was on my way to becoming one of them, a Kham-pa, but the shopkeepers who were my language resources became increasingly disinterested. Conversations, if I could have one, centred more and more on my presence in Lithang. With good reason, they wanted to know why I stayed behind when hundreds of Chinese soldiers had continued to Batang. Had I become sick? Was I too exhausted to continue? Why was I not in the same uniform as the soldiers? Was I returning to China soon?

There were hard stares, whisperings and snickers from doorways and upper floor windows when I walked through the streets. The same boys who had been so curious and helpful in my first few weeks had now begun to watch me from a distance.

'Go home, *gyame*!' they began to taunt, 'we don't want your commie ideas poisoning our air and water!'

Daily, the undercurrent of distrust and revulsion toward me grew. It was as if the community as a whole had decided to make me the target of their long-ingrained distrust, if not hatred, of the Chinese.

I'd been warned. Comrade Li had said this would happen. Several others in Chengdu were more scathing. They said the Khampas were a particularly volatile race of barbarians, not to be trusted.

Feeling ostracized, I eventually went to see Dawa and Thampa. They were happy to see me, but Thampa was preoccupied. He didn't tell me, but I presumed there were unpleasant issues regarding the transfer of authority to Nawang, who was due to arrive soon. Dawa, however, was sweet and fed me well. They hadn't received any news from Yangchen nor did they know how Thupten's quest was going. Dawa said she had heard rumours that I was having difficulties with the townspeople and, again, suggested I stay with her.

'It is very tempting, Dawa-la,' I replied, 'but I must decline again. I need to show that I can be strong.'

'You are a wise and brave young man,' Thampa said with a sigh, 'and you are right, the people are testing you. If you stay and withstand their worst, they will eventually accept you.'

Encouraged, I returned to the tavern that evening to find Tenzin waiting to see me. He gave no explanation for his long absence, but announced he was going to Dartsendo to arrange a caravan for his father's return.

I felt like engaging Tenzin to see where he stood in regard to Phuntso's idea of a home-grown Tibetan revolution.

'Comrade Tenzin,' I began, 'I've seen how fiercely independent the people here are. They are not only hostile and disrespectful of us Chinese but they don't like Lhasa very much either, because the taxes they pay in either direction have never materialized in any direct improvement of their lives. There is no infrastructure, no public education, no clinics, and no services of any kind.'

'Yes, comrade,' Tenzin responded awkwardly, 'but that will change soon. The Party will begin providing these things and the people will be grateful, I'm sure.'

'That very well may be,' I countered, 'but I'm beginning to wonder about the presence of the PLA in such large numbers. The people see them as a threat; that they are headed to Lhasa to occupy and establish Party rule.'

'No, that can't be. They are building roads, helping to implement policy.'

'Perhaps,' I said. 'Did Comrade Phuntso ever tell you about his hopes for Tibet? I'm sure he did when he visited your school.'

'Yes, he talked about bringing communism to Tibet.'

'Of course; but he is all for a home-grown brand that will leave Tibet an independent and equal partner in the Worldwide Brotherhood of Communist Nations. What do you think of that?'

When Tenzin remained silent, I had to assume he'd not given it much thought.

'Rabten,' I asked after Tenzin left the tavern, 'what do you think of that young man?'

'Tenzin?' Rabten responded quickly, 'he's been avoiding you. I would have thought he'd want to be your friend since he says he's a communist like you.'

'Yes, that occurred to me, too. Hopefully his father will encourage him to be a better communist.'

'That would be expected,' Rabten agreed, 'but doubtful.'

'What do you mean?'

'Nawang is an opportunist, if you know what I mean. He recognized the shifting of power before the rest of us and took advantage of it. He did his best to manoeuvre himself into his present position of authority by pleasing Party leaders in Chengdu.'

'People like that are useful for a while, but I'm sure Party leadership will see through them sooner or later,' I responded.

'Hopefully.'

Rabten was a shrewd observer of human character. I appreciated his candour. He was often my sounding board and consultant on a variety of topics. We had developed a relationship I could rely on, a true friendship. He, along with several others, were of the opinion that the PLA was waiting for orders to move toward Lhasa.

And then I heard the news!

The People's Liberation Army had crossed into Tibet proper at Chamdo, attacked the Tibetan Army and claimed victory.

I felt betrayed.

The peaceful revolution I'd hoped for seemed out of reach. The aggression of the PLA was uncalled for. Why had they attacked the tiny Tibetan Army?

As the news spread, my presence in Lithang was even more suspect. People avoided me; they would not talk to me.

I began to stay in my room at the tavern. Daily, I sank deeper into despair. I grew sick of my room, sick of living in the tavern. Rabten's servants treated me like an outcast. Smells from the kitchen assaulted me. I stopped going to the window in my room because I was nauseated by the human faeces, rotten food, and dirty rags I saw discarded in the street below.

The only time I came out of my room was when the man shackled to a heavy yoke came to the tavern on his daily visit. Since it was impossible for his hands to reach his face, I had been making it a point to help him. I fed him *tsampa* and helped him drink tea or even some *chang*. I would also take a jug of water and wash him. He was a thief, he told me, and had to endure the wooden yoke for a year.

My kindness to him was ridiculed by passers-by. Still, I persisted. But as I grew more and more alienated, I caught myself feeling the thief deserved his lot in life.

This thought shocked me.

'Rabten,' I confessed one day, 'I am beginning to hate it here. The people dislike me and I am beginning to dislike them. I came here to show people a better way of life yet my own life is falling apart. What is happening to me?'

'Chuang-la,' Rabten said sympathetically, 'we all have good days and bad days. Don't lose heart. You'll find your place if you persevere.'

That afternoon, at Rabten's suggestion, I attempted to shake my gloom with a brisk walk in the countryside. I was

97

grateful that despite the community's growing hostility toward me, I could count on Rabten's support. The walk helped clear my head and I returned to the tavern with a good appetite. I asked for a bowl of *thukpa*, a soup with meat and vegetables and a plate of *momo*, potstickers. A short time later, the cook delivered the soup with an angry grunt. I had a hard time forcing it down; the meat was rancid, the vegetables old and mouldy. On the verge of vomiting, I rushed outside. Passing through the curtain hanging in the doorway, I bumped into a tall and powerfully-built nomad coming in. I glanced up and saw his red face and eyes; he was very drunk. He shouted as I pushed past him to the street.

'Watch where you're going, *gyame!*' he blurted with a slur. I heard him pull his sword from its sheath and turned in time to see it come down toward my neck. Instinctively, I deflected the sword by catching hold of his arm and, using his own momentum, forced him past me. He sprawled to the ground in an undignified heap.

Exclamations of surprise were expressed by several onlookers, his nomad friends included. My attacker gave me a look that immediately reminded me that embarrassing a fierce Khampa warrior was a dangerous thing to do! I had made a big mistake!

He got to his feet, retrieved his sword and came at me again. This time, he attempted to thrust the sword into my belly. Once again, my reaction was swift. The proud warrior found himself rushing past me and smashing into the stone wall of the tavern. Now he was truly enraged, and fumbled in the folds of his *chuba* to retrieve a pistol. Keeping his distance, he aimed at my chest.

'Enough!' roared an authoritative voice, 'Dorje, put it away!' I recognized Lobsang as he stepped through the crowd to stand between me and my assailant. Dorje lowered his weapon but continued to glower at me. I recognized him now. He was with Lobsang when we'd met during my first weeks in Lithang.

'So you are still here,' Lobsang said as he turned to me. It was an accusation. He said it as if the mere fact of my presence had caused the incident and summarized how the entire country—from these people in the street to the nomads living in the mountains and grasslands—felt about me. My assailant was merely acting on the unconscious desire of every Khampa to be rid of me and my kind.

At that moment, I agreed with him. I should not be here! This was their world. I had no right to be here. Try as I might, I would never enter it, never see life as they do. What did I think I was doing by coming here? They didn't want a revolution. They didn't want social or economic change. How could I have thought I could tell them anything that would change their minds? And, now, did I really want to?

'You remember me, I see,' Lobsang said. Everyone's eyes were on him, waiting to see how he would handle me. Though he was not a welcome visitor among the townspeople, I sensed they were on his side against me.

'Yes, of course, I remember you,' I recalled the threat he had delivered. I remained wary while remembering to maintain self-confidence in every situation—something Master Tashi insisted on.

'That was impressive,' Lobsang said. 'What you did to Dorje, I mean. He's a good fighter but you made a fool of him.'

99

I glanced at Dorje and said to him, 'I didn't mean to push you out the door. I was rushing out because I was feeling ill. I needed fresh air.'

Dorje continued to glower but put his pistol and sword away. Lobsang took Dorje by the arm and led him into the tavern. The crowd dispersed quickly but I noticed my former gang of young boys gaping silently with renewed awe.

Not wanting to go into the tavern with Lobsang's gang inside, I began wandering the streets, thinking over what had just happened and feeling isolated, unwanted. Lobsang might have been impressed with my ability to defend myself, but it didn't change his attitude toward me. I wasn't wanted here!

I had to acknowledge, though, that it took courage to face a man insulted enough to want to shoot me. As a result, my mood brightened enough for me to chuckle over the sight of Dorje sprawled in the street and then smashing into the wall. It quickly sobered me, though, to realize how lucky I'd been. What if Lobsang hadn't intervened and Dorje had pulled the trigger? Or all of Dorje's friends had turned on me? I would have been finished!

Not knowing where to go; just wanting to get as far away from the tavern as I could, I hurried down the street, turned a corner and collided with Thupten.

'Thupten!'

I was so happy to see him, I grabbed him in a bear hug.

'Comrade Chuang!' Thupten gasped in my grip.

'You're back!' I stated the obvious, 'when did you arrive?'

'Just now! First thing I heard was about your fight at the tavern. Are you alright?'

'I'm fine, it was nothing,' I said modestly, 'I accidentally bumped into a drunken nomad in the doorway. He got angry and pulled his sword on me.'

'I hear you defended yourself with your bare hands. The young eye witness was quite impressed!'

'An instinctive response,' I replied simply. 'Something I learned as a boy, it's called jujutsu. I didn't realize how useful it could be.'

'I'm glad you're okay. How are you otherwise?' Thupten's penetrating eyes searched mine, and he quickly discovered my malaise. 'You lack your usual enthusiasm.'

I didn't speak. He took me by the arm and led me up the street. The gang of boys, still watching me, followed at a distance.

'Let's go see Dawa-la and Thampa-la,' he urged, 'I have news for them.'

I was grateful for Thupten's concern and company.

Key to Understanding

When Thupten and I showed up at her door, Dawa apologized for the mess; they were packing to move to Gyawa, their home village. In another week, Nawang would arrive from Chengdu and Thampa wanted to be out of the way.

Despite being stressed, Dawa was eager, of course, to hear Thupten's news. While we enjoyed tea and refreshments, Thampa and Dawa listened solemnly as Thupten described his visits with each of their relatives in Lhasa. These relatives had left Lithang a generation or more ago, and said they had no claim on the property in Gyawa; they had given no directives and there were no objections to getting rid of it.

When the conversation turned toward Kalimpong, Dawa, as if bursting to ask, blurted, 'Any news of Dechen?'

'Yangchen says your daughter is away and doing well. She didn't say more than that.'

Both Dawa and Thampa were crestfallen. I could see the emptiness this news caused them.

Thupten continued to relate how Yangchen was delighted to hear I was in Lithang. Her brother, Palden Rinpoche, listened to details of my proposal while Yangchen beamed with enthusiasm. After several days of discussion, the Rinpoche and Yangchen both sent their blessings to Thampa and Dawa with their encouragement to ask me to establish a cooperative in Gyawa.

Thampa and Dawa insisted I go with them to Gyawa. They wanted to follow my advice and ask the villagers what they thought of the idea of forming a cooperative. Saying they would be leaving in three days, they bid us good day and resumed their packing.

Greatly excited, I returned with Thupten to the tavern where Thupten, Rabten and I, over bowls of *chang*, began a lengthy conversation.

'Understanding is the key,' I was saying. 'If I can't understand your culture I won't be much help, will I? I need to think like you do.'

'I think you've come a long way, Chuang-la,' Thupten observed. 'You've been here over four months and mastered our language. You have a good grasp of our way of life but the only area you don't understand yet is our religion. Perhaps you'll understand that one day, too.'

'Religion?' Rabten remarked scathingly, 'why should he try to understand that?'

'Well, yes, I agree with Thupten,' I interjected, 'I need to understand why it has such a huge influence on all that you do.'

'That's right,' Thupten affirmed.

'I hope a deeper understanding will provide the wisdom I'll need to suggest a way forward for all of us.'

Both Thupten and Rabten nodded their heads slowly.

'That's what I appreciate so much about you,' Thupten said, 'I've known you for such a short time but I already see that you are a wise person.'

'No, I'm still struggling,' I said, 'but with your help I'm finding my way out of discouragement and despair.'

Rabten and Thupten nodded again sympathetically.

103

'I'd like to be able to generate enthusiasm for an orderly, peaceful revolution,' I continued. 'We cannot thrive unless we can cooperate. It is the good and the kind-hearted who, in the long run, will create a world in which we will want to live. The strong, the ruthless, and the competitive are those who dominate and oppress others. We don't want a society based on separation and fear.'

Rabten and Thupten remained silent, wanting to hear more. I took a more personal approach.

'What has distressed me the most here,' I observed, 'is the level of verbal and, too often, physical abuse by landlords and aristocrats.'

'It's true,' Rabten observed sheepishly, 'but not all of us are like that. I treat the people working for me more like equals, or even family, rather than servants or slaves. I give them a place to sleep and food to eat for their work. By the way, I found out what my cook served you that made you sick. I sent that cook away. The assistant has taken over now.'

'Her food was always tastier,' I acknowledged with a chuckle.

'I'll let her know,' Rabten responded.

'I was not being critical of you,' I said to Rabten. 'I know how you treat people, like family.'

'But it's true what you say about the abusive behaviour of the upper classes generally,' Thupten affirmed. 'They hold their place in society by right of birth, and own vast holdings of land.'

Rabten was quick to join in and said, 'They control the government. They collect the taxes and use the income to manage their huge estates. They travel to Lhasa, to India, to China and beyond. It is not unusual for aristocratic, or even merchant family members, to be educated abroad and to know what goes on in the world.'

'Many aristocrats,' Thupten agreed, 'when exposed to ideas that are foreign to most people in Kham, do little to change things for the well-being of people here. They see no reason to change the status quo. They have it good, so why introduce ideas, services, and infrastructures that will upset things?'

'Nawang and his son Tenzin are examples of this,' Rabten agreed. 'They have been exposed to communism, but unlike you, are disinterested in positive social change.'

'That's consistent with what Comrade Li told me, and with my own observations,' I said, 'modernizing means change and, of course, that will upset the balance. The wealthy want to hold on to their wealth; they want to control the changes so they can maintain their positions of privilege. They are the class that opposes communism most.'

'It is to Thampa-la's credit,' Thupten observed, 'that he doesn't want to oppose communism. He is in favour of change if it will bring a better way of life for everyone.'

'Now,' I pressed in another direction, 'the nomads. I have learned that they exist outside the system of the villages and towns. They are a completely different breed of people. Am I right?'

'Yes,' Rabten agreed. 'Their dress, their behaviour, everything about them speaks of independence, self-reliance, and a natural existence close to the elements. Whenever groups of nomads wander around our streets, we townspeople get out of their way or we hide inside our walls and houses. And like the cowards we are, we shout abuses at them from the safety of our homes!'

105

Thupten had a good laugh.

'The main difference between nomads and townspeople or villagers is housing. Nomads don't care for permanent dwellings; they prefer tents so they can move with their herds. They follow the cycle of seasons and move to high pastures in the summer and sheltered valleys in the winter,' Thupten said more seriously, adding, 'they have regular places they go to but no permanent structures. They are hardy and self-reliant. They live off their herds; they hunt and gather food in the mountains. They live by an ancient code dictated by the environment. This puts them in conflict with the values of villagers, townspeople and traders.'

'For example, if a caravan passes through their territory, they "gather" what is needed from the passing caravans by demanding payment for the right to pass. They consider this acceptable behaviour. Of course, the caravans don't really appreciate this, and arm themselves for protection. Fighting is often inevitable, but the scale of violence is usually checked by Buddhism.'

'Nomads are highly religious people,' Rabten added, 'more so than townspeople.'

'That's right,' Thupten continued, 'nomadic raiders seldom inflict injury or cause death. Traders and travellers, however, see the situation differently; to prevent extortion and robbery, armed patrolmen use deadly force. This naturally creates bad blood between townspeople who own caravans and the nomads whose territory they must traverse.'

'That's helpful to understand,' I noted.

Rabten explained how some nomadic families' wealth far surpasses that of the landed aristocracy. How vast herds brought them unimaginable wealth, power, and prestige.

'You could say Lobsang is the king of Chengtreng,' Rabten observed, 'he and others like him have no need for civil authority.'

Thupten and Rabten helped me understand how government officials knew better than to interfere with these rugged and independent tribal kingdoms. If they tried to force them to pay taxes, it would be easy enough for someone like Lobsang to raise an army of warriors and make the official regret the demand. But these nomadic kings rarely become marauding warlords.

'They are religious people beholden to the monks,' Rabten added. 'The monks are the only group in Tibetan society who manage to keep the nomads in check by reminding them of the Buddhist principle of non-violence.'

'It amazes me,' I said, 'to see nomads prostrating as they go through town on their way up to the monastery and, reaching it, circle it many times before entering the courtyard.'

'True,' Rabten noted, 'some travel for days in this fashion from the high grasslands. Some go on pilgrimage all the way to Lhasa and even farther west to the sacred mountain called Gang Rinpoche, or Mount Kailash, repeating "*Om mani peme hum*" the whole way.'

'What does "*Om mani peme hum*" mean?' I wanted to know.

'You'll have to ask Palden Rinpoche, Yangchen's brother,' Thupten said.

'Is Palden Rinpoche the expert Dawa suggested I ask about Buddha dharma?'

Connections to Jiachen were arising again; she had a grand uncle who was a learned spiritual teacher, someone Dawa suggested I talk to about religion.

'When can I meet this Palden Rinpoche?' I asked.

'He likes to keep his movements to himself,' Thupten said, 'so I don't know if or when he'll come back here.'

I looked out the tavern window. The afternoon sun still warmed the street below. An elderly woman sat on the steps of the building across the street, spinning a prayer wheel and chanting what I assumed to be '*Om mani peme hum*'. In her left hand, she held a string of beads with which she kept track of her repetitions.

Om mani peme hum
Om mani peme hum
Om mani peme hum

It seemed a superstitious and pointless practice to me; a waste of time. Time that could be spent more productively!

'This third group,' I said coming out of my reverie, 'the monks and lamas in the monasteries, how can they afford to live in such large and ornately decorated buildings filled with expensive idols? There seems to be plenty of wealth there, too.'

'Like the aristocrats,' Thupten stated sarcastically, 'through usury and holding large tracts of land and vast herds. One way or the other, they accumulated property, and coerced people into tilling the soil and herding their animals to pay back loans.' After a pause, he continued, 'They also get paid in kind or in cash for religious services at important life-stage rituals such as births, weddings, funerals or to bless the ill and pray for good fortune. The lamas travel around the countryside to perform these services. Offerings to the monks and lamas are considered to bring great spiritual merit, so the people are eager to do it.'

'What makes someone want to be a monk or a nun?' I asked.

'It is the custom,' Thupten offered. He was not as caustic as Rabten about religion. 'Every family sends at least one son or, less frequently, a daughter to join a monastery or nunnery. The reasons vary from family to family. Sometimes, a child will join against the family's wishes. Other times, a child is forced against his or her will. Sometimes a child is taken from a family by a monastery against the child's and family's will. This happened to my youngest brother. I see him now and then. He lives up there in the monastery, and is quite happy now.'

'I understand that the abbot of Lithang Monastery,' I said, 'is a powerful political figure as well as a spiritual leader.'

'Powerful politically, yes,' Rabten agreed, 'but I'm not so sure he's all that interested in the spiritual. What I know is that here in Lithang, he has had direct influence over all civil decisions. Lord Andrutsang has always been shrewd enough to bow to his authority. It would be wise for the Communist Party in Chengdu to at least acknowledge his authority. Hundreds of Gelugpa monasteries all over Kham are under the Khenpo's control.'

'Gelugpa,' I said, 'what is that?'

'A branch or school of Tibetan Buddhism,' Thupten explained. 'There are several others, the Nyingma, the Kagyu, and the Sakya. Each has its own traditions and teachings based on philosophical leanings, but the Gelugpa is the largest. The Dalai Lama belongs to this tradition. The main reason Lithang is an important place is because three Dalai Lamas out of 14 have come from this area. One of them, the seventh, built this monastery.'

'The shed he was born in is just down the street,' Rabten added.

'I've seen it,' I said. 'A very humble, dark hovel. Hundreds of years old, I was proudly told by a nomad paying homage at the place.'

I was beginning to see how the monasteries were able to influence all levels of society. At the very top was the Dalai Lama, who held both secular and spiritual authority over every Tibetan. The secular administration in Lithang was thus beholden to Kunchen, the *Khenpo* of our monastery, the Dalai Lama's representative.

Despite Phuntso's warning to stay away from religion, I was beginning to guess that it might be the clergy who were the key to social change in Tibet! Change would never happen unless the religious institutions also wanted social change. They alone were in a position to influence the nomads and, perhaps, even the aristocracy. Revolution would have to be supported—no, promoted by the clergy! This was far too much to ask. Communism and religion were worlds apart.

I might as well ask a yak to be a horse!

Moving to Gyawa

In high spirits a few days later, I rode out of town on my chestnut mare with Thampa, Dawa, Thupten and a caravan headed south to Gyawa, the Andrutsang ancestral village. The fresh air, new landscapes, and enthusiastic companions made it easy to be optimistic. I would meet this new challenge with confident and cheerful energy.

'This is a dream come true!' I exclaimed to my riding companions. 'I can hardly believe how things have fallen into place. First, meeting Phuntso in Chengdu, then finding you three in Lithang. How lucky!'

'Don't forget Yangchen,' Dawa reminded me.

'Of course,' I acknowledged. And Jiachen! I said to myself.

Around noon, we crossed a low pass beside a rocky butte famous for a small cave where the great Buddhist teacher, Padmasambhava, or 'Guru Rinpoche', is said to have spent time in retreat. Dawa wanted us to stop and make an offering at the shrine. I watched with great interest. It felt as right to venerate the ancient teacher as it did to stop and enjoy the expansive vista from the pass. I took the *lungta* offered to me and tossed them into the sky with everyone else.

'*Lha Gyalo! Lha Gyalo! Lha Gyalo!*' we shouted as the *lungta* glittered in the sunlight overhead.

Saddle-sore and weary, we arrived at Gyawa village in the late afternoon. The trail emerged from the forest among barley fields in a wide valley. Villagers came out to greet Thampa and Dawa. They bowed and offered all of us silk *khata*. Thupten was very happy to be reunited with his family; his wife Pema and two young children offered me *khata*, too, and graciously invited me to stay with them.

Thupten and Pema's house was similar to houses I'd visited in Lithang, smaller and less decorated though. It was three stories-high; the ground floor stored tools, saddles, and harnesses, and had animal stalls used during the winter. The next floor, up a steep wooden staircase, was living quarters for the family. The main room was the kitchen with comfortable seating on carpets and cushions near the hearth, where the family spent most of its time. It was the centre of conversations, eating, daily chores, and even sleeping. Two other rooms were on this floor; one for guests and storage, the other was always used as a shrine for daily offerings to the Buddha. Several *thanka*s decorated the walls. The top floor had one small room above the stairwell, which Pema said would be mine. The flat rooftop surrounding the room was a nice open space for enjoying the sun while doing chores on warmer days. Their house, like every other, was surrounded by a high stone wall that provided a courtyard for many activities as well as sheltering animals.

Village houses were grouped together, surrounded by fields. Yaks and horses grazed on slopes above the village or near the river. Boys or young women watched the animals. Young children were free to play, the older ones watching over them.

The day after we arrived, Thampa called a town meeting to formally introduce me.

'My name is Chuang Wei Ming,' I began, 'I am from Shanghai in China. It's far away from here but the water in this stream flows into the Lithang River, which flows into the Yangtze, or the 'Dri Chu' as you call it. So you see, I grew up by the same river as you.'

People were politely attentive and interested in my simple geography lesson. I felt encouraged.

'I guess you've already heard about me. You may even have heard the rumour that I defeated a Chengtreng warrior with my bare hands. Young boys in Lithang think I have supernatural powers!'

I paused and looked at Thupten, who was chuckling.

'Well, sadly I don't have any magical powers. It would be nice to have them, of course. I was lucky because my attacker was very drunk and slow. It was easy to avoid his sword.'

'That's not exactly true,' Thupten spoke up. 'He does have some impressive skills. Being a modest man, he doesn't like to boast.'

'What I came here to do is to help you find ways to make your lives better. If you agree, I will live here with you. But beware, I ask lots of questions. I hope you will not be angry with me if I ask too many.'

Now I had their attention. Humour, especially at my own expense, was a tested way to gain interest and trust. I had prepared for this moment by thinking up a story that echoed what I knew of Gautama Buddha as a young man. I hoped it would capture their imagination while introducing some socialist ideas.

I began telling the story...

There was once a king, who was showing the marvels of his vast kingdom to his beautiful young queen. They travelled in great comfort on the back of an elephant all over their

113

kingdom. Every day, they journeyed a few miles and set up camp near a village or town, where their subjects welcomed them with a feast and entertained them at night with joyous singing and dancing. The queen was delighted and, of course, deeply in love with her king.

One day as they passed through a village, the queen saw a very thin woman begging. 'What is the matter with that woman?' she asked as she pointed, 'she looks so thin and tired.'

'She's hungry and she's asking for food,' the king tried to explain, but the queen did not know how people could be hungry and so skinny. The next day, she saw a man on his hands and knees beside the road, vomiting. 'What is that man doing?' the queen asked the king.'

'The man is ill,' the king said.

That night, the joyful entertainment did not interest the queen. She was thinking about what she had seen.

'The next day they passed a field where people were tilling the soil. A big man was shouting and whipping them when they stopped to rest.

'Those people,' the queen asked indignantly, 'what are they doing?'

'They're working,' the king said. 'They work to grow food. The man with the whip is making the people work harder.'

A great sadness came over the queen and did not leave her.

'What is the matter, my dear?' the king asked his beloved queen once they returned to their palace and her mood had not changed.

'Things are not right in our kingdom,' she said. 'All our people should be happy. Everyone should have enough food to

114

eat, they should not be sick, and they should not be beaten by cruel men to make them work harder. I can't be happy again until these things stop happening.'

As you can imagine, the king was in a terrible situation. How could he be happy if his queen was unhappy? He had to find a way to make his people happy. A dark mood settled over the palace, trouble spread all over the kingdom. The people grew unhappy because there was no way to stop hunger, disease, and oppression in the kingdom.

One day a stranger came from a land far away. He had heard about the troubled kingdom and its unhappy queen.

'I have a solution,' the stranger said. 'People are unhappy because the powerful and rich in the kingdom do not share their wealth. If the rich start sharing their wealth and if everyone shares what they have with each other, everyone can be happy. The people will be happy if they see that their own happiness depends on the happiness of others.'

The queen was very interested in what the stranger had to say. She said to the king, 'If you love me and want to see me happy again, follow the stranger's advice and do one thing just for me.'

'Of course, my dear,' the king agreed because he loved her very much, 'what can I do for you?'

The queen told him, 'Set the example.'

'Set the example in what way?' the king asked.

'We must give away what we own. We have far more than we need. We can give our fields to the farmers who work on them. We can give our herds to those who care for our cows and horses and sheep,' said the queen, adding, 'we can give our houses to the homeless and we can feed the hungry and take

115

care of the sick. There is so much we can do to make other people happy. If we start doing this, other rich people will have to follow our example. After all, you are the king and the people will follow you.'

'That is an interesting idea, my dear queen. I will do as you wish,' said the king.

I ended the story there and shrugged my shoulders.

My audience, I saw, was engaged with the story and made the connection to themselves. I invited Thampa, as well as Dawa to join me in front of our audience. People began to stir and whispered quietly.

'You can see how Thampa-la and Dawa-la are like the king and queen of my story,' I suggested. 'These two have seen the injustice and suffering that many rich and powerful people have caused. They have decided to do something about it. Not all landlords are as understanding and compassionate.'

I turned to Thampa and Dawa and asked them, 'Am I right?'

'That is a good and true story, Comrade Chuang,' Thampa replied, and Dawa nodded her head. 'You say that Dawa and I are like the king and queen, but you are like the wise stranger. You have helped us see what needs to be done so we can all live happily. It is true that Dawa-la and I cannot be happy unless all of you are happy.'

There was an audible stir of interest among those listening. I felt encouraged.

Thampa, equally encouraged, turned to Thupten and gestured that he join them.

'I want my life-long friend, Thupten-la, to tell you what we would like to do. Thupten-la?'

'As you know,' Thupten spoke with confidence, 'our fields have belonged to the Andrutsang family for many generations. The rest of us live here to work in their fields and watch over their herds. The Andrutsang family has been good to us but we all know the system we live under is not as it should be.'

'We are caught in a trap set by rich and powerful noble families and, yes, even some lamas. Most of us owe money to other noblemen or even to some lamas. To repay these debts, we are forced into working for them. If we can't pay back borrowed money, if we can't pay taxes, if we can't work when it is demanded, we face harsh consequences,' he continued. 'Some of us grow desperate and steal an animal or grain so our family can eat. Punishments are cruel and far too unfair. What is the justice of cutting off a man's hand if he steals a bag of *tsampa*? How can he provide for his family then? How can he work to pay off his debt?'

There were sighs and shakings of the head among the villagers. Everyone knew of people who suffered from terrible injustices. Phuntso told me that few people would publicly identify the system as unjust but in their hearts they felt it keenly. Thupten was among the few who were brave enough to voice dissatisfaction with the status quo.

'What Thampa-la and Dawa-la have agreed to do is to give you all the fields and herds. Instead of trying to divide it up fairly, they will give their property to the whole village. This way, all of us will own the fields and herds together. We will form a cooperative and share what we produce. We will all live as equals in this place we call home.'

A middle aged man stood up. Thupten immediately acknowledged him and let him speak.

'Thupten-la, I understand what is being proposed but if we turn everything over to a cooperative, won't we just end up working for the cooperative? Who will own the cooperative?'

'That's an excellent question, Jampa-la,' Thupten said. 'The answer is quite simple. We own the cooperative. It will be ours. It is called a cooperative because we will cooperate to manage it. We will make decisions together, we will work together, and we will all share what we produce. All the families in the village who join the cooperative will own it.'

'How will we do that?' Tashi asked.

'First we have to decide, as a village, if we want to accept Andrutsang's offer or not. We don't have to decide right now. We can take time to talk about it and understand how a cooperative can help us live better lives. Comrade Chuang knows about cooperatives, and can help us understand how we can make it work for us. After we learn about it and think about it, we can meet again to make a decision. What do you think?'

'I think that's a good idea, Thupten-la,' Jampa agreed. There were several voices in agreement.

I stood up at that point.

'There is no need to rush into a decision,' I said. 'Let's learn all we can first. You can teach me about your village and I will be happy to teach you how a cooperative works.'

'Our courtyard or our great room,' Thampa announced, 'are available for village gatherings like this. We can have discussions and learning sessions. Dawa-la and I are happy to answer any questions about the inherited relationships we have had with each of you. Please feel free to come and ask us anything. We want to make sure everyone is happy and able to live free of past obligations to us.'

The first time it snowed, I was excited. It began to stick and build layer upon layer. I'd seen flurries earlier that fall but nothing stayed long on the ground. This was real snow that crunched when you walked on it; snow you could pick up and squeeze into a ball. I joined in when snowballs began to fly. Several village boys used me for target practice, and ended up losing when Thupten came and helped me out.

I'd seen pictures of snowmen in Western magazines as a boy, so I diverted the boys' attention from the battle by rolling a larger and larger ball of snow. They got the idea quickly, and soon we had a jolly round figure they immediately called a snow-Buddha.

It snowed for three days straight. Then the wind howled up a blizzard for another three or four days. It was impossible to go outside. On the second day, I borrowed a small brazier from Pema to warm my hands and bring a hint of warmth to my little room.

I had been sending regular monthly reports to Comrade Li but kept my doubts and questions to myself. My supervisor only got a general report of my movements and the developments here. Like many well-educated Shanghainese, I was completely bi-lingual and wrote my personal journal in English. It was an extra precaution lest my journal find its way into the hands of any less open-minded Chinese comrades. It was a risk, too, since writing in English could also to be used to prove I was a spy.

Things were not progressing smoothly in Gyawa. I could not deny it. Several of the families I visited saw no benefit from the suggested changes. Understandably, they feared reprisals from the powers that be. I had no way of reassuring them that it would not happen.

'This is the way things are,' they would say, 'how can we change our *karma*? We are born to our lot in life, what can we do about it except obey those who are higher born? All we can do is accumulate merit in this life so that in the next life, we have a better chance of being born among the wealthy.'

They accepted their lot too easily, and I regarded this religiously motivated attitude as an impediment to progress. *Karma*, as it was popularly understood, was a powerful idea used by the nobility to maintain their dominant position. Likewise, the monastic system encouraged the popular understanding as a way of maintaining its position of moral authority. The people were ensnared in a sticky web of deceit perpetrated by those who considered themselves of higher birth.

'This lie needs to be exposed,' I wrote in my journal. 'The people need to be enlightened! Science is on my side; human society, at least in educated societies, has evolved beyond superstition, beyond blind acceptance of religious dogma. We have to come to grips with life in the material world and make the best of it. Hocus-pocus about next lives cannot be proven. Therefore, they cannot be real! They only exist in the people's collective imagination, not in reality!'

'A person's worth,' I continued writing, 'is determined by his or her work to make life better and happier for others. Banking up merit for the next life...how ridiculous! The poor are enslaved because they conform to this collective deceit.'

In my small room, I reached a point of absolute faith in the ideals of communism. I believed it possible to create a society in which every member enjoyed equal access to society's resources, and was free to develop, grow and enjoy life to his or her full potential.

120

I was acutely aware of the main obstacle to overcome: the power the clergy and the aristocracy held over the people, manipulating them with false ideas. That was an area in which I needed to put more thought. I needed to find common ground between Mao's version of communism and Buddhism. This, I felt, was the central dialectic of Tibet's struggle. Out of this struggle, perhaps, something that transcends both might emerge.

Progressive ideas had been planted; I waited for our cooperative to germinate, the first sprout to appear. Meanwhile, I spent my time as a scientific investigator, studying the various functions of the entire village to analyse traditional work patterns. I found some activities were culturally determined. For example, it was mostly the women who worked in the fields. The work was hard and I thought women should be spared this kind of difficult physical activity, but the division of labour was universally accepted. When I questioned the practice, I learned there were good reasons behind it. The women were left with the farming because the men were too often called away to fulfil obligations to noblemen, to whom they are indebted.

I immediately saw how these external obligations would be a source of tension once the cooperative got underway. How would we deal with debts owed by members of our community? Could we be bold enough to tell monks and noblemen that our members would no longer serve them? To make a fresh start, we would need to consider all of these issues, and truly liberate our members from these burdens. Nearly every family was indebted to money lenders or merchants beyond the village. I was astonished to discover how many generations back some of this debt extended.

For the most part, despite hardship, I found most families happy, and relationships, healthy. Daily tasks included milking, grinding barley into *tsampa* flour either at the watermill or on a millstone turned by hand in the house, carding wool, weaving cloth or a carpet, making felt, ropes and bags, repairing tools, finding and preparing firewood, keeping a fire burning in the kitchen hearth, churning milk into butter, making butter tea, cooking meals, cleaning pots and bowls, making *chang*, and countless other little tasks that keep a household going. Daily life demanded constant activity.

Popular Tibetan culture was rooted in an oral tradition. Knowledge was passed from generation to generation orally. I had a habit of paying attention to sayings, stories and songs. Women, especially, would recite songs and stories to the children of the house. These recitations functioned to bind the family members together as well as give voice to the accumulated knowledge of previous generations, and assure the continuation of the culture. Practical knowledge as well as moral patterns and social taboos were thus instilled in every child. Of course, the patterns of language, manners of speech and local dialects were taught and maintained in this way, too.

Dawa enjoyed telling me stories. In her stories, magical powers were a repeated theme...as were demons, gods and goddesses related to specific locations. Often, the stories reinforced the superiority of Buddhist deities over spirits of the natural environment. I interpreted this as the battle of civilizing forces, such as Buddhism, against more ancient indigenous spirits. The aboriginal Bon religion was a nature religion with gods, goddesses, demons, and demonesses who were imbedded in the natural landscape. In Bon, the demonic forces needed to be appeased while gods and goddesses demanded praise and honour. Misfortune was sure to befall the family or village community that ignored or inappropriately related to these forces. Surely, from what I could see in the religious lives of the ordinary people, this mentality of appeasement and praise continued to control their lives. The deities of Buddhism merely replaced the more ancient forces of the environment.

Stories that impressed me personally were the ones related to a particular local site such as the Guru Rinpoche cave at the pass into the Lithang valley. Padmasambhava, otherwise known as Guru Rinpoche, had meditated to battle demons who inhabited the surrounding mountains and the expanse of the Lithang grassland valley. With his magical powers, he transformed the demons into protector deities of Buddhism. In this way, he assured that Lithang would become an important centre for Buddhism.

Besides stories about religious teachers, there was also one very popular story about an ancient king named Gesar. More recent than Guru Rinpoche, Gesar was considered a reincarnation of Padmasambhava himself. He ruled a kingdom in a part of Kham called Ling and organized a society based on Buddha dharma, the teachings of the Buddha, in which all his subjects benefited socially, economically, and spiritually. Since no one really knew the actual location of Ling, I wondered if King Gesar had actually existed or if his story was a fictional means of cultural teaching. In every situation, whether in deadly combat with his enemies or at home in his palace, King

Gesar was the perfect example—the role model and hero of every Khampa warrior. He showed that the courageous warrior is decisive in action yet compassionate.

I have to admit, the legend of King Gesar greatly intrigued me; I wondered if the society he set up was similar to the one we were hoping to create.

The rest of the winter was bitterly cold. I was unprepared for the raging snow storms that kept me indoors for days at a time. My room upstairs was too cold and isolated, so I was grateful when Pema moved me to their spare room next to the kitchen, where I could relax in the company of Thupten's family. I enjoyed listening to Pema with the children. She recited traditional sayings in the form of rhymes and little songs. Her children, a boy of seven and a little girl of four, loved to repeat these saying and songs.

One time, the little boy, Sonam, was crying as he came up the steep staircase. He ran to his mother and told her a demon chased him. Pema hugged Sonam tightly and looked at me with a wink. She began to sing:

> *On the tall snowy peaks,*
> *The little lion cub is playing,*
> *Oh big mountain be very gentle*
> *Till the cub has grown his mane*

On another occasion, while I was busy writing, Pema sang a song I suspected was directed at me:

Babbling brooks are noisy,
But the ocean is quiet,
Those with little learning are proud,
The truly wise are humble

I was puzzled at first because I assumed I was the babbling brook, but she laughed when she realized I'd taken her the wrong way.

'No, Wei Ming, you're the quiet and humble one. I like that about you. You have all this knowledge and understanding but you are humble about it. You ask questions where others would be telling people what to do and how to think.'

Another day, Thupten and I were having a serious discussion while Pema was brewing a kettle of tea. Thupten turned to watch Pema and began reciting a saying:

One, the best tea from China,
Two, the purest yak butter of Kham,
Three, the whitest salt from the Changtang,
All three from different places,
Mixed together in a copper pot.
Yet, how the tea is brewed,
Is up to you, oh tea maker!

Pema scooped some tea with her ladle, dipped her ring finger in the tea and flicked it at Thupten. Thupten pretended to be drenched and they both laughed heartily. Thupten explained that Pema was blessing him with this gesture. Pema then proceeded to likewise bless me with a flick of her finger soaked with tea.

Creating a Cooperative

In March, we gathered for a meeting to start the cooperative. Throughout the fall and winter, Thupten and I talked with people about the management of collective resources, had open discussions about transparent decision-making, and voting procedures.

'The time has come!' Thupten declared. 'I think most of your questions have been answered. It is time to make a big decision about the future of our village. Before we put it to a vote, I think we should hear from Thampa-la.'

Thampa stood up. Smiling pleasantly, he turned to Dawa and, offering his hand, encouraged her up to stand beside him.

'I know you all agree it is time for change in our society. We know how corrupt our old system has become. Too many people are poor, heavily burdened, and uneducated; the lamas use people to work their fields, carry their loads, and build their mansions while justifying it by telling falsehoods. Most of them go from place to place encouraging the people to give them money, or they loan money at high interest rates.'

Thampa was getting emotional, and paused to gain self-control.

'How many lamas spend their time teaching Buddha dharma? How many of us have been taught how to meditate? Most monks these days never meditate and don't know how to teach it,' he nearly shouted.

'How many of your sons have been taken from you at an early age to end up working at the monastery more like slaves than students of Dharma? And the sweet, good looking boys—where do they end up? In an elder lama's bed!'

Thampa stepped forward; he was really worked up now. 'Do you see what I'm saying? Too many lamas are corrupt; they are more interested in making themselves and their monasteries rich than in seriously following and teaching Buddha dharma.'

I was getting an earful! Thampa's revelation of the monastery's dirty laundry had never crossed my mind.

'As for the nobility! They willingly follow the example of the lamas in every respect. They use people as animals, and worse. While making sure the animals in their vast herds are fed and looked after, they mistreat the people who care for their herds.'

Red in the face and beginning to sweat, Thampa continued, 'If a man or woman steals or tries to run away, they see nothing wrong with cutting off their hands, putting out their eyes, or crippling them by cutting their tendons. They don't go so far as to kill anyone because they are "pious" followers of Buddha dharma. They live in luxury and travel to foreign places because they have grown rich at the expense of the poor.'

'The lamas tell us that the rich, including themselves, deserve their position in life because of the good deeds they have done in past lives or even in this life,' Thampa-la continued, 'at the same, time they tell the poor that they deserve their lot in life because of their evil past lives or that they are truly evil in this life. These are the falsehoods that prop up the lamas and the noble families of Kham, and all of Tibet.'

Thampa was exposing the deceptions of the religious in terms the people clearly understood. I would never be able to do that!

'If I say too much, forgive me,' Thampa admitted. His breathing had become rapid as his anger built up. 'Of course, I believe in Buddha dharma but I do not believe the lies some of the lamas tell us. I do not believe the rich deserve to be rich nor the poor deserve to be poor.'

Calming himself, Thampa looked at me and concluded his speech.

'We no longer live as King Gesar taught us. You also know there is a new government in China that wants to make many changes in the way we live.'

Calmer now, Thampa looked at me to bring our focus back to our immediate situation. 'Our friend and comrade, Chuang-la, suggests they will try to make us live like they do in China. We are not strong enough to stop the Chinese from imposing their way of life on us, but Chuang-la thinks we can make changes we can live with while also satisfying the communists.'

I nodded in solemn agreement.

'We should try Comrade Chuang's experiment,' Thampa concluded, 'because it is more like the enlightened kingdom of King Gesar. If we are successful, our example will help others in Kham, and all of Tibet, to see the benefits of making positive changes.'

'Well said!' Thupten murmured as he got up to stand beside Thampa. To the gathered members, he said, 'Thampa-la and Dawa-la, like the rest of us, have seen and understand the cruelty and injustices inflicted on people by the nobility as well as by many of our lamas. And he is wise to compare our vision here in Gyawa with the kind of society King Gesar established.'

Thupten stepped aside to indicate that Thampa had not completed what he wanted to say.

Thampa continued, 'Dawa-la and I wish to express our deepest gratitude and beg your forgiveness for any mistreatment you or your ancestors received from our family.'

He was very emotional. Tears gathered and, with both hands, he wiped his face before continuing. He looked at several people in personal acknowledgment and appreciation of their presence.

'As the traditional owners of the fields and herds in this place we call Gyawa, Dawa and I voluntarily and officially release our claim to ownership. We willingly give all our property to Gyawa Cooperative—if you agree to establish it.'

Though choked with emotion, Thampa and Dawa were bathed in a luminous glow, both warm and joyful. It brought a lump in my throat, too. Sunlight seemed to brighten, or perhaps the clouds parted for a moment, while we were all lifted together in hope for a better future.

'Let all who depend on the land and water and air of this place,' Thampa declared dramatically, 'both people and animals, join in cooperation to build a way of life that will allow all of us to be happy, and to thrive as in the time of King Gesar!'

'*Lha Gyalo! Lha Gyalo! Lha Gyalo!*' several shouted with excitement.

Indeed, it felt like we had climbed a difficult mountain trail and reached a pass! Beyond lay a wide open landscape of new opportunities!

Our gathering lasted most of the day. After expressions of gratitude to Thampa and Dawa, the members of the village unanimously agreed to form Gyawa Cooperative. That formalized, Thampa and Dawa signed a statement officially transferring the property. There was a mid-day meal and celebratory rounds of *chang*. In the late afternoon, everyone gathered to make Gyawa Cooperative's first decisions; they unanimously chose Thupten to moderate our meetings and, since the cultivating season was nearly on us, we needed to organize work assignments.

'In a very few days, I'm told,' I said in an effort to make a suggestion, 'the fields will need to be cultivated. We will be very busy and it will put us in a new situation. Since we have many people for this work, we need to decide how to get it done efficiently. How will we organize and coordinate our daily work assignments?'

I sat down. I didn't want to influence the discussion.

Thampa immediately got up and several people gave him a puzzled look, but they quickly realized he wasn't trying to reassert any authority over them.

'How shall we do this?' Thampa said confidently, 'Do we need someone—and there is no reason it must be a man—to help us decide who works in which field so that the work is done efficiently and people are assigned fairly, or do we need to have a daily general discussion about work assignments?'

'These general discussions are good, but it will take too long every day to arrive at a decision. It would be better if someone we all agree on took on the responsibility to organize work assignments,' he added.

'It should be you, Thupten,' someone suggested. Several others agreed.

'No, it should be Pema,' a woman suggested. 'After all, who bosses Thupten around?'

Though there were chuckles and smiles all around, they took the suggestion as valid. After all, it was the women who did most of the field work, even though the men handled the oxen for ploughing.

Pema was a good choice. She had a strong personality, and was a well-respected opinion leader among the village women.

'We all know it is the women who run our homes and do most of the work in the fields,' Thampa affirmed.

Dawa leaned toward Thampa's ear and whispered. I could not hear what she said but Thampa nodded.

'Dawa-la suggests we ask both Thupten-la and Pema-la to be our work leaders together,' he said, 'Thupten-la can save face this way!'

There was general laughter and good-natured agreement about this.

'No,' Thupten said, 'you have already chosen me as moderator of our meetings. Besides, Pema knows more than I do! She's our best work boss. You should choose her!'

There was more laughter as Thupten took Pema's hand and pulled her to the front of the crowd to stand beside him.

Given the positive attitude during the meeting, I was confident the people would abide by this decision. Everyone had a 'let's see how this goes' attitude about the cooperative; even those who previously seemed resigned to their subservience to the greater system. I felt everyone wanted the cooperative to work.

Pema, with the help of a few other women, organized groups of 10-to-12 people and divided tasks in each group according to skills and strengths required. Groups worked a field and moved on to the next once it was cultivated. They managed ploughing, breaking up the clumps of earth, spreading and turning fertilizer into the soil. Other groups were responsible for bringing fertilizer to the fields. Because of this division of labour, work went quickly and a spirit of camaraderie prevailed.

Each evening after work, everyone gathered for a communal meal. So long as the labour required many hands, it was more efficient to have one kitchen. Eating together created a festive occasion and an opportunity to laugh as well as discuss the day's work, share useful ideas and plan the next day's activities.

I'd been assigned to a work detail with Dawa. Once she saw I hadn't a clue what I was doing, she took pity on me. Though I watched carefully, I was clumsy and ineffective in the use of rakes and spades to break up clods of ploughed earth, or to spread and turn fertilizer into the soil. I accepted Dawa's suggestions, tried them and found her method effective. Soon, I was working like the others.

'How is it, Dawa-la,' I asked after I realized she was working with the same ease and skill as everyone else, 'that you are able to work so well with your hands even though you belong to the aristocracy?'

Dawa laughed.

'We Gyatotsang are part of the aristocracy but, like the Andrutsang family, we treat the people in our village with respect. We do not put ourselves above them and we work in the fields like anyone else. It was only when I moved to Lithang that I stopped digging in the dirt like this.'

'Are there other aristocratic families that stay in the village and work alongside the workers?'

'In this part of Lithang, along this stretch of the river, I know several who have managed to stay connected to the land. Like the Gyatotsang and Andrutsang families, they have kept the old ways taught to us through the stories of King Gesar.'

'The way you talk about this ancient king makes him sound like one of your ancestors,' I observed. 'Is he?'

'It was so long ago, a thousand years, but yes, we like to think there is a connection. But who can say? It doesn't matter now.'

Thampa arrived with a basket of yak dung on his back and dumped it where Dawa pointed.

'From governor to dung carrier,' Thampa said with considerable humour. 'I much prefer this!'

'I need to alter your *chuba*,' Dawa observed, 'you're already losing some of that belly.'

Then Dawa turned to look at my clothing. I was in my usual Party work clothing; blue pants and shirt, drenched with sweat and smudged with dirt. She just shook her head.

Despite the cool breeze, the sun was strong. Sweat dripped from my face onto my hands as I worked, making my grip slippery. Working like this had long been my desire, or perhaps my 'fantasy' would be more correct. Thupten and Thampa had tried to dissuade me but I insisted. I admit to having second thoughts once my hands got dirty, developed blisters, and sweat streamed off the tip of my nose!

A refreshing bowl of tea with *tsampa* was most welcome at noon.

'For us women,' Dawa explained as we shared our mealtime, 'this cooperation is not such a new idea. We have always helped our neighbours prepare and harvest their fields in exchange for their help in ours.'

133

'That's an important point,' I said. 'Women, by nature, are more cooperative than men.'

'Pema immediately liked the idea of forming a cooperative,' Dawa continued. 'We talked to all the other women and once they were convinced, we worked on the men to make them see its overall benefits, and how it fit our traditional way of life.'

I had to acknowledge that Pema and Dawa had brought the men of the village around to accepting the idea of our cooperative. How many times had Jiachen lectured me on the role of women in the Revolution? How many times had she insisted she could be a leader as strong as, or stronger, than a man? At the time, I was confused by her rhetoric; she was questioning things that had never entered my mind. How far ahead of me she had been!

'I promise to be aware of women's contributions to the well-being of the cooperative,' I responded with a smile. 'And I promise to help other men understand, too.'

It was clear that Yangchen had instilled strength in her daughter as much as in Jiachen. Even Yangchen's other daughter, Nuying, was strong in her own way.

I was smiling to myself.

'Why are you smiling?' Dawa-la demanded.

'Perhaps the Tibetan revolution should be led entirely by the women!'

'Absolutely right! If our revolution succeeds it will only be because of the women,' exclaimed Dawa-la.

'You are a true revolutionary, Dawa-la!'

We both laughed and got back to work.

I could not help thinking of Jiachen as I worked. She would have loved it here. This thought got me daydreaming about what our life together would have been if we had married. I don't know why, but I was sure Yangchen would have brought us here and we would be doing exactly what I was doing now. I sighed and dismissed these thoughts as sentimental.

The next day I was sore and achy; my work slow. Dawa complained of aches and pains, too, so we were a sorry pair. We were both too tired to carry on much of a conversation.

Tired as I was on the second and third days, I appreciated the physical labour. My hands were blistered from the constant grip and pressure of the hoe; the work was mesmerizing and kept me focused on what was immediately in front of me. I loved the smell of the earth as it was exposed, the pungent smell of the animal dung fertilizer as it was dumped from baskets, and the mixture of soil and fertilizer as we turned it in.

'Wei Ming,' Dawa called out from behind me as we walked to a new field.

I stopped and waited for her to catch up.

'You are ruining your clothes with this work! How many changes of clothing do you have?'

'I have three sets. One I keep for special occasions.'

'You could at least wash out your shirt!'

'Do I smell so bad?' I asked, suddenly self-conscious.

'Well, yes, I suppose you do, but I don't mind body odour as much as I'm concerned that you'll ruin your clothes. Where will you get new ones here?'

'I suppose a tailor in Lithang could do it.'

'Perhaps, but even so, those clothes are not suitable for this work.'

'What do you suggest?'

Dawa only smiled.

After the communal evening meal, Dawa invited me to follow her and Thampa to their house. She disappeared while Thampa and I enjoyed a bowl *chang*. She returned and lay three *chuba*s on the table beside me.

'Here, Wei Ming, these are Thampa-la's. He has plenty. I noticed you two are about the same height and thought you could wear them.'

'Oh no, Dawa-la, I can't do that,' I protested.

'No, you must wear them when you work.'

Thampa looked surprised and a bit embarrassed.

'Really, Dawa-la,' Thampa objected, 'why do you think he'd want to wear my old *chuba*s?'

Dawa ignored him.

'Here,' she ordered me, 'put this one on. Go on, take off your shirt.'

I complied. It was made of homespun wool. A *chuba* is a robe that comes to the knees, and the sleeves nearly touch the ground. A high collar can fasten together to keep out a cold wind if necessary and the front, doubled over, is kept in place with a long band of cloth wrapped around several times. Above the waistband, the robe puffs out to create a huge pocket where odds and ends such as a drinking bowl, knives and small tools, bags of *tsampa*, and valuables can be carried. The sleeves are rolled up but in warm weather, with one or both sleeves tied around the waist, the arms are free. Most of the men working in the fields were bare skinned to the waist, though some wore shirts.

Dawa handed me a pair of trousers. I unfastened and dropped my pants without exposing myself and pulled up the trousers made of the same course material. I expected wool to be scratchy but it was surprisingly soft and comfortable.

Once I was dressed, Dawa and Thampa admired my sudden transformation.

'You look like one of us now,' Dawa exclaimed. 'But to make it complete, you need a hat to cover your short hair.'

She disappeared again and returned with a fine golden fox fur hat and gave it to Thampa, who could more easily put it on my head.

'Ah yes! A handsome Khampa, at last!' Dawa bubbled with an almost childlike enthusiasm. She led me to a corner of the room where a full-length mirror hung on the wall and made me look at my transformed self.

'I see what you mean,' I said. 'Perhaps I could be mistaken, at first glance anyway, as a Khampa. In any case, it allows me to show my solidarity with you. Thank you, both of you!'

'You must take all of these and wear them,' Thampa agreed enthusiastically.

'Yes, the *chuba* and trousers, but I cannot take the hat. It looks expensive and would be too hot to wear in the fields.'

Until now, I'd seen the *chuba* everywhere, of course, but assumed they would eventually be replaced by the worker's uniform worn by communist comrades everywhere in China. Now that I was actually wearing a *chuba*, I could see just how practical and suitable it really is for this environment.

I appeared at our gathering in the *chuba* the next morning.

'Comrade Chuang has become Chuang-la!' someone said in a loud voice. There were several cheers of approval and lots of laughter.

'It really suits you, Chuang-la,' someone said in a loud voice.

'After all the changes you are going through,' I said, 'why shouldn't I make changes, too?'

137

'What changes, Chuang-la?' some else joined in. 'We still have our fields, our animals, our work, our homes, our songs and jokes; we even have our Buddha dharma.'

Several people were nodding appreciatively.

'The only change,' Thupten interjected, 'is that we really own all of this now. We are living like our ancestors once lived in the days of King Gesar.'

'I've heard so much about this legendary king,' I said. 'I hope one of you will tell me more about this wise leader.'

'We know someone who can do that, don't we?' Dawa shouted.

'Yes, our Palden Rinpoche!' someone called out.

'That's right,' Dawa responded.

People began talking among themselves and I could hear phrases and words repeated around me: 'Rinpoche', 'Gesar', 'Buddha dharma'. I even heard 'Chuang-la' several times.

When it looked like people were ready to go, I stood and asked for their attention.

'Before we go out to the fields this morning,' I began, 'I'd like to say how pleased I am with the way things are going. Our fields are nearly ready for planting. Pema tells me we are waiting for rain.'

'Yes, the first spring rains,' Pema agreed.

'That means our first growing season is about to begin! We won't know how good our experiment is until we harvest crops in the fall. What I already know is how good it feels to work with you. We are working hard together and growing closer as a community. I want to thank you for trusting me.'

I bowed deeply, repeatedly in everyone's direction.

Moved by my speech, Thupten gave me a bear hug.

'Your ideas have brought us together and made Gyawa Cooperative possible. It is we who should be thanking you!'

It was Thupten's turn to bow. He bowed to me, and then to everyone else as I had done.

'Not my ideas, Thupten-la,' I said as he stood up. 'These ideas originated in the minds of great revolutionary thinkers and, by the way all of you so eagerly adopted them, I'm beginning to see that similar ideas are also part of your own tradition.'

'Wherever they originate,' said Thupten, 'we appreciate you for your courage to come here from Shanghai to share your enthusiasm. We call you Chuang-la, not because you wear our *chuba*, but because we accept you as one of us.'

'Thank you!' I said with emotion. 'I'm honoured and I hope you'll see me as someone not just trying to look like a Khampa. I'd like to really be one of you.'

A woman in the crowd shouted out, 'Only a Khampa wife can do that for you!'

This brought laughter and merriment as they gathered their tools to go to the fields.

That night after work, Pema handed me a bowl of *chang* with a stern expression as we sat in her kitchen.

'She's right, you know! You need a Khampa wife!'

I wasn't in a mood to consider something as serious as that.

'Don't be ridiculous,' I retorted, 'she was making a joke.'

Pema frowned. She respected my mood but I could tell she meant what she said.

139

'Besides, I'm already married,' I said under my breath recalling what I'd told my father. Unfortunately, Pema heard me.

'Already married?' she gasped. 'You never told us that!'

I couldn't avoid the topic now.

'Actually, no, I say that because I may as well be married to communism. It is my life now.'

'That's ridiculous,' Pema echoed my word. 'You don't marry a way of life, you marry a person!'

She suddenly got decisive.

'Ok, we're going to find you a wife! You'll get married and then you'll be one of us.'

'No,' I protested.

'Why not?'

'I was deeply in love once.'

'Yes, I know,' Pema acknowledged, 'to Yangchen's granddaughter, Jiachen.'

I didn't need to tell Pema about Jiachen but found myself doing so anyway. I needed to relive those memories.

'We met in a courtyard at university. We were in a line to register for classes. I was standing behind her. We suddenly both looked up toward the east where we saw a brilliant flash of light. Turning to each other, we both said, "Did you see that?". That's how we started talking. Later, we found out it was the atomic bomb exploding on Nagasaki that ended the war with Japan.'

I could tell Pema probably didn't know what a university was and had never heard about atomic bombs, or Japan for that matter, but I went on without explaining.

'We were both going to be doctors. She was very beautiful, bright, and strong-willed. Our attraction was immediate and mutual. A few months before we were to be married, she led a protest march against the nationalist government and became a martyr. I was there. I saw her get shot!'

I looked away and stared into the fire for a few minutes.

'I was devastated without her,' I continued after a while, 'but her friends helped me through the worst of it. Gradually, I understood why she was so dedicated to the communist revolution, and I became a Communist Party member myself before Mao's forces entered Shanghai. My father, a wealthy banker, tried to force me to leave with my family to Hong Kong and marry a friend's daughter. I refused. I stayed in Shanghai when they left. I haven't heard from them since.'

'How tragic!' Pema commiserated. 'You must have been deeply in love. It is good that you continue what she began.'

'That's why I say I'm married. I continue our relationship through dedication to the Revolution she died for. It is something she wanted me to do. Just before she died, she told me to "liberate the people".'

When I said that, I realized it didn't sound right but I couldn't remember exactly what she said.

Thupten had been listening intently. He nodded and smiled sympathetically when I looked up to see him watching me.

'Pema-la, I think we should honour Chuang-la's wishes,' he said looking at me with a flicker of humour, 'but if he finds a pretty Khampa girl and changes his mind...well, we will be very happy.'

Breaking the Cycle

As the summer progressed and the crops grew, work details continued with weeding, taking herds to the summer grazing lands, making butter, shearing sheep, carding wool, and a host of other productive endeavours. Trading caravans were organized to market some of our products in exchange for tea and other necessities from Lithang, and places like Dartsendo, Batang and as far away as Lhasa as well.

During that summer, District Commissioner Tsering Nawang sent a message saying he would be making an official visit to Gyawa Cooperative. We welcomed the visit as an opportunity to discuss the issue of debts owed by our members to people outside our village. Too many people were requesting leave to fulfil obligations related to debts. We needed lenders to release our members from these obligations.

Thampa suggested it was not out of the question to repay the accumulated debt of every member of the cooperative. It was to our advantage, as well as our responsibility as a true cooperative, to intervene on behalf of every member and release them from these oppressive obligations. Generously, Thampa and Dawa offered funds from the sale of their property holdings in Lithang. This put us in a position to be able to pay off the debts of our members. We would suggest to Commissioner Tsering that a communist government could endorse such transactions, and make the repayment of all debts legally binding. We would make the case that the lenders were being fully compensated and must release the debtor from any further obligation.

At the scheduled time, Commissioner Tsering, dressed like a Chinese Communist Party member, arrived with an entourage of officials including two Chinese advisors. I had not heard of any Chinese officials in Lithang, but discovered they had recently arrived and had suggested this visit to Gyawa Cooperative. They told me privately that they had heard good things about me and, on Comrade Li's suggestion, wished to inspect the cooperative and help me in any way they could. I did not want to discuss anything official with them even though they pressed me to divulge information about my plans for the cooperative.

'It is not my place to speak for the cooperative,' I informed them. 'If you have questions, please raise them directly in our general assembly. The people have authority here. I am merely an advisor.'

I don't think they believed me, nor do I think they could understand the position I had taken. They assumed that I was in charge of the cooperative. I tried to explain that I was following communist principles by giving power to the people; the revolution belonged to them.

'As a Party member, Commissioner Tsering, of course, has our confidence,' one of them stated in explanation of their presence in Lithang, 'but we are here to see that necessary policies are put in place.'

'It is good you have come to see us,' I responded. 'The cooperative has something to discuss that will require

143

Commissioner Tsering's approval and the full support of the Party. Come, let's join the others to discuss the matter.'

I think they expected me to put the issue to them first, so they would have a chance to formulate a response before our general discussion. Reluctantly, they followed me into our meeting room in Dawa's courtyard, where nearly everyone in the village had gathered.

Thampa came downstairs to join us a few minutes later with Nawang. From Thampa's bearing, I realized something of consequence had transpired between them.

It was Thupten who opened the meeting and welcomed Commissioner Tsering and the other officials. As there was only one matter to discuss with our visitors present, he introduced it right away.

'As an independent cooperative we feel obligated to struggle for the liberation of each of member who is bound by previous circumstance. Several of our members have asked for leave in order to fulfil obligations related to debts incurred in the past. As you are aware, this means they will be away from our cooperative for several weeks at a time. During this time, as most of you can appreciate, we suffer a loss of manpower, and those called away suffer the indignity of forced labour.'

I noticed that a Tibetan official was quietly translating for the two Chinese officials.

'We want to repay the loans with our own resources; if one of us is in bondage, we are all in bondage. Until everyone is free of obligations outside our cooperative, we cannot function to our full potential.'

Thupten then asked an elderly man named Tashi to stand and outline the details of our proposal.

'We have resources available to repay the loans of each member who has an outside debt,' Tashi said confidently. 'We offer to return the full amount originally borrowed. Since it is not possible to come to an agreement about the value of labour already provided, we think it is more than fair if we regard it as interest paid. You will agree this is generous.'

Tashi paused a moment when Nawang turned to confer with the two Party officials. When Nawang looked back, Tashi continued.

'We want to know if our comrades in Lithang will support this proposal,' Tashi continued. 'We are well aware that money lenders will complain not because our offer is generous but because their source of free labour will disappear. We ask that an official be present to record and validate transactions with all lenders; merchants, noblemen, or lamas alike. We want these transactions to be legally binding. Lenders must be bound by law to recognize our legitimacy. We want our members to be liberated from this kind of oppression.'

There was silence for a moment as we waited for the translation to be completed and while Nawang conferred with the two Chinese officials. One of them signalled that I should join them. I declined. I could see how my refusal angered them and I wondered if it would influence their decision. In the end, it did not matter as I had made my point that the cooperative was independent of my control and the request did not originate from me.

'What you request is praiseworthy,' Commissioner Tsering announced, repeating, no doubt, what the two officials had said to him. 'It fits within the broad guidelines of communist principles. This is exactly the kind of liberation the people require; freedom from conscription for forced labour and bondage to oppressive moneylenders. We will ask the various lenders to come to court where you will repay them the appropriate amounts and the district court will record the transactions. Provide a list of borrowers, lenders and the amounts involved and the court will see that this matter is settled. We want Gyawa Cooperative to be able to proceed without outside pressure. It is a great experiment you have started and we hope other communities will follow your example.'

That was easy, I thought. I looked at Thampa for a clue as to what might have transpired before the meeting. He sat distracted, with a long face.

Our first harvest season was underway. Thampa, Thupten and I were preparing loads of sheaves to carry to the threshing floor from the fields. The sun was hot, we were sweaty. We took a break when Dawa arrived with cool drinking water. As I lifted my bowl to drink, I noticed a lone horseman approaching on the trail from Lithang.

Thupten and I looked at each other, both thinking the rider was bringing a message from Nawang's office and hoping it would finally be some good news about the process of repaying our cooperative members' debts. Only two loans—token gestures, small loans to local shopkeepers—had been fulfilled so far. We were discouraged that none of the big, wealthier lenders had been called to court. Our members were still feeling obligated to leave the village to provide services.

As the rider approached, I thought he was Chinese. He wore pants and shirt, had modern-style short hair and shiny black shoes. Thupten went toward the trail to meet him.

'Tenzin,' Thupten called out, 'what brings you here?'

It was Tsering Tenzin, Nawang's son.

'I've come to see Comrade Chuang.'

Apparently he did not recognize me, even though I was quite close to him. I worked bare-chested with my *chuba* around my waist like other men around me, and my hair was longer now.

I noticed that Thampa was not happy to see the young man, and gave Dawa a furtive glance. Dawa, however, was busy noticing the irony of the situation.

'One man takes the uniform off; another puts it on,' she said pointing to me. 'Most amusing!'

Suddenly Tenzin recognized me.

'Ah, yes, Ama-la,' he said with a self-conscious laugh, 'it is amusing, isn't it?' He turned to me and added, 'It is you, isn't it, Comrade Chuang?'

Tenzin was already managing to irritate me. I tried to check my reaction and hoped my words would not betray my true feelings.

'Amused that I adopt the ways of your people? I dress like this to show solidarity as much as for practicality. The *chuba* is better suited to this climate and lifestyle.'

'Yes, of course, comrade,' Tenzin began but Thupten interrupted him.

'Then tell us, why do you wear a foreign attire?'

'I wear it,' Tenzin replied proudly, 'because I'm a member of the Communist Party.'

When he dismounted, Tenzin put out his hand for me, and grasped it in the non-Tibetan, and non-Chinese, Western way.

'I've been hearing so much about your work!' he gushed. 'What you have achieved is truly amazing. Did you know that your accomplishment is known throughout China? Even Chairman Mao is aware of the success of this cooperative.'

'I doubt that, comrade.'

'No, it's true. I heard all about you while studying in Chengdu.'

'We've only just begun, and we won't know how successful our experiment is until our harvest is over.'

'No, you are inspiring many young volunteers to start cooperatives in distant parts of the motherland.'

'It's true, Chuang-la,' Thupten agreed. 'I'm guilty of spreading your story a bit myself. I sent a message to some friends in Chengdu telling them what you've accomplished.'

I glowered at Thupten. I didn't want this kind of attention, and changed the subject. I focused on Tenzin's attire once again.

'I'm still not sure why you are dressed like this,' I said as I flicked his shirt sleeve. 'You don't have to go so far as to change your dress just because you're a Party member! Tibetan members of the Party should maintain cultural identity while whole-heartedly embracing communist principles. As for me, once I started wearing the *chuba*, I understood how it connected me with the people. While living here, I feel I must adopt the local dress and culture.'

'I'm not sure you're right, Comrade Chuang,' Tenzin said bluntly.

'Of course he's right!' Thupten said emphatically.

I noticed that Thampa was walking away and Dawa was hurrying after him. I wondered what was going on.

'So, Comrade Tsering,' Thupten began in a more official capacity, 'what is the reason for your visit?'

'It's not a visit,' Tenzin informed us while taking a letter from his pocket. 'It's an assignment. This is from Comrade Li of the Tibet Work Committee in Chengdu. The letter asks Comrade Chuang to mentor me. I'm here to help him and to learn as much as I can.'

I looked from Tenzin to Thupten, trying to hide a sudden flare of anger. This was the last thing I wanted, a shadow! Most of all, this shadow! Turning this insincere and shallow young man into a true revolutionary would be a challenge!

Dawa picked up the kettle from the fireplace and refilled our bowls with *chang*. Thupten, Pema, a few others and I were in Dawa's kitchen to officially welcome Tenzin.

'Mother wishes you'd spend more time in Lithang,' Tenzin said to Dawa quietly as she poured *chang* into his bowl.

Dawa nodded and smiled politely, but gave no reply.

'And your father?' Thampa interjected to deflect from Dawa's discomfort. It was obvious he, too, was having difficulty with Tenzin's presence. 'Is he enjoying his new responsibilities?'

'Yes, but he's so busy he hardly has time at home.' Tenzin sounded proud. 'I think that's why Mother misses Dawa-la so much. She's often alone.'

'That's understandable,' Dawa agreed. 'I'm sure she wants you to bring home a daughter-in-law. Are they planning your marriage?'

'Ah, yes, about that...' he began sheepishly. 'I've been eager to ask when your daughter is returning home.'

149

'Dechen?' Dawa stepped back, alarmed.

Thampa suddenly flushed with anxiety.

'Father has an agreement with Thampa-la that Dechen and I will marry.'

Dawa fired a 'how dare you!' glare at Thampa.

'I, I merely agreed with Nawang-la long ago,' Thampa fumbled, 'that they might be a good match for each other. They were both children!'

'No,' Tenzin insisted, 'it was more recent.'

'There is no agreement!' Thampa exploded.

'That's not what Father understands.'

'I'm sorry. He misunderstood me!'

I noticed Dawa was confused as she looked from Thampa to Tenzin.

'I don't see what advantage this alliance is to your family, Tenzin,' Thampa was saying. 'In any case, my daughter is unlikely to ever return here.'

Clearly surprised and confused by Thampa's response, Dawa stood up and glared down at Thampa.

'This is what you've been keeping from me?' Dawa exploded at Thampa. 'Every time this young man's name is mentioned, you cringe and try to hide your face from me. What's going on?'

'That's enough,' Thupten intervened calmly. 'Please settle this issue privately.'

Tenzin threw up his hands apologetically.

Dawa continued to glare at Thampa. There would surely be a heated discussion in this kitchen after we left!

The room was quiet while we sipped from our bowls, hoping the mood would change.

'Tenzin, let's not get off on an awkward start,' Thupten said eventually. 'Whatever hopes you might have for the daughter of this house must not interfere with your responsibilities.'

'I understand,' Tenzin agreed. 'I'm sorry. Dawa-la asked and I couldn't help responding.'

'What you've said suggests,' Thupten observed, 'that your father might be putting a price on the help he offered us last summer.'

'What do you mean?' Tenzin responded defensively.

'I'm sure he has told you about our method of clearing the debts of our members. This has been happening far too slowly. Is there a possibility he thinks the agreement of your marriage to Thampa-la's daughter would encourage him to proceed with the plan?'

'What?' Tenzin looked genuinely surprised, but perhaps it was Thupten's insight that startled him.

'It's either that or he lacks the clout to bring the wealthy and powerful to court!' Thupten was getting angry.

'There's...there are no conditions I'm aware of,' Tenzin stammered nervously. His manner revealed he was not being completely truthful.

'I hope that's the case,' Thupten concluded, and stared hard at Tenzin to let him know his suspicion remained.

'So,' I intervened, 'about your mentorship, Tenzin. I'm happy to do as Comrade Li requests but you must understand we all take part in the work of the village here. As you saw when you arrived, I work alongside everyone else. We will expect it of you, too. Do you agree?'

'Ah, yes, of course, Comrade Chuang,' Tenzin responded after a moment's hesitation. We could tell he was not very enthusiastic to do manual labour like the rest of us.

151

'Very well then.'

The arrangement for Tenzin's housing was complicated. Neither Pema nor Dawa wanted him to stay with them so we fixed up a vacant house, and arranged for him to have his meals with the family next door. Tenzin may have felt ostracized but didn't complain.

Once the crop cycle was over for the winter, Pema had not assigned me to any physically demanding work groups. On stormy days, I spent time writing my journal and studying. When the weather was good I visited families and conducted education and training sessions—always shadowed by Tenzin. Together, we learned that almost everyone was appreciative of the way things had gone over the past year. The harvest was abundant, people felt their basic physical needs were adequately met, and they recognized the multiple benefits they enjoyed from participating in the cooperative. Tenzin seemed genuinely enthused by what we heard, and my attitude toward him began to change.

One afternoon, Tenzin and I climbed up a hill for an overview of the cooperative. I was curious about his training and what he knew about communism. As a way of starting a conversation, I mentioned I was reading two of Mao's essays: 'On Contradiction' and 'On Practice'. Contradiction was the term Mao used for Karl Marx's dialectic theory.

'Mao states that cycles of social progress evolve through a series of contradictions,' I explained.

Tenzin's disinterested expression made me suspect he knew little of Mao's philosophy.

'When one class of people is in power,' I continued despite his apparent lack of interest, 'they subjugate others for their own material gain. The suppressed class eventually reaches a point of dissatisfaction and revolts. Mao states that this conflict drives social evolution. He says it happens by violently overthrowing the class in power. Compromise and reconciliation, Mao believes, is impossible.'

I could not tell what Tenzin was thinking.

'The once-subjugated class rearranges society and the economy. Inevitably, however, a new elite group emerges and takes control. This has been the pattern of civilization for thousands of years and I fear it will happen in China.'

Now I seem to have gotten Tenzin's attention. He was looking at me quizzically but remained silent.

'I'm convinced we can break that cycle by creating communities like this one,' I said, pointing to the village below us. 'The cycle of one group taking back power and setting up a new power elite must be broken if we are to evolve beyond violence and achieve happiness for all people. That cycle is not social evolution.'

A furrow formed on Tenzin's forehead. I was pushing the limits of acceptable thought, I knew, but I felt he should be exposed to our philosophy if I was going to be his mentor.

'We did not recreate this community by violently overthrowing the land-owning class. We began by making careful observation of the socio-economic structure of the existing community and making suggestions about new ways of self-organization, as recommended in Mao's 'On Practice'. Once the entire village, including ancestral landowners Thampa-la and Dawa-la, understood the benefits of cooperative living, we

153

restructured our lives so that we all shared the bounty of this land equally.'

Tenzin was about to interrupt but I was too intent on getting my point across.

'As you've seen, Tenzin, the people are content. They collectively own the means of production and enjoy the security that all will have food, shelter, and clothing. Other than the change in ownership, they live as they have for generations; they have their families, their own homes, their culture, and religious tradition. In my opinion, this is as it should be.'

'Yes, comrade, the people are generally happy,' Tenzin tentatively agreed, 'but, as good as it is, it's...'

'It's what?' I prodded when he hesitated.

'Well, the Party considers this a first step, a softening-up stage. It's true they praise your work but they regard the willingness of the Andrutsangs to give up their property unlikely to be repeated by other landowners.'

'So,while publicly praising our cooperative,' I asked, 'are you assuming they will, in fact, have to implement things their own way?'

'I can't only guess but from what I've seen of the communes we were shown near Chengdu, that would be the model they aim for here, too. They operate on a much more regimented basis. Ideas of private ownership do not exist. Everyone lives in dormitories and everyone eats in a community dining hall. Children live in a separate boarding school. Families living in private homes, we were told, are a thing of the past.'

'I've heard of these extreme communes. How did visiting them make you feel?' I asked.

'To be honest, I wouldn't like to live like that.'

We were both silent for a while. The sun was nearing the horizon behind us. I could see where our little stream flowed into the Lithang River. To the east, the river bent and the forested mountains beyond were bathed in an enchanting golden green.

I had to assume Tenzin was sending reports about me back to Chengdu but I saw no advantage in keeping my views to myself.

'My hope,' I continued, 'is that the Party will take seriously the success of our cooperative and implement a system like this as the norm for Kham. Families need to live in their own homes; parents and children together. All other aspects of village life can be communal; work in the fields, herding animals, production of goods and tools, schooling, training, and so on. Otherwise one oppressive system will simply be replaced with another—as you've seen happening in the communes!'

'Yes, but all houses are not of equal size and value,' Tenzin pointed out testily. 'To make it fair you'd have to tear everything down and build houses proportional to family size.'

His curious response jolted me and I must have looked at him with surprise. He laughed self-consciously hoping to make a joke of the statement.

'What's the point of doing that?' I asked, exposing myself further. 'Why not make good use of already existing structures, physical as well as social? What's wrong with living in families? What's wrong with houses of different sizes when a large one can have many functions? For example, Thampa and Dawa have made their large house available for meetings, classrooms, and guest quarters.' Pausing for a moment, I continued, 'They only occupy two rooms. It's important to ensure that

155

everyone's basic needs are met. I hope our cooperative can become so successful that we can modernize our housing, buy trucks and farm machinery, set up a hydroelectric power system, start a school, and even set up a health care system.' 'These are dreams, I know, but I'm sure we can begin making progress in that direction soon. This year, we produced more than we needed,' I pressed.

'The mood of the Party,' Tenzin observed, 'seems to be that we need to "wipe the slate clean", as they say. The revolution will be a success once everything tainted by the older civilization is removed.'

'I see,' I responded angrily. 'Don't you see what's happening? The Party is already emerging as the new elite class. They are making decisions without consulting the people themselves! No. Communism is for the people, not the elite. It begins with the people, one community at a time, and must conclude with what's best for all the people.'

I didn't mind what Tenzin thought of me. The results of my beliefs were right there before us in the village below. I started down the hill immediately; I wanted to distance myself from Tenzin who I saw as a pawn of the Party in every way. I could not mentor him in the way I thought he should be mentored; he was incapable of seeing things our way.

Thupten, Thampa and I accompanied our caravan to Lithang to sell our surplus. It was my first time back to Lithang. As we were busy making sales, I was startled when a booming voice filled the street. I realized it was a public address system. The

Chinese visitors had brought a radio and set up a public address system so the entire town could hear daily news reports. Along with everyone else, we learned that a Tibetan delegation from Lhasa had signed a Seventeen Point Plan for the Peaceful Liberation of Tibet.

Following this announcement, the town was buzzing with discussion. The most common opinion was that the delegates had been held captive in Peking and forced to sign the agreement. No Tibetan would acknowledge that Tibet had ever been part of the 'big family of the motherland', nor would members of the delegation ever sign such an agreement unless forced to do so. A few were more pragmatic and said that as long as China recognized our distinct culture and our freedom to practice Buddha dharma, as the Plan declared, what difference would it make if China took our taxes or if the 'sweet-mouths' of Lhasa continued to rob us?

Despite my growing sense of betrayal, I held on to what Comrade Phuntso had told me—the highest Party leadership would honour the cultural integrity of the people of Tibet.

Commissioner Tsering Nawang informed us, when we asked about the announcement that the agreement applied to the Tibetan area administered by Lhasa and did not apply to Kham.

'Since Kham has already been assimilated into Sichuan Province,' Nawang informed us, 'the same land reform program implemented in the lowlands of Sichuan are scheduled to be introduced in Lithang district beginning in the spring.'

I was horrified but tried my best to remain calm, my expression, unreadable.

'The people, for the most part, remain unaware of the implication of Kham's assimilation,' I said as evenly as I could manage. 'In fact, I'm not sure I know what this will mean for the people of Kham. Don't you think it would be in everyone's interest to know what changes to expect and how they will be introduced?'

'We are letting them know!' Nawang replied defensively. His manner was more revealing than he realized. It was clear to me that he was getting nowhere with the local aristocracy. Force was the only option available to meet the timeline of the Party!

I sent a letter to Comrade Li to state my opinion that the land-owning class might be persuaded to voluntarily surrender land, herds, and property through an adequate program of education. More importantly, I explained that educating and gaining the support of the religious community was the key to reforming Tibetan society. Unlike Phuntso, I had come to the conclusion that we must open a dialogue with this all-important sector of society. The people, including the upper classes, would listen if the Party honoured Buddhist teachings about alleviating the suffering of others.

Regarding Nawang, I indicated he was a poor choice as district commissioner because he lacked the ability to influence the aristocracy and, most of all, because he disregarded entirely the political significance of the abbot of the Lithang Monastery. Both the aristocracy and the religious communities were gatekeepers of social change.

I never got a reply.

When Thampa, Thupten and I returned to Gyawa, we noticed tensions within the community. As winter set in, tensions increased. Disagreements stalled our large group decisions and some families stayed away from our meetings. Thupten, Pema and I spent much of our time negotiating the uncomfortable terrain between opposing factions. One family in particular felt that they had been unfairly treated. They raised one issue after another. First of all, they complained that their house was substandard and in need of repair. The issue of home repair was raised at a general meeting, and it was agreed that funds and labour would be provided to make the requested repairs. But once that was done, the same family complained that they no longer had freedom to acquire things on their own, and that their cash allowance was inadequate. These kinds of complaints spread to other families in the village like poison.

Other than the boredom of winter, the only difference in our community—I hated to even think it—was the presence of Tenzin. I recalled Tenzin's description of communes near Chengdu and his comment about the relative size of houses. Could he be planting discord? Had he been sent to disrupt the cooperative? Was he attempting to prove that my ideas would not work?

'Perhaps we should invite Tenzin to have his meals here,' I suggested to Pema.

She exploded immediately, 'Why?'

I was about to explain when Thupten intervened.

'To keep an eye on him. I don't see it as a mere coincidence that he has been taking his meals with the family that complains the most!'

159

'Oh, yes, you're right,' Pema said in agreement. 'I find him arrogant, lazy, and often devious. He puts questions in people's minds that weren't there to begin with.'

'From the beginning, I suspected he's not here to learn from Comrade Chuang as much as to keep an eye on us,' Thupten observed.

'And perhaps to disrupt our experiment,' I said, giving voice to my own suspicions.

'Ok, I agree,' Pema relented, 'if he eats and spends more time here, I'll be able sort him out!'

The three of us had a good chuckle. We knew Pema would handle things her own way.

Tenzin started eating with us and Pema made sure he was put to work with a detail she supervised whenever he wasn't with me. Even during the winter months, there was hard physical work to do. Pema made sure he was assigned to jobs that would get him dirty. We could tell Tenzin was growing increasingly discontent; he resented having to work like everyone else, complained about his clothes getting dirty, and was sullen at meals with us.

'Here,' Pema said as she handed him one of Thupten's *chubas*, 'wear this.'

Tenzin made a face and declined. 'No, I'm not going backwards! Absolutely not!'

How Pema managed to hold her tongue I have no idea.

A couple of weeks later, a messenger arrived with a letter for Tenzin. We suspected it was in answer to a message he'd sent to his father. Tenzin claimed that he'd been called to Lithang on urgent family business. We were greatly relieved when he left. He did not return that winter, and once spring arrived, we heard he had gone to Chengdu.

Unsurprisingly, complaints began to diminish and people were happy once again in Gyawa.

Over the course of Gyawa Cooperative's second year, there was an ever-increasing presence of Chinese Party members and PLA soldiers in Lithang district. The military encampment in Lithang grew larger by the month. Rumours of hunger among local people reached us, and I realized the presence of the Chinese troops was to blame. Not enough food could be produced in these highlands to feed both the local people and the growing number of soldiers and camp hangers-on. Diseases such as influenza and TB from the lowlands began to spread among the Khampa who had no immunity. Many people got sick; many died.

A more positive development was the completion of a motor road all the way to Chamdo along the northerly trade route. Another road was being built through Lithang to Batang, and onwards to Lhasa. The section as far as Lithang would not be completed for at least another year.

A motor road would certainly change things. It would be good for us, and I looked forward to the cooperative buying its own truck, perhaps more than one. We could then begin transporting goods to markets further away, and go as far as Chengdu to buy modern farming equipment, pipes for water supply to each house, generators and fuel for electric lights, and gradually bring in other things to improve our lives. We would show the way forward to better living; something everyone could aspire to and achieve through cooperative effort.

On the other hand, distressing news came from the south. In Gyalthang, an area of rich valleys and forests to our southwest, the presence of the PLA was deeply resented. We heard tales of troops forcibly collecting livestock and grain to feed themselves. The most outspoken aristocrats and wealthy merchants were terrorized by selective arrests, and publicly humiliated or ruthlessly killed in front of the entire village.

Non-Tibetan tribes—the Lolo, Naxi, and Miao—also to the south of us, were put through the same nightmare. We heard the fierce Lolo resisted valiantly for as long as they could, but were eventually outnumbered and defeated.

This kind of news distressed me greatly. It was clear to me that non-Han peoples were being treated unfairly as second-class citizens. The Han were never good at honouring the independence and unique contributions of other cultures. Societies were only good if they looked up to the Chinese as superior; this, the Tibetans would never do!

Places to the west of Lithang such as Chamdo and Batang on the Dri Chu, and other important centres to our north and east were also subjected to PLA coercion. Of course, this kind of news only enraged the Khampas.

Our cooperative did even better the second year. I could only assume, for whatever reason, the Party was still watching my experiment, and had instructed the PLA to stay out of Gyawa and the surrounding areas. It was even possible that Party officials in Lithang were applying pressure on Nawang and wealthy moneylenders to accept repayment of our members'

debts. I hoped that if Comrade Li was behind this, he would continue to have clout among the Party leadership in Chengdu. Whatever the real reason, by the end of that second year, all our people were free of debt and eager to give all their time, talents, and energy to the success of our experiment.

After the harvest, we began to tackle larger projects such as repairing the ancient irrigation system. No one alive remembered it being used. Sections of it still existed, so all that was needed was to rebuild the missing sections.

In our third year, we began irrigating more fields close to the village for sizable vegetable gardens. We were prosperous. People from far and near began to show interest in what we had achieved. Our members proudly promoted our success when people came to see for themselves. When our members travelled, they told people about our cooperative experiment. We were soon well-known throughout Kham.

It was my fourth winter in Gyawa. Thampa and Thupten were visiting me in my small room on the top floor of Pema and Thupten's house. We were huddled around the charcoal brazier. I took a moment to add some charcoal, and blow it into the embers to encourage more heat.

'I'm assuming,' I said to continue our conversation, 'that I am still here helping you because Comrade Li is an influential member of the Communist Party. When I met him in Chengdu, I was impressed with his understanding of the Tibetan people. I am hoping he is on our side, and is quietly promoting our experiment. I think he has faith in our approach. So, let's take heart!'

I smiled confidently, even though I felt a tinge of anxiety that I might be declared a 'counter-revolutionary' or a 'revisionist', and hauled away at any minute for 're-education'.

'In the meantime,' I added, 'we must develop a strategy. We need a deliberate plan to spread our story of success to encourage other communities to make changes before reforms that are inappropriate for the people of Kham are forced on us against our will.'

'I agree, Chuang-la,' Thupten said. 'We need to create a will to change. We need to explain the revolution to all levels of society. Most of all, we need the willing participation of the upper classes and the lamas.'

Thampa cleared his throat as if he had something important to say.

'Thupten helped me understand that communism,' he began, 'at least Marxism, as you've said, and Buddhism are not that different when it comes to living in the world. Both philosophies see the importance of eliminating suffering caused by oppression, and both think equal distribution of resources is a good thing. This is what swayed me more than anything else.'

'That is an excellent point,' I agreed. 'The idea that Buddhism and communism want the same outcome for people is an important concept.'

But Thampa continued to be pensive. 'That is an important insight but it was not the final reason for our decision to relinquish our holdings. It was Palden Rinpoche's suggestion that King Gesar would approve of the cooperative that finally convinced us.'

'King Gesar?'

There was that old story again. What incredible power it must hold on these people!

'King Gesar was wise,' Thampa continued. 'All the people were happy and shared the wealth of his kingdom. Rinpoche said that if the cooperative was modelled on the Kingdom of Ling, it would be successful. All that you have suggested is in agreement with the way Gesar would have us live.'

So there it was. The key to the hearts of the people of Kham and all of Tibet! Even more important than the commonality between Buddhism and communism, the story of King Gesar would have to be the way to promote a true revolution among the Tibetan people!

Part Two

Lithang
1954

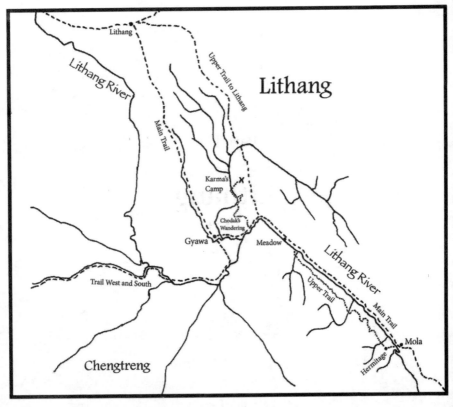

Southern Lithang with Gyawa and Mola

On the Way to Mola

During the spring of our fourth growing season in Gyawa, a friendly letter from Comrade Li suggested I leave Gyawa Cooperative and use my gifts to inspire people to form cooperatives in other villages. He called me a visionary; staying in one place and managing the affairs of one cooperative was not an adequate use of my abilities. Li's letter was a confirmation of my own feelings. I wanted to visit other villages, talk with opinion leaders, and see what could be done elsewhere. Several of Thampa and Dawa's peers among the aristocracy were interested in what we had accomplished.

I felt Gyawa Cooperative would continue to do just fine without me. Our method of decision-making gave everyone a voice and a vote. We had not set up a management committee, nor was I the authority figure; I did not control decisions. I thought I had made this clear to Comrade Li, but he was sending Tenzin back to Gyawa and assured me he had 'complete confidence' that Tsering Tenzin could 'supervise the collective'. I had no trouble reading between the lines; the use of the word 'supervise' suggested authoritative control, and the word 'collective' instead of 'cooperative' indicated to me that the Party was planning to implement their own social system through Tenzin.

I wondered if Comrade Li had, indeed, written the letter. Perhaps his influence was waning! Whatever the situation, I had to be more careful now.

When I told Thupten, he immediately objected; the idea that Tenzin, who had caused so much trouble before, was returning to the cooperative annoyed him greatly. Thupten was doubly vexed when I explained Comrade Li's implication that Tenzin would 'supervise the collective'. We both realized how unlikely it was that Tenzin would shake off his arrogance and take a supportive role, as I had.

Another alarming turn of events, from my point of view, was the appointment of Commander Deng Li Peng, a military officer of the PLA, as acting commissioner responsible for all of southern Kham. The military and civil authority for the districts of southern Kham, including Lithang, Daocheng, Derong, and Batang, were now in the hands of one man.

Most of the people of Gyawa had left for summer horse racing festival in Mola, a township south of Gyawa. Dawa and Thampa had been gone a week; they went to help Dawa's relatives prepare for the important festival. This year, instead of being held on the Lithang grasslands west of the town, the festival would take place in Mola. Thampa explained that the ever-increasing presence and watchfulness of PLA gave everyone an uneasy feeling about holding the festival in Lithang. It had been cancelled altogether the past three years but this year, the Gyatotsang clan—Dawa's people in Mola—were more than happy to revive their ancient tradition of hosting the annual festival. Publicly, it was announced that the Lithang festival was cancelled again, but privately, invitations were sent out to villages and nomadic clans who had traditionally participated in the Mola festival. Gyawa was one of these communities and excitement was high; it was rumoured that Palden Rinpoche was back and had made special preparations in celebration of ancient Khampa traditions.

Before she left, Dawa came to see me and insisted I attend the festival in Mola; I would be able to meet Palden Rinpoche and ask my questions about religion and King Gesar. The event would also give me a chance to meet nomads and villagers from all over southern Kham. I readily agreed, and looked forward to attending as an appropriate way to transition to my new mission.

Ahead of schedule, Tenzin arrived with his father, Nawang, and other dignitaries. It was not an official visit because they were passing through on their way to attend the festival in Mola. They had heard about it, despite the secrecy around the event. Pema let Nawang, Tenzin, and their friends stay overnight in Thampa and Dawa's house since it was vacant. To Thupten's chagrin, Tenzin began strutting around the village, greeting people as if they were old friends and making it clear he would return soon to replace me. Though I'd thought it appropriate to bring Tenzin up to date on the cooperative's activities, he deliberately avoided me.

The next morning, Tenzin, Nawang, and the other VIPs from Lithang, along with several others from Gyawa—including Thupten, Pema and their children—proceeded me on the trail. Feeling nostalgic, I lingered in my room to tidy up and store a few belongings—extra clothing, my papers and journals—in a wooden chest Pema said she would keep for me. I did not know how long I would be travelling from community to community, so I took a bare minimum with me. I was the last person to leave Gyawa for the festival. Only a few people stayed behind to feed the animals and keep an eye on things.

The warm air was full of the earthy scent of freshly ploughed fields, pine trees and the songs of birds. Above the forested hillsides, snow still covered the peaks on either side of the Lithang River Valley.

I turned back for a last look at Gyawa. The buildings of town were gleaming with fresh whitewash, and I was filled with a deep satisfaction; we had accomplished so much over the past three years. I laughed when I realized I had, like a proud parent, mixed feelings about leaving; there were reasons for both pride and trepidation.

At the bend in the river valley, I directed Chestnut to take a short side trail up the hill to get a view of the entire stretch of the valley that cradled Mola Township. It was a wide U-shaped valley with cultivated fields along the Lithang River. Most of the villages—and there were many in the township—were on the eastern side of the valley because the river cut close to the western edge, leaving little room for fields or villages. Dense forests covered both hillsides above the valley, thinning half way up the slopes into sparse bushes and high grassland pastures. The western hillside, referred to as the 'horse-grazing' side, was considerably steeper than the eastern 'cow-grazing' side. The lower end of the valley was abruptly terminated by a ridge covered with trees. I guessed it was the terminus of the glacier that carved the wide valley: a mound of rock and soil pushed there by a creeping glacier long ago. The river was diverted and forced through a gap in the towering cliff that had been carved by torrents of water when the ancient glacier melted away.

With a deep, refreshing breath of air, I cleared my head and spoke gently to Chestnut.

'Are you ready?' I asked, more to myself than to Chestnut, 'because I have a good feeling about this new adventure. Let's go!'

When Chestnut and I re-joined the main trail, she began to run as if responding to my excitement, but in reality, I think she wanted to catch up with other festival-goers who had left Gyawa before us. I slowed her down after a while and we walked at an even pace; I wanted to enjoy this temporary solitude, this gap between my experiences in Kham so far and those yet to come. I enjoyed the sights, smells, and sounds of the valley, heightened by my sense of freedom from responsibilities.

I began to drift into a daydream about taking the revolution all the way to the heart of Tibet in Lhasa. There was so much to accomplish in the future! I sincerely believed this next adventure would get me closer to fulfilling Jiachen's wish to liberate her people, and I was, at last, entering her ancestral homeland. Surely, that was what she had said; she wanted me to 'liberate' her people.

Full of these mindscapes, I wasn't aware when Chestnut wandered off the trail to graze in a lush meadow. The grass tickling her nose made her snort, and I was startled. Suddenly, I saw I was no longer on the trail. I laughed at myself and, instead of leading Chestnut back to the trail, I dismounted and let her continue grazing. It was a beautiful meadow. I took the opportunity to stretch my legs. Chestnut had chosen well!

I watched Chestnut graze; the grass she was eating was so green and alive with vitality. I walked around, the grass swishing and curling around my feet and calves. Hearing the roar of the river nearby, I went to watch the water tumble over rocks. I looked up to the forest on the hillsides above and watched trees dancing to the rhythm of the wind. Gradually, I felt a deep humming enter my body from the ground... as if the earth herself was singing with pleasure and, with a waft of fragrance and dazzling brightness, I was enfolded in an immense feminine presence. She stood with me on the meadow, her feet in the grass but her face looking down on me from the sky above. I can only relate to this form by calling her Kwan Yin, the mother of compassion, a goddess of incalculable power and understanding. Her face was intimately familiar to me; her voice, inside me, unmistakeably repeated Jiachen's parting message: *'Awaken! Awaken! Awaken!'*

And then she was gone! But in her wake, I saw my surroundings transfigured. Wherever I looked, things were transparent, crystal clear, and totally known to me. I felt oneness with whatever I looked at. Were the trees nearby really transparent? How was I able to see through them! Were they singing a joyful response to the forest on the hillsides above?

I looked at my hands; I could see right through them! A tear of joy dropped into my upturned hand. It was a molten pool of radiance reflecting the entire universe spilling its brilliance everywhere. In it, I could see everything from multiple points of reference. Light and radiant joy expanded endlessly, filling everything! The world and all its forms laughed with primordial delight in shimmering, clear, spacious light. Everything connected; all being, all things were united and moved by love. Everything felt inseparable, always interconnected; an unbroken stream of existence!

And she continued to say to me, *'Awaken! Awaken! Awaken!'*.

I looked again at Chestnut grazing; now I could taste and smell the grass she nibbled, I shared her awareness of the cool breeze, the insects buzzing round her sweating shoulders, and I even knew her 'thoughts' about me watching her—'Just a few more bites! Please!'

Whether this ability to see and know 'from the inside', as it seemed to me, lasted a long time or an instant, I could not tell but the experience collapsed with the thought that it was happening to me, to Chuang Wei Ming. Up to that point, there had been no thinking, no judging. With this ego-awareness, what had been translucent grew more opaque, what had been radiantly joyous subsided to the dull, normal mode of my usual orientation to the world; this was both a great disappointment and something of a relief. I was relieved that the world was 'solid' again.

Gradually, I realized I was back to 'normal'; doubts overpowered my thinking mind. Had I lost my grip on reality? How could this have happened? Wasn't I a rational, grounded person? There had to be a rational explanation. Had something caused me to hallucinate? Could I have ingested something? Had I been poisoned? Perhaps I was going mad? Was the anxiety of venturing into something new too much for me? Was I unstable?

I desperately tried to pinpoint any physical or psychological reason for this apparent lapse of sanity. Was there really such a thing as transcendent beauty and goodness beyond my understanding? Had I imagined seeing Jiachen? Could I have been brought to tears by an apparition?

My tears returned. I was filled with the beautiful sorrow of separation and longing; they were tears of love. Oh, how I missed Jiachen. Had she really appeared to me? Had she grown in her transcendent existence; was she the feminine presence who'd appeared to me as the goddess of love?

175

Shaking my head, as if to clear it, I went to Chestnut. Rested, she was eager to run. I let her gallop.

Was I going crazy?

I didn't want to acknowledge what had happened. I hoped never to go through anything like that again, and vowed not to let anyone know it had happened. People might think I was going crazy.

Desperately, I tried to tell myself I was not crazy. I had quite a revelatory emotional experience induced by heartache for my long-lost beloved. I hadn't encouraged it nor welcomed it; it had just happened.

Even so, it had been a powerful experience, and soon I had a wide grin on my face. I couldn't help it.

I rode on. I let myself into 'the flow' with Chestnut. We rode as one. I was reminded of galloping through the marshes as a boy, moments from the past when I'd been 'outside myself'; riding and shooting arrows with Master Tashi, and private moments with Jiachen. And suddenly I knew these extraordinary experiences did not mean I was going insane. I'd had them before!

I allowed the thrill and joy of my 'hallucination' to return and linger. I allowed exhilaration knowing it came from Jiachen; she was near me again and had spoken to me.

I allowed love.

Messenger of the Gods

By the time Chestnut and I caught up with the others travelling to the festival from Gyawa, we were nearly there. The trail left the river, and we followed it up to a wide grassland. Over five hundred tents were pitched in a randomly organized settlement.

I dismounted at the same time as Thupten and Pema at a large ceremonial tent, and an attendant took Chestnut from me. It was fitting that Thampa and Dawa greeted Pema and Thupten, who had once been tenants on their land, as enthusiastically as they greeted me. Dawa introduced us to her relatives, Samphel and his wife Zema. Samphel was dressed in a fine silk *chuba* trimmed with spotted leopard's fur. He was tall, powerfully-built but not corpulent like Thampa. A fox fur Khampa hat framed his proud face. Zema, standing beside Samphel, had on a multi-coloured silk *chuba*. She was tall, elegantly graceful and, I thought, very beautiful. The two of them together were the image of noble grace and confidence.

'Welcome to Mola,' Samphel said with sincerity. Turning to me, he added, 'We have heard so much about you. Dawa speaks very highly of you, as does my great aunt Yangchen.'

From this introduction, I was able to piece together the family connections. I knew that Yangchen had two brothers. Palden Rinpoche was the elder and Jampa was next, but he'd died many years ago. Samphel must be Jampa's son and patriarch of the Gyatotsang clan.

'We've heard about the cooperative, of course,' Samphel continued, including Thupten and Pema, 'but if you hope to convert us, expect to be disappointed.'

I smiled politely and held my tongue. Thupten was brave enough to say, 'We don't want to convert anyone, we only want to give dignity back to the people who deserve it.'

Samphel was taken by surprise and was about to respond, unkindly I would have thought from the look he gave Thupten, when Zema intervened to prevent a confrontation, 'Let it be. They've travelled far today to enjoy the festival.'

Turning to me, Zema added, 'Come with me. Refresh yourself with some *chang* inside our tent.'

Thupten and Pema excused themselves to set up their own tent.

'I'm glad you've finally arrived,' Dawa said to me as she followed me inside Zema's tent. 'There's a special performance beginning soon. You'll enjoy it.'

'Oh? What sort of performance?'

'A traditional singing drama we call *lhamo*,' Zema said.

'From the story of King Gesar,' Dawa added. 'Palden Rinpoche has organized it.'

'Wonderful!' I was immediately interested.

Dawa picked up a bundle of clothes and said, 'I brought these for you. You'll need to dress up for the festival. Find a place to change.'

It was a new silk *chuba*, bright green over a white silk shirt, blue pants, a red waist band and the golden fox fur hat Dawa had tried to give me once before. Once I put it on, I felt like any respectable Khampa ready to celebrate the festival!

❦

I followed Dawa and couldn't help noticing that the spell of ecstasy from my encounter on the meadow continued; everything I saw and heard remained brilliant, crystal clear, and filled with meaning.

The stage was an open area in front of a large white tent. It was set up in a natural amphitheatre at the base of the sacred hill, the ridge I had seen that abruptly ended the Mola Valley. There was plenty of sloping grass where people made themselves comfortable in family groups around the outdoor stage. Prayer flags, stretching overhead from the white tent, fluttered gracefully in the late afternoon breeze. The day had been warm so the breeze was refreshing, not cold.

There was no need to ask who the elderly but vigorous-looking man might be when he stepped into view on stage; everyone around me murmured with great respect.

'Rinpoche! Palden Rinpoche!'

He wore the robes of a monk but unlike most monks, his greying hair was long and tied round his head with red tassels like any Khampa man. He had a thin beard, too. His eyes sparkled when he smiled and his presence brought a radiant happiness to his audience, including me.

He played a six-stringed instrument, a *drangyen*, and began singing. The words of his song escaped me. Dawa said the words were an ancient form of their language that came to chosen singers of Gesar's story.

'Palden Rinpoche will interpret the song after he sings,' Dawa informed me. When Rinpoche concluded his song he bowed and, taking a few steps forward, addressed us.

'Good people of Kham, listen well to this story of your ancient king, Gesar of Ling,' Palden said. He didn't translate the song as Dawa expected. Instead, he proceeded to introduce the drama.

'Pay attention as Goddess Manene descends through clouds to awaken the young Gesar, and to remind him that he has a noble purpose.'

Saying this, Palden Rinpoche stepped to the left of the stage, put his *drangyen* down, and picked up a small drum and horn. He began a slow rhythm with the drum but our attention was on two young women, each holding an end of a long, gauzy length of white cloth between them, dashing across the area designated as the stage. They held the cloth so that it covered them from head to knees while it billowed between them as they ran toward us. Behind them, another pair of young women brought a brilliant red cloth, slightly shorter in length, toward the audience and stopped directly behind the first pair. More pairs, each holding a slightly shorter cloth than the previous pair added green, gold, and blue in a series of the five Buddhist colours; five veils across the stage. After a pause, four more pairs emerged and repeated the first four colours: white, red, green, and gold; a total of nine veils tapered from the front row of the audience to the opening of the white tent. This created a truly graceful and novel effect. The audience responded with gasps of delight as well as of discomfort. I was told later that this was not a traditional *lhamo*, it was an innovation disturbing to those who expected to see a traditional performance.

Our view of the tent opening was veiled but did not fully obscure the lone figure who pressed through layer after layer of coloured veils as she came toward us. This could only be Goddess Manene moving as if floating through clouds!

Each pair of young women wrapped Manene in their veil as she moved through them until she stood still before us, her outline majestic and intriguing. Then each pair, one by one, unwrapped her and carried the veils away. First, the longest white veil floated away to the right of the stage. The second veil, a brilliant red cloth, flowed away to the left. Eight veils vanished in this way, to the right and left, leaving a golden veil covering the goddess from head to toe.

When the golden veil was removed, we were dismayed to see her face still heavily veiled in white. We wanted to see her face!

She spoke.

'I am Manene, messenger of the gods. I descend to this world with an important message.'

This voice. These movements. The grace and fullness of her figure. They reminded me of someone...

Behind her veil, the goddess glided to one side of the stage looking earnestly out across the audience. Though it was clear she could not see through her veil, she searched for someone, perhaps someone able to hear her message. Disappointed, she glided to the other side. I watched in suspense.

I tried but failed to peer through her veil. Who is it?

The magical appearance of the goddess combined with the lingering translucent clarity experienced on my way here was playing tricks on me.

It was Jiachen! I was convinced.

Off to one side of the stage, Palden Rinpoche began playing his *drangyen* and the radiant goddess sang the lines she had only spoken before.

'I am Manene, messenger of the gods with an important message...'

181

Searching back and forth, she stopped abruptly in the middle of the stage and stepped forward, close enough for me to touch her.

There was no doubt who she pointed to suddenly.

She was pointing at me!

'...for you!'

She sang directly to me in her golden voice.

'The time has come! It is time for you to accomplish your mission in this world, to awaken my people!'

Several people in the audience drew their breath of surprise. No one was as surprised or as stunned as I was. It was as if the goddess recognized me! And, pointing to me, she said what Jiachen had said to me, 'Awaken my people'. This was no coincidence; it was Jiachen! It had to be!

I looked at Dawa. Deeply intent, she was mesmerized by the young woman playing the part of Manene.

I looked at Thampa who, thinking it was a good joke, chuckled and slapped my back as if to say, 'why would the goddess choose you, a foreigner!'.

'You are to join together,' the goddess continued singing, **'the ways of Heaven, Earth and the Human to create an enlightened society, a people of goodness, courage and dignity.'**

A hushed, attentive energy stirred the crowd. Though she continued to look at me, the audience was intent on her message, on her radiant presence.

As was I.

'You are to show that life in this world can be lived with a bodhisattva's wisdom and compassion. Young man, you are on treacherous ground in a corrupt world. Your

mission is to overwhelm the demons who dazzle minds and tether bodies.'

Turning to the rest of the audience, Goddess Manene delivered the rest of her message to them.

'Like Gesar's, his pure heart will fly straight through this world like an arrow but his acts will seem strange to deluded minds. He will use worldly means guided by primordial wisdom. Together, you will face demons and their unwitting slaves who are determined to pervert the face of liberation.'

She paced to the other side of the stage.

'Tread the path he shows you as windhorse warriors!'

The ninth pair of women with the golden veil rushed in to encircle and hide the goddess from us again. Palden Rinpoche's rattling drum slowed while the golden veil carried the goddess back into the white tent.

When his drum was silent and placed beside the *drangyen* and horn, Palden Rinpoche went backstage and immediately returned with the goddess. He led her right to where I was sitting with Thampa and Dawa, in the front row. With a flourish, he removed the veil from the beautiful goddess' face. People around me immediately recognized her and gasped in surprise.

Yes, it's Jiachen! It was definitely my beloved Jiachen. But it couldn't be!

My mind reeled, my heart pounded.

'This wonderful singer,' Palden Rinpoche announced, 'the young lady who played Manene, is Dechen, daughter of our beloved Thampa-la and his lovely wife Dawa-la.'

What? Could it be that Jiachen and Dechen were identical twins? No, it couldn't be; Dechen was Dawa's daughter, not Nuying's.

I looked at Dawa, then at Thampa. They were both overcome with joy and pride, but also, I thought, confused by Dechen's presence. They had not expected to see her, let alone hear her sing as beautifully as Goddess Manene in the story of King Gesar!

'You look surprised,' Palden said so everyone could hear, as if he was reading our thoughts. Addressing the entire audience, he continued, 'You heard Dechen returned from America a few years ago. You heard she stayed a few months and returned to America again. Well, she got as far as Kalimpong. She thought she could not fit into our way of life again but her heart said otherwise. Unable to leave, she came to see me and explained her dilemma. I suggested she study Buddha dharma and she eagerly agreed. She was a good student and her understanding was profound. She soon asked to go into retreat under my care.'

Palden Rinpoche looked at Dechen, as if asking permission to continue. Dechen nodded subtly.

'While on retreat,' he continued, 'she often entered a trance. It was soon clear to me that she is a true *babdrung*, a Gesar singer. But because of her Western education, she brings us wonderful gifts such as the idea of using coloured veils to represent clouds. She insists that we use our common language when reciting the Gesar story instead of the ancient language few of us understand. I am also impressed that she sees Buddha dharma and the legend of Gesar with fresh eyes and I'm convinced that through performances like this, she can teach us how we can all live in an enlightened society like Gesar's Kingdom of Ling.'

Palden finished his praise of Dechen, and bowed low before her to show us his high esteem for her. Still bowing, he backed away like a servant.

Dechen stood alone on stage, her arms spread wide in the gesture of blessing, and beaming with joy. Her beauty and presence lifted our spirits.

Then, she moved toward her parents with her arms still outstretched.

I saw Thampa struggling to stand so I got up to help him. Dechen happily embraced her parents while I stepped back. Though I was curious about her, I didn't want to intrude on the family reunion. And, indeed, Dechen ignored me even though I'd been sitting with her parents and she had singled me out during her performance.

I found myself craving her recognition, and I had to laugh at myself for thinking she was Jiachen and she should know me. I was telling myself there was no significance for me personally in what had happened in the performance. Anyone could have been the recipient of the goddess' call for the sake of the drama. Or perhaps she was in one of those trances Rinpoche mentioned and had no idea who she had pointed out. But then again, I acknowledged in a panic, if she really was in a trance, choosing me may not have been by chance.

In the midst of these thoughts, I saw Yangchen emerging from the white tent. She hurried toward me with her arms outspread! It was like seeing someone from home! She embraced me with unconditional, grandmotherly love.

'I'm so happy to see you, Wei Ming!' she exclaimed. 'I knew you were here, of course. Thupten told me when he came to Kalimpong. Jiachen would be so proud of you!'

'So good to see you, too,' I said. 'I hoped you'd be here with your brother!'

'Come,' she said taking my hand, 'I'll introduce you.'

185

I thought she was going to introduce me to Palden Rinpoche but Yangchen led me toward Dechen.

'Dechen, my dear,' Yangchen said gently, 'this is Wei Ming. The young man your sister loved.'

Your sister?

What was Yangchen saying? Were they truly sisters or did she mean sister as in sister-cousin, a term interchangeably used here?

I was so astounded that Dechen's response escaped me.

Yangchen saw my confusion.

'Let me explain,' she said. She glanced at Dawa a moment and Dawa nodded as if to say she could continue. 'Jiachen and Dechen are twin sisters. Dawa is their mother. Dawa and Nuying were visiting me in Chengdu while both were expecting babies. Nuying's baby died at birth but Dawa had twins. To save Nuying from bringing sorrow to her Chinese husband, I encouraged Dawa to give one of the girls to Nuying. That's how Jiachen was raised in Shanghai, and how I came to live with her.'

All I could do was look from Yangchen to Dawa, from Dawa to Dechen, and from Dechen back to Yangchen. It was too much. My heart was about to burst with emotion. Dechen reminded me so much of Jiachen! Dechen watched me sympathetically but said nothing. I had to acknowledge she was not quite like Jiachen, even though she looked and behaved in surprisingly similar ways.

I turned away and walked a few steps, before Yangchen followed and took my hand to console me.

'I'm sorry, Wei Ming,' Yangchen said. She held my hand while I tried to sort my feelings out.

'This is the man Manene has chosen!' I heard Rinpoche. I turned to see him pointing at me.

'What? My dead sister's Chinese communist lover?' Now, it was Dechen who was confused. She sounded angry! 'How is that possible?'

She had no sympathy for me now. Her angry eyes flashed all over me!

'I'll have nothing to do with him,' she said hotly to Rinpoche.

'Dechen,' Rinpoche pleaded, 'calm down! Yangchen and I will explain everything, but right now you need to go with your parents.'

Angry with Rinpoche, Dechen abruptly turned away. She readily accepted that Thampa and Dawa should be her primary focus. But Thampa was upset with Dawa.

'Did you know she was here?' Thampa nearly shouted.

'No, of course not!' Dawa glared at Thampa.

'Ba-la, don't be angry with Ama-la,' Dechen intervened. 'She didn't know I came back with Yangchen-la and Rinpoche-la. Nor did she know where I was. I was in retreat when Thupten came, and Yangchen-la didn't tell him I was there. Don't start blaming anyone.'

A host of mixed emotions played on Thampa's face: anger for not knowing she'd returned, relief that she was back, jealously of Palden for being with her for so long, curiosity about what she felt about giving their property to the cooperative, but finally, delight trumped all of those feelings. He embraced his daughter and turned to take Dawa's hand to form a ring; the three of them—father, mother, daughter.

This unfolding drama proved as interesting as the preceding performance for the gathered crowd. It was a more familiar, intimate performance. Thampa laughed with delight

187

as he looked around the circle of so many people empathetically enjoying his delight.

Then, suddenly, there was Tenzin! He was dressed for the festival in a fancy *chuba* like everyone else. He stood in the closest ring of onlookers staring at Dechen with wide-eyed, undisguised desire. More alarming still was seeing Thampa reach out and draw Tenzin into their family group!

'Daughter,' Thampa said full of delighted excitement, 'you remember Tenzin, don't you?'

Bewildered to see who her father had suddenly included in their family reunion, Dechen reacted angrily and stepped away from the tight family circle.

'No, Ba-la! I told you before, I make my own decisions!'

Dechen and Dawa regarded Tenzin scathingly.

Searching Dechen's face, Thampa struggled to understand her reaction. He threw a questioning glance at Dawa before settling his imploring eyes on Palden to intervene and correct his daughter's attitude. Palden willingly complied.

'You sent your daughter away at an early age, Thampa-la,' Palden reminded him as he stepped to Dechen's side. 'She has returned to her people, transformed and ready to serve them in her own way. You will need to accept her for who she is now.'

Thampa nodded with sad acknowledgement; tears filled his eyes.

Nawang angrily came to Tenzin's side and spoke sternly to Thampa.

'You'd better make sure your daughter understands our ways!' Nawang threatened, his angry face inches from Thampa's. 'We do not take broken agreements lightly!'

Nawang took his son by the arm and pulled him away. Father and son pushed through the crowd, jostling people as they went.

'Please, everyone,' Palden Rinpoche raised his voice for all to hear, 'return to your tents and enjoy your dinners. Enjoy your own families, and let this reunited family have some privacy.'

The crowd began to disperse noisily in all directions.

Yangchen remained with me. She took me by the arm to introduce me to the Rinpoche.

'This is my brother, Palden. I have been with him in Sikkim since I returned from Shanghai. I went there when he sent me a message that Dechen was with him. I wanted, of course, to know my other granddaughter.'

'I've heard about you,' I said as I bowed respectfully to Rinpoche. 'You are the one everyone tells me I should talk to when I ask them about Buddha dharma or King Gesar!'

'I'd be very happy to enlighten you about both,' Palden replied with a good-natured laugh. 'I've heard about you, too. We'll talk later. I have things to attend to now.'

Palden hurried off into the white tent that served as the backstage area. Dechen was going with Thampa and Dawa to their tent. Dechen had her arm around Dawa but continued to glance angrily at Thampa.

Yangchen suddenly laughed gently. 'As you can see, she is as independent and strong-willed as her sister!'

I could see what she meant.

'Come,' she said, 'I think you should stay with us. After all, I'm your grandmother. Almost. It is so good to see you, Wei Ming!'

189

Again, she laughed delightfully. I noted that both Palden and Yangchen liked to laugh and spread joy!

'This has been an incredible afternoon!' she exclaimed. 'So many revelations!'

She took me by the arm again, and led me toward a smaller tent behind the large white 'backstage' tent. It was a simple black tent of woven yak wool in the style of the nomads.

'One more thing I need to tell you,' Yangchen said as we walked. 'It was always Jiachen's dream to bring the Revolution to her people here.'

Yangchen saw my surprise and began to giggle.

'Yes,' she added, again as if reading my thoughts, 'I remember you telling me the last thing she said to you, communicating directly to your heart. Tell me again, what did she say?'

'She said, "Lib...", I mean, "Awaken my people!".' It was clear to me now that she had said 'Awaken' and not 'Liberate', though I was not sure why this distinction was important.

'That's right, she wants you to accomplish what she was not able to.'

We stopped walking and I searched her face as I grappled for understanding because she spoke of Jiachen in present tense, as though she still lived! 'That's what lovers do,' she continued, 'love is stronger than death. The connection remains and she has been guiding you.'

Thoughts, let alone words, were unable to form in my mind!

'Sometimes things don't work out as expected,' Yangchen said, disregarding my utter bewilderment. 'Jiachen's vision was limited. She had difficulty accepting spiritual reality until it was too late. She's making up for that now.'

The Legend is Alive

Palden Rinpoche's campfire crackled. We sat opposite each other under heavy wool quilts, holding warm bowls of chang. Yangchen was in the tent, asleep already. I stared into the fire puzzled by what Yangchen had said about Jiachen guiding me. How? Had she put ideas in my head? Had she brought me to Kham? Was none of this by chance?

Yangchen spoke as if death was no barrier between us. If that were so, how was it I had not always felt Jiachen's presence? Had I closed myself to her, dismissed her with my busy days, my rational this-worldliness, my self-centeredness?

Though Jiachen was often on my mind, today, in the meadow, her presence returned to me overwhelmingly. Then seeing Dechen, who was so like Jiachen, I was reminded of her tangible form, her breathtaking beauty! Now all I could feel was the acute pain of our physical separation.

An ember popped. I watched sparks soar into the darkness above and merge with the expanse of stars.

And what did Yangchen mean when she said Jiachen was making up for her limited vision? What was that about?

I conceded that Jiachen was as rationally idealistic as I had become. As a good communist, we both acknowledged that religion is based on superstition, and that real salvation comes through social struggle and economic progress in this material world. Why consider something that could never be proven scientifically? The spiritual domain was only as real as a daydream, a figment of imagination.

And yet I had experienced something earlier in the day that taunted my determination to discredit spiritual reality. Everyone here, from Yangchen and Palden Rinpoche to Dechen, took the spiritual dimension of life for granted.

I was, thankfully, distracted from my thoughts when Palden added a log to our fire.

'The legend is alive,' Palden said suddenly. 'It is kept alive by gifted men and women who add to it each generation. How? By entering Gesar's Kingdom in a trance.'

I must have revealed my scepticism with a wry smile.

'So Dechen is one of them?' I said as sarcastically as I could. 'She, ah, visits Gesar's kingdom? In a trance?'

'Yes, of course,' Palden said, ignoring my derision. 'As she did today.'

'Why? How? In her trance I mean, why did she point to me?'

Clearly amused, Palden tried not to laugh as he said, 'She apparently didn't know who she pointed to. You saw how angry she was when I told her it was you. How that happened, I can't say. Perhaps there's an explanation, perhaps not. You'll have to decide for yourself.'

He obviously knew something.

'You must have some idea, Rinpoche!'

Palden shook his head. He wouldn't explain.

I tried another approach. I wanted to unravel this mystery.

'So Dechen came back from America,' I said, reviewing what Palden had told the audience, 'but couldn't fit in.'

'It wasn't so much that she couldn't fit in,' Rinpoche responded, 'it was more a matter of needing to study Buddha dharma and unlearn mental habits from the West. Not so different from what you've done. You've had to unlearn a lot of your Western ways of thinking, too. Am I right?'

'My Western ideas?'

'Yes, of course. You had a Western style education just like Dechen did, and you adopted communism, which is a very Western ideology. While you and Jiachen fell into communism, Dechen was enthused by Western ideologies, tempered a bit by her hero Mahatma Gandhi, who believed non-violence is the natural and obvious result of our union with the sacred.'

I was impressed by the lama's grasp of the world, and grew excited at the prospect of an intelligent discussion with him.

'So now that she's back,' I pressed on, 'you've organized this program to reveal Dechen as a...ah... a *babdrung*.'

'Right. We want to go all over Tibet reminding our people of Gesar's wisdom. And if you ask me, it's just what's needed right now.'

'Oh? Why's that?'

An ember in the fire popped and sent sparks into space again.

'We believe Gesar is very much alive and continues to teach us. His message, if heeded, will keep our people strong, and give us courage and dignity as forces of change press upon us.'

'Forces of change? You mean our communist revolution?'

'No!' Palden responded immediately, then tempered his tone a bit. 'Actually, I don't have anything against communism. In fact, I have been very much in favour of the things you've

193

done in Gyawa. It is all in accordance with Buddha dharma. Equality, sharing resources and participating in labour, community-wide decision making—these are all good values, and exactly what King Gesar promoted a thousand years ago.'

I nodded in appreciation of Palden's acknowledgement of our shared values.

'You said the legend of King Gesar would "give us courage and dignity as forces of change press upon us". If you don't object to communism, what forces of change do you mean?'

Laughter, hoots, and whistling from nearby intruded on our conversation. People were having fun clapping, dancing, and singing.

'I should have said,' Palden replied a little louder, 'we must fortify our people with dignity and courage so they can welcome the forces of change. Gesar speaks to every aspect of our lives; social, political, economic, and spiritual.'

'Is Gesar the founder of your civilization?' I matched Palden's volume to be heard.

'You could say that, I guess. He gives us a vision for an enlightened society.'

Keenly interested, I moved around the fire, and closer to the old lama so we could continue conversing over the noise of the singing and dancing.

'Just like Chairman Mao!' I offered with zeal, 'Mao created a vision for the New China by establishing an enlightened society based on economic and social equality.'

Palden vigorously shook his head with a frown. 'What you mean by enlightenment and what we understand by that word are very different, my friend. Ours comes from the heart, from within.'

'Communism is of the heart, too! We passionately devote our lives to the cause. There are thousands of people like myself who are working day and night to change society for the better.'

'I applaud you. Sincerely, I do,' Palden said with a sad smile. 'Unfortunately, your revolutionary enlightenment is focused on **externals**. You don't understand enlightenment as we do.'

'Of course, I do!'

What was this old lama talking about? Couldn't he see the benefits communism brings to the people?

'The enlightenment communism brings,' I boldly declared, 'is the light of reason. The rational, scientific approach that organizes life so that all of us share the fruits of our labour.'

There! Surely he could not disagree with that argument.

'Yes, it is possible to know an infinite number of things with the mind and organize the world around us,' Palden responded calmly, and watched my reaction. 'I'm talking about wisdom, the wisdom of the heart which includes, but goes beyond the reach of the mind. The rational way of thinking identifies, categorizes, and thus separates things. Our enlightenment sees everything in unity, in non-duality. There is ultimately no separation; all things are holistically one. Everything in existence is united at the deepest level, which we can perceive with heart-mind. In this way of perceiving the world, contradictions are overcome. The rational mind is the wrong tool to use for understanding this dimension of our existence. The acknowledgement of this is missing from communism.'

Not able to understand, nor prepared to think through what he was saying, I changed the subject.

'Is the Gesar song written down somewhere?' I asked. 'Has it been translated into Chinese? I'd like to study it.'

195

'No,' Palden laughed, 'it is transmitted orally from the heart by special ones like Dechen. It is not written down, nor should it be.'

Again, not willing to understand what he was talking about, I diverted the conversation.

'I think you know why Dechen pointed to me in her trance,' I said pointedly. 'Was Goddess Manene actually choosing me for something? If so, what for?'

'Oh, that!' Palden laughed. 'No, really, I don't know yet. We'll have to wait and see.'

Palden Rinpoche curled up under his quilt and prepared to sleep by the fire. I did the same but couldn't sleep right away; I was sorting out the events of this most confusing day.

I lay awake gazing at the stars. It was my first time sleeping in the open.

<hr>

The next morning, I was urged to participate in one of the festival activities. I'd been warned that I would not be allowed to stand around and observe; participation was a must! As an accepted member of Gyawa, I was no longer considered a visitor. When Thupten said I would be riding a horse and shooting at a target, he laughed and said it would be fun even if I couldn't hit the target. It would entertain the crowds. I guess he expected me to be the local clown.

I played along. In front of hundreds of onlookers, I let him show me how to hold a bow and shoot an arrow. I made a scene of being clumsy and ignorant. Thupten and Tenzin laughed, encouraging others to laugh and enjoy my attempts to fit in.

With a bow in hand, I had memories of Master Tashi with tinges of nostalgia for the days spent with him on the marshy delta plains outside Shanghai. The days before communism! In the days of capitalism when families like my own ruled Shanghai. When I lived a privileged life that gave me opportunities to learn from someone like Master Tashi.

I took a practice ride on Chestnut along the row of targets, deliberately fumbling with my arrows and missing every target.

'Not even one?' Thupten said with mild dismay when I returned.

Tenzin hooted with delight! His practice run had demonstrated he could hit each target. Not accurately, but at least he hit them.

I had no idea what the stakes of this competition might be, but I decided to accept the challenge because there were several other riders, besides Tenzin, who did quite well in their practice runs.

The competition began and most of the dozen or so competitors had completed their runs; only Tenzin and I remained. I noticed Dechen arriving to watch us. She stood with several of the young women who had helped with the drama performance. Tenzin noticed, too, and made a grand bow in Dechen's direction before he started his run. Better than any run so far, Tenzin's arrows hit near the centre of each of the six targets. He gloried in the attention he imagined Dechen was giving him but when I looked back at Dechen, I could see her eyes were not on him; they were on me. I imagined her companions were telling her with great amusement how the clumsy foreigner had fumbled his practice run.

It was my turn; I was the last competitor. I ignored Dechen. I ignored Tenzin. I ignored the crowd because I remembered something Master Tashi had taught me: 'There is only the target. There is no you, there is no bow, there is no horse. There is only the arrow and its target. Let the arrow and target be one.'

I let Chestnut run and did as my master had advised. I flowed with Chestnut's movement under me, as we had run together the day before. I fixed my intention on the first target. With six arrows in my right hand, I sank an arrow in the centre of the first target and turned my attention to the next one, the next and the next, until I'd passed each target and my hand was empty.

When I turned my horse back toward the waiting crowd, I grabbed a second bunch of six arrows I had tucked between my thigh and the saddle. I faced the target and let loose an arrow that split the first arrow in two. The crowd watched in stunned silence. I proceeded at a walking pace to the next target, faced it on the horse, split my arrow and moved to the next target. An official ran from one target to the next behind me, exclaiming, 'The first arrow in the centre of each target is split by the second!'

Palden was now standing beside Dechen. He watched me intently as I emerged from my flow-induced state and approached the onlookers. Palden showed little surprise about my achievement, and Dechen observed me with level detachment. But Thupten, along with everyone else, was astonished by what I'd done. When I dismounted and handed him Chestnut's reins, his mouth was wide open but unable to speak. Samphel, and even Tenzin's father, Nawang, stood nearby staring at me, trying to understand what they'd just witnessed.

'Well done, Wei Ming!' Palden said so Dechen could hear him. 'You've shown your true colours now.'

Tenzin gave me a defiant glare. He was angry his skills paled in comparision to mine, and jealous that Dechen was watching me; a situation that would be awkward if encouraged.

'I was lucky!' I responded to Palden. I was feeling the intensity of every eye on me.

'No,' Palden countered with certainty. He raised his voice so everyone could hear. 'That was not a matter of luck. You are skilled. You know how to hold the arrows in your hand and how to shoot from the right side of the bow like an ancient warrior. Tell us, where did you learn to ride and shoot like that?'

I shook my head trying to deny my skills. I was sure Yangchen knew about Master Tashi and may have already told Palden. Jiachen had joined us to ride and hunt on several occasions before she became all-consumed by the Revolution. I guessed Palden was trying to get me to reveal the source of my training for everyone else to hear.

'It so happens,' I explained as I glanced about, 'that as a boy I had a Tibetan riding and shooting master in Shanghai.'

'Oh?' Palden said deliberately showing surprise and curiosity. 'What was his name?'

'I called him Master Tashi.'

'Tashi?' Palden repeated. 'Yes, that's a Tibetan name.'

Tenzin suddenly got on his horse and galloped through the crowd, scattering people who shouted at him with displeasure.

I spent the rest of the afternoon as the centre of attention at the archery run, where I demonstrated and taught several young riders how to shoot arrows from the right side of the bow in rapid sequence. It proved to be an opportunity to get to know several young men and their fathers who, I determined, were mostly leaders of the small villages of Mola township and nomadic clans from the surrounding grasslands.

As the sun rose the next morning, people were already heading for the open field. It was the day of the main event of the festival, the horse race. Riders would take banners and prayer flags to the top of the sacred mountain, the ridge that cut across the valley and diverted the river. Putting prayer flags in the wind up there was not so much a competition as a journey to the sacred peak, where the riders gained blessings for their families. Most of all, it was a celebration of the horse and its rider, a ritual continuously observed since ancient times.

Again, I was told to take part. Thupten explained to me that the only objective was to reach the summit where I must plant a banner, and join in with the others in the jubilant victory shout to the gods. Despite the non-competitive nature of the experience, it was still a race and the first to the summit received special blessings from the gods. That was reason enough for most of the riders to try to ride faster than anyone else. Well, I thought, I didn't believe in the gods so it would be prudent if I didn't reach the summit first.

Tenzin galloped past on a shiny black horse as I leisurely led Chestnut from the corral to the field. I recognized Tenzin's horse as one Nawang had brought with him from Lithang. It was much taller and stronger-looking than the local mountain variety. But horses from the lowlands generally did not do well at high altitude. My chestnut mare was a hybrid. She was a little taller than a full-blooded mountain horse and ran nearly as well in these mountains.

Tenzin's haste and confidence both amused and dismayed me. I felt sorry for him; he so desperately wanted Dechen's attention. He was determined to have her. If the traditional match, the arrangement between Nawang and Thampa, was out of the question, it made sense that Tenzin would do everything he could to impress Dechen in the hope she would change her mind about him. If Dechen was like Jiachen, I knew she would not find desperation attractive!

Palden came up beside me, leading a small, white mountain stallion. It was a fiery thing, not used to staying still and probably wishing it could fly!

'Your mare will not do,' Palden said. 'Ride this one instead.'

'Oh, no thanks, Rinpoche, I'll ride my own horse.'

'No, you must ride this one,' Rinpoche insisted. 'You must receive the blessings of the sacred mountain gods.'

'I don't need the blessings, Rinpoche. Let someone else have them. I don't believe in the gods.'

I had no choice as it turned out. Palden simply took the reins of my horse from my hand and replaced them with those of the little white horse. His spirited animal reluctantly followed me, and gave me a hard time when I tried to mount its low back.

Once again, the crowd was laughing at me. I must have looked foolish trying to control the horse. My long legs nearly touched the ground and, once I put my feet in the stirrups, my knees were up near my ears! I had to get off while a young man adjusted the length of my stirrup straps for a better fit.

I was the last to join the line-up of hopeful riders. As if waiting for me, Palden Rinpoche walked out into the middle of the field, directly in front us. He raised his arms and everyone, even the horses, immediately grew silent. It was remarkable how much respect this man commanded.

'This race honours our ancestor King Gesar of Ling. Today, you ride as Gesar's windhorse warriors! *Ki! Ki! So! So! Lha Gyalo!'*

The horsemen and the crowd joined him in one voice.

'*Ki! Ki! So! So! Lha Gyalo!*

'*Ki! Ki! So! So! Lha Gyalo!'*

When Palden lowered his arms, the horses leapt into action. I was swept along with them on my little white stallion. I thought we'd knock Rinpoche over but we flowed around him like river rapids around a rock.

I found that I didn't need to urge or guide my little mount. He did what he wanted to do. He was in fierce pursuit of the leaders of the pack. Among the leaders, across the flat stretch of the open field, was Tenzin on his black charger. By the time we reached the foot of the sacred mountain, I was there among the lead group.

Thanks to my northern Chinese ancestry, I was as tall and big-boned as a Khampa. With the exception of Tenzin, who was short but rode a tall horse, the rest of us looked huge riding our small horses. How could these little animals move so fast with such big loads? And my little horse was doing so well! I was astounded.

On the uphill climb, I thought we would surely fall behind, but we kept ahead of the main pack. We reached the top of the ridge, and the race suddenly began in earnest. The ridge top was wide enough for two or three horses abreast, and my sure-footed steed made the most of the rocky, uneven terrain.

I didn't know his name but I found myself talking to my little white stallion as we flew past several others.

'That's it, Little White!' I shouted encouragingly, 'you can do it! Get past two more!'

A competitive streak took over me. I now wanted to win! In this new mindset, I ordered Little White to run faster!

'Faster! Come on! Run!'

Little White stumbled and we fell behind. I immediately saw the link between my desire to win and Little White's progress. Master Tashi's voice came back to me, 'Don't think, and don't demand. Just ride. Give your horse your full attention and let it run.'

I apologized to Little White, released my own expectations and let him run; we began to 'flow' together, just as Chestnut and I had been able to do in the archery run. We gained on the riders ahead of us once again. Little White passed one, then another. Only the tall black horse being ridden by Tenzin was ahead of us.

Tenzin turned his head and looked at me in surprise. Anger flooded his face, he beat his horse savagely to keep ahead.

'This is not your race, comrade! I'll never let you win!'

He raised his whip as if to lash Little White across the face, but we leapt to the side. Tenzin's whip met empty space and the force of his violent motion made the tall black horse stumble. I looked back and saw Tenzin land face-first in a juniper bush.

Suddenly, Little White and I were at the peak of the sacred mountain. Other horses surrounded us. I was encouraged to dismount and plant my banner at the centre of a centuries-old heap of *mani* stones. Other banners were planted around mine, and the victory shout was raised.

> '*Ki! Ki! So! So! Lha Gyalo!*
> '*Ki! Ki! So! So! Lha Gyalo!*
> '*Ki! Ki! So! So! Lha Gyalo!*'

Our shout rang up the valley, and echoed back and forth from the flanking mountainsides. When the last echo faded away, our shout was answered from the encampment below. Once again, the echo reverberated while the world stood still to listen.

Tenzin stood where he'd fallen. He was covered in twigs and dirt, and he was furious! He did not come to the peak to add his banner but threw it to the ground, and sulkily led his black horse down the backside of the mountain.

He'd lost face.

Again.

The afternoon was a continuation of horse riding and stunts for the enjoyment of the crowd. The gathering of nomads and villagers lined both sides of the race track to watch. *Khata* were tossed into the raceway by young women for riders to sweep up from the ground. Some would lean over backwards so far they nearly fell off their horses, but managed to stay on and scoop up several *khata*s.

Again, Thupten demanded that I participate. I watched carefully as the other riders swept up the *khata*, and decided I could try it. I noticed, too, that Tenzin did not ride his tall black horse. That would have put him too high off the ground to reach the *khata*. He rode a smaller mountain horse, low to the ground. These horses had been trained to counterbalance their riders when they leaned far over to one side.

I had no doubt Little White would be up to this task, but I was worried I wouldn't be. Giving in to shouts of encouragement from Thupten and several others, I gave it a try. Little White took off and we raced toward a *khata*. Trying to emulate how the other riders gripped the belly of their horses with their legs, I leaned over the side to retrieve the *khata*.

The next thing I knew, I was rolling in the dust! Little White continued running without me! I heard bursts of laughter and shrill whistling from the crowd.

I'd made their day! The foreigner had eaten some good Khampa dirt!

King Gesar of Ling

Although I'd anticipated my life taking a completely new direction after I had entered Mola, I didn't know how to deal with what was happening to me now. Since that curiously disturbing experience on the meadow, I was aware of an intense vitality to everything. The air seemed to be fresher, water tasted sweeter, colours were brighter, and sounds were crystal clear. Most of all, my heart was lighter. Whatever activities I got involved in, despite my initial reticence, became all-absorbing, fulfilling and successful—except for the *khata* episode, but that was fun, too.

Wherever I went, I was treated like a hero by young and old alike. Curious children followed me just as the young boys had befriended and followed me in Lithang. Chittering young women watched me from a distance. Older women took me by the arm and offered me a bowl of tea or *chang* when I passed their tents. The men would bow or slap me on the back as I walked past. I longed for the anonymity I had in Gyawa. I didn't like being a celebrity.

The only logical explanation I could come up with about the way the people were treating me was that I had defied expectations. I'd interfered twice, as Tenzin insinuated, by outperforming every local participant. Rinpoche went around repeating how I'd been trained in ancient warrior arts by Master Tashi, a Tibetan in faraway Shanghai. I never dreamed, when

Master Tashi was teaching me, I'd ever be put in a situation like this! This was the second time his training had benefitted me; jujutsu had returned to me instinctively when attacked by the enraged nomad in Lithang, and now the riding and shooting skills had manifested.

Caught in a web of my own thoughts, I paid little attention to Palden Rinpoche sitting with me at our campfire as we had the previous two nights. When I looked up from the mesmerizing glow of the embers, I couldn't help notice how perfectly still he sat; so fully present and alert. I admired his skill and suddenly realized how much he reminded me of Master Tashi.

Wondering where Master Tashi was now, I looked up at the night sky ablaze with brilliant stars. How I loved the night sky! In the city it was never noticed. Here, with no electric lights shining into polluted air, the stars seemed close enough to reach out and touch. My Western education told me they were trillions upon trillions of miles away, but that didn't matter. They seemed closer here in Kham.

I looked at Rinpoche again. He rested upon the earth with equanimity; like Master Tashi, a fount of wisdom. I wanted to tap into his experience and learn what I could. I wanted his help; if communism was as close to Gesar's 'enlightened society' as he claimed, surely he would help me ignite a Tibetan revolution.

'The legend of King Gesar is very long,' Rinpoche began suddenly as if anticipating my desire to hear the story. 'To tell you the whole story would take a great amount of time, months perhaps. I will only give you an outline this evening.'

'That's all I need,' a replied with a grin. I'd been looking forward to hearing this story.

207

'Gesar incarnated powerful mythic forces connected with Shambhala, a sacred transcendent world. He is considered a manifestation of Padmasambhava, the Great Guru Rinpoche. By nature he is like Manjushri, an eternally youthful divine prince. In the future he will be Ridgen Rudrachakrin, the final Shambhala king who will establish a new Golden Age here on earth.'

'Wait a minute!' I objected, 'I don't understand what you're talking about. Incarnation, mythic forces, Shambhala, transcendent worlds, and future golden ages leave me confused. I'm not used to being bombarded in this way.'

'Fine.' Rinpoche agreed with a smile. 'Since you don't know much about these things, I'll keep it simple.'

Rinpoche began again and related the complex story. This is how I understood it:

King Singlen of Ling was a week and timid man. His queen, apparently, was barren, so Singlen conceived a child with one of the queen's servant girls. The king had a younger brother, Todong, who was jealous and thought he should be king. He couldn't kill his brother, but hoped to be king after Singlen. When Gesar, Singlen's heir, was born, Todong conspired with the queen to destroy the servant girl's child. Gesar, however, was bestowed with magical powers. Everything the jealous uncle and stepmother tried to do backfired, and the little boy only grew in strength. The uncle and the queen eventually managed to have Gesar and his mother banished to the wilderness, where they survived by living as simple nomads.

When Gesar became a man, Manene appeared to him and revealed his destiny to him. The future king was given the magical horse, Khyang Go Karkar. Together, young Gesar and his horse found a vast treasure hidden inside a sacred mountain. The treasure included magical armour and weaponry to protect him in his future battles.

Gesar returned to his father's kingdom on the magical horse and arrived just in time for the summer horse race. Gesar learned that King Singlen, his father, had gone on pilgrimage to India 10 years ago, and had not returned. Since it was assumed the king was dead, Todong was holding this race to decide who the next king would be. He had proclaimed that the winner of the summer horse race would become the next King of Ling, and would also marry Sechen Dugmo—the most beautiful woman in the kingdom, the daughter of a wealthy merchant.

Gesar, knowing just how devious Todong was from stories his mother had told him, assumed the race was rigged. He entered the race looking like a wild man from the wilderness, and he was told he could not take part looking like a beggar. So, after all the riders started, Gesar acted like his horse couldn't help itself and took off after them. Being on a magical horse, Gesar was soon riding side by side with Uncle Todong. Gesar shouted, 'Hello, Uncle'. Todong recognized Gesar, and was filled with rage. He struck at Gesar's horse to discourage it, but Khyang Go Karkar merely leapt ahead. Todong tried to catch up but Gesar was first to cross the finish line. Gesar was declared King of Ling, and married the beautiful Sechen Dugmo.

As king, Gesar waged war against the demons to the North, East, South and West. He was a warrior king who won 18 wars altogether. These included wars in Yunnan, the jungles of Assam and Northern Burma, kingdoms of the Himalayan Mountains from east to west, and even to the plains of India to the South; in Mongolia to the North; against the Persians and Turks in the far West; and to the East, of course, he confronted the Chinese and subdued the demons he encountered there. These wars brought turmoil, but eventually, lasting peace and Buddha dharma to many people.

Two hundred years earlier, Padmasambhava, the great Guru Rinpoche, established Buddha dharma in Tibet by defeating the powers that held the local people captive across its mountains, valleys, forests, and grasslands. Gesar, who was sent to continue the struggle against these forces, as well as against demonic forces from outside Tibet, raised an army of hundreds of thousands of warriors. He was assisted by commanders who were themselves enlightened beings. Together, they brought about peace, openness, happiness, and enlightenment to all people.

Gesar's army was an army of heroes, both men and women, who relied on the skills of non-violence. In battle, they stood before their enemies and faced poisoned arrows, flaming spears, and swords. They did not strike first, nor did they turn and flee. With patient awareness, they were able to catch incoming arrows with their hands, deflect a flaming spear, and rely on the strength of their shields and armour. If the forces against them were too strong, they fell in battle, but they accepted this willingly if others were protected by their sacrifice.

I was amused by learning that the rest of the lengthy story of King Gesar of Ling is mostly a series of great songs of war. Each warrior sang of his or her heroic battle and began with an invocation to Guru Rinpoche, or another deity, followed by an introduction of him or herself. Their songs included a description of battle and the reason for fighting.

It is more accurate to say they fought against anthropomorphized demonic forces. Rinpoche pointed out that people in positions of power are motivated by envy, pride, greed, and hatred. These were the 'demons of the four directions', the demonic forces that Gesar and his warriors battled. Rinpoche emphasized that Buddha dharma teaches compassion toward the people corrupted by these forces; thus Gesar counselled his warriors to battle against these powers rather than the people ignorantly consumed by them. These wars, therefore, not only brought order and happiness to Gesar's own people, but spiritual liberation to those whom they battled by releasing them from negative forces.

Gesar was not only a warrior; he was also a great teacher. He imparted profound teachings to those closest to him during his lifetime; things he'd learned as a result of conquering his own mind during many years spent in solitary meditation. As an enlightened king, he taught with great wisdom about the nature of mind. His greatest achievement was to establish an enlightened society among the people of Ling; a society in which all excelled in the understanding and practice of Buddha dharma.

Palden Rinpoche, after gazing silently at the embers for a while, finished by saying, 'The enlightened society Gesar established in Ling is a legacy the songs keep alive. It is my hope we can recreate just such an enlightened society.'

Overcome with strong emotion by the power of Rinpoche's story, I found myself trying to find a way to connect Gesar's legend to my own mission.

What was its relevance to our present situation? Was there a way to use this story to help all the people at this festival, for instance, to willingly accept the social and economic reforms the Party would insist on? Without Rinpoche's support, I would not have access to the people. And without reaching mutual understanding about the nature of my mission, I would not get his support. I was about to open my mouth and begin a conversation along this line of thought when Dechen appeared out of the dark, and sat on the carpet to Rinpoche's left.

'You are quite mistaken if you think you will succeed here as you have in Gyawa,' she declared abruptly. It was as if she'd been reading my mind.

'Why would it not work here?' I asked as evenly as I could. When she did not respond, I continued. 'I'm sure you and Rinpoche have ideas of your own. Tell me about them and let's see if we can find a way to help the people of Mola township adjust to what's sure to upset the current social structure. In my opinion, it is best to accept the new reality, understand it and find ways to make it work for everyone.'

Yangchen emerged from the tent and joined us. She put her hand on my shoulder for support as she sat down beside me.

Seeing Yangchen comforting me, Dechen's tone also softened, and she continued, almost apologetically.

'What you've done in my parents' village so far is praiseworthy but, ah, at the same time, somewhat limited.'

'Thank you,' I replied, 'I'm grateful that you supported your parent's decision to share their land. It is a courageous and noble thing they have done.'

I smiled graciously and tried to be unruffled by Dechen's apparent ability to read my mind. I glanced at Palden to see him watch our exchange with amused interest.

'I'm open to any ideas you might have,' I continued, 'that would make my efforts, ah, less limited.'

'Don't presume I'm going to help you!' Dechen was fiery again. Without giving me time to respond with an equal retort that was on the tip of my tongue, Dechen turned on Palden Rinpoche with an equally fiery demand. 'And I don't understand why you and Yangchen-la asked me to come here tonight!'

'My intention in getting the two of you together,' Palden said with a raised and authoritative voice, 'is certainly not for you to argue!'

'You're right, Rinpoche,' Dechen acknowledged and continued with a deliberate display of sarcasm, 'I apologize Perhaps you don't realize we're dealing with a Chinese communist masquerading as a Khampa! Has this escaped your notice? I'm quite bewildered that you are even sitting here with him!'

I was more amused than upset.

'You remind me of your sister!' I chuckled with a grin.

'I never knew her,' Dechen said dismissively.

I suddenly missed Jiachen deeply.

'I'm not Jiachen!' Dechen shouted, sensing my emotions.

'Enough!' Palden exploded. 'I know this is awkward for you but you must realize the two of you have been brought together by circumstances beyond your control. Yangchen and I need you to listen to us a moment.'

'This is very important,' Yangchen said once Dechen's anger subsided. 'As Palden-la says, you have both been brought to this place for a reason. We are sure about both of you. And Dechen, there is no mistake about Wei Ming. He's the one Palden and I have been looking for. It has been more than adequately confirmed.'

Dechen looked as astonished as I was bewildered by Yangchen's statement but there was no opportunity to ask for clarification. Before either one of us could speak, Thampa, followed by Nawang and Tenzin, stumbled into the firelight. Thampa was uncharacteristically blustery and it was obvious the three men were intoxicated.

'What're yer doin' 'ere?' Thampa demanded with slurred words. He looked only at Dechen.

Palden, Yangchen, Dechen and I stood to meet the angry men.

'We had something to discuss with Comrade Chuang and Dechen,' Palden said mildly.

'S'after dark. M'daughter sh' be 'ome.'

Tenzin reeled forward in drunkenness. He pointed at me and shouted, 'There! Didn't I tell you?'

Thampa moved toward me as quickly as his thick frame allowed. He pushed Dechen aside to get to me. I was shocked by his aggressive behaviour; he'd never behaved like this toward me before.

'What're yer intentions with m'daughter?' Thampa demanded, drunk and angry.

'Ba-la!' Dechen was just as shocked, 'what are you doing?'

Thampa turned on Dechen and screamed furiously at her, 'Shuddup!'

People came running from their tents and campfires; a crowd quickly encircled us. I glanced briefly at the curious, shocked faces illuminated by the firelight.

'If you will listen to me for a moment, Thampa-la,' Palden said soothingly.

Dawa broke through the circle to get to Thampa's side and put a hand on his arm to calm and reassure her husband. Thampa acknowledged Dawa's presence and noticed the circle of people his behaviour had drawn. He looked at me and his manner softened as if he was coming to himself again; the Thampa-la I thought I knew.

'The other day,' Palden began when he had Thampa's attention, 'your daughter gave her first public appearance as a *babdrungma*.'

Palden hesitated a moment while he gestured toward me.

'I was as surprised as anyone when Manene singled out this man from the crowd. Your daughter was in a trance. She did not consciously make the choice. Goddess Manene chose this young man.'

The crowd murmured in response.

'Then he proceeded to demonstrate skills,' Palden continued, 'as if Manene had truly awakened the ancient warrior ways in him.'

I noticed Dechen look at Rinpoche, then at me trying to guess what Rinpoche was about to reveal to everyone.

'That's why Yangchen-la and I called Dechen here tonight. We were explaining the uniqueness of this situation to them both. Now all of you will know, too.'

The crowd was stunned. All eyes were on me and I must have looked as confused as I felt.

Tenzin's anger was not abated. He stepped toward Palden, venting.

'I really don't care what you say! He's a Chinese communist and communists don't believe in bullshit like this! Goddess Manene, indeed! This whole damn festival's been rigged! By you, old man!'

One could hear the gasps! People were shocked at Tenzin's disrespect for Rinpoche.

Palden Rinpoche laughed.

'Rigged? Where have you seen shooting like that? Who could have rigged something like that? And the horse riding? I understand your big horse stumbled and you ate some dirt!'

Nawang must have thought Tenzin had gone a bit too far. He quietly put a hand on his son's shoulder to spare further embarrassment.

'Just a moment, son,' Nawang said to Tenzin. Then he spoke in the strong public voice we were used to hearing from officials. 'Comrade Chuang won the archery run and the race to the peak fairly. We all concede that. But how is it possible to know about the performance? She could just as easily pretend to be in a trance as to actually be in one. It's your word against our disbelief.'

Tenzin shook his father's hand off his shoulder.

'That's not the issue here!' Tenzin exploded. 'I want to know why this old man is encouraging Dechen to associate with the foreigner! She's been promised to me!'

There it was! He persisted in this claim.

The crowd gasped.

I saw Dechen bristle; she couldn't hold her tongue any longer.

'I've communicated my answer to your fantasy of a so-called marriage arrangement,' she said evenly to Tenzin, who was now standing directly in front of her. 'Stop pressuring my father. He does not make decisions about my life. I do. Understand?'

'Beloved people of Kham,' Rinpoche interrupted, ignoring Tenzin's bluster, 'I must tell you about the purpose of our *lhamo*. I believe, as Goddess Manene proclaimed, that this young man from Shanghai will fulfil a sacred mission. It is our plan to take this *lhamo* to people all over Kham. I wanted to ask Comrade Chuang to join us because Yangchen-la and I believe he may be a *babdrungpa*, able to play the part of Gesar. However, he is not yet a follower of Buddha dharma and has much to learn.'

It was my turn for astonishment. I think I stood with my mouth wide open and my mind in total shock.

This was getting out of control! *Babdrung*? Me? What sort of asinine scheme is this about me joining their drama troupe?

Nawang interrupted my introspective reeling by turning his incredulity on Palden Rinpoche.

'Surely you can find someone better than a Chinese communist to join your *lhamo*. Why not my son! He'd make a good Gesar, don't you think?'

'No!' Dechen blurted out. She'd had enough. 'I'm not as convinced as Rinpoche-la about this communist, but there is no chance Tenzin can be involved!'

217

Nawang coldly turned to Dechen, 'As your future father-in-law, I don't like the idea of your involvement in this Gesar *lhamo* if Comrade Chuang is to be part of it!'

'So be it,' Palden avowed suddenly. He stepped in between Nawang and Dechen, who was on the point of turning her wrath on the man who claimed to be her future father-in-law. But he surprised me by remaining calm. 'Comrade Chuang will not be part of the *lhamo* if you, as Lithang district commissioner, allow Dechen and me to perform our *lhamo* in Lithang or anywhere else we wish to go.'

Nawang stepped back and took a deep breath. 'Permission granted,' he said magnanimously. 'You may come to Lithang and perform for us but my offer to accept my son as part of your *lhamo* will continue to stand. You must never include Comrade Chuang. His participation would be regarded with disfavour by Khampa and Chinese alike!'

Before anyone else could respond, I felt obliged to state my position in this matter.

'I have no intention of performing in anything whatsoever! My only purpose for meeting Palden Rinpoche is to learn about your traditions so I can promote communist values in a way suitable to your local situation.' I paused for a moment. 'I applaud Palden Rinpoche's intentions to bring your history alive through performances about the life of your ancient King Gesar. Perhaps there is a way that the story of King Gesar, with its emphasis on creating an enlightened society, could help explain the benefits of forming cooperatives. It would be wonderful if we could work together but I don't think I'm really a *babdrungpa*, do you?'

A few weak chuckles rippled around the crowd, and Rinpoche took charge of the situation.

'Now please,' Rinpoche said, 'return to your tents!'

People began to disperse. Dechen left with her parents. Even Nawang and Tenzin staggered away. Yangchen, Palden and I were left alone by the fire but I was too numb to engage in conversation.

Dechen

The festival was over. With the first light of morning, people took down their tents and packed caravan animals for the journey home. Nawang approached me and insisted I return to Lithang with him. Commander Deng and other officials from Chengdu wanted to meet me, he said.

I bid goodbye to Yangchen and Palden Rinpoche. They had been very good to me. They invited me to visit them at Rinpoche's hermitage on the hilltop, west of Mola, when I returned from Lithang.

I saddled Chestnut and joined Nawang, Tenzin, Thupten, and Pema as they headed up the Lithang River Valley. Coincidentally Thampa, Dawa, and Dechen were leaving at the same time. Thampa had insisted that since Dechen was back in the area, she should spend time with her parents in Gyawa. She dutifully obliged them.

As the two parties rode along together, it was clear that tension between Dechen and Tenzin continued. Tenzin rode sullenly behind Dechen, staring at her back. I wanted nothing to do with them, and tried to stay out of the way. But even so, I was curious. I watched as Tenzin managed to get alongside Dechen. I could hear their brief exchange.

'Dechen,' he began hopefully, 'I'm sorry about last night.'

Dechen pretended not to hear.

Tenzin tried a different approach.

'Now that you'll be in Gyawa, we can get to know each other. I'd like that because, well, I think if you got to know me, you'd change your mind.'

Dechen turned to give him a withering look.

'I won't change my mind, Tenzin. Give it up!' She spurred her horse and left Tenzin behind.

She rode past Nawang and her father at the head of the line.

As Dechen passed him, Thampa urged his horse to keep pace with her. Unconsciously, I allowed my horse, Chestnut, to pass Tenzin and Nawang, and follow Thampa to separate the quarrelling parties.

'Wait, Dechen,' Thampa called out, 'where are you going?'

Dechen let her father ride up beside her and said, 'Getting away from Tenzin!'

'I was very drunk last night,' Thampa said apologetically, 'I'm sorry.'

'I know, I know. Nawang put a lot of pressure on you.'

'True. But even so,' Thampa sighed. Growing stern, he added, 'Please listen to me, Dechen. We shouldn't turn down this offer.'

'Just stop, Ba-la. I said "No" and there's nothing more to say! You got us into this mess. You can sort it out.'

'I don't think it's so easy. Tenzin is very determined and Nawang thinks we have an arrangement. They are quite vindictive, that clan. And now they have powerful connections.'

'Yes, they'll turn to their Chinese overlords.'

Thampa turned to see Tenzin right behind me.

'It's to your advantage to show Tenzin more respect.'

'You wanted me to spend time with you so I agreed to come. You didn't tell me Tenzin would be living in Gyawa when

221

I agreed. I may change my mind if Tenzin continues to pursue me and you keep pressuring me about him. Let me make it absolutely clear to you again: I will not marry that man. Do you hear me?'

'I hear you,' Thampa replied quietly.

Dechen suddenly urged her horse into a gallop, and disappeared up the trail.

Tenzin had obviously heard that last comment and looked quite dejected. He noticed me riding beside him and gave me an angry glare, believing, I thought, I was to blame for Dechen rejecting him.

Wanting to distance myself from Tenzin, I deliberately lagged behind. Soon, everyone was far ahead of me and I was riding alone. Distracted, just as I'd been on my way to the festival, I came to the same grassy meadow of my mystical experience. I deliberately directed Chestnut off the trail and dismounted to stretch my legs. I found a rock and sat down to enjoy the surroundings again. Willing the same vividness and timelessness to return, I began paying close attention to the sounds and smells, to the grandeur of the view. A hint of the clarity of perception returned but not the full translucent vibrancy.

I heard a horse approaching at a gallop. I looked down the trail and recognized Dechen. Impulsively, I leapt up and ran to the trail. I got there just as she galloped around the bend. She was forced to slow down quickly.

'Out of the way, communist!' she shouted, 'What are you trying to do? Let me by!'

'Oh!' I said as I realized that I had unconsciously blocked the trail. She reminded me of Jiachen shouting slogans.

I stepped aside to let her by. Her horse, Little White, had slowed to a walk. He flicked his ears forward in recognition. I walked beside him.

'How did you get behind us?' I asked looking from Little White up to Dechen.

'I was off trail waiting for the group to pass.' She urged Little White to go faster.

'I'm glad you came along,' I began panting as Little White's quickening pace forced me into a jog. 'I want to apologize for the trouble Tenzin is causing.'

Dechen regarded me quizzically.

'Do you plan to run beside me all the way to Gyawa? Where's your horse?'

I was torn between wanting to get my horse and staying with Dechen so she wouldn't ride ahead.

'Yes, no; I'm not running all the way. I'll, ah... Can you wait for me? You shouldn't ride alone.'

Dechen laughed, 'Alright. Get your horse!'

Dechen followed me back to the meadow. She let Little White graze as she waited for me to get Chestnut.

I saw Dechen take a deep breath and look around enjoying the meadow. I mounted Chestnut and we sat on our horses, admiring the place.

'It's a nice place, isn't it?'

'Yes, it is,' she agreed. 'I feel a joyful lightness here like the presence of a goddess.'

The way she looked at me caught me off guard. Could she know I'd seen Jiachen here?

I wondered what had induced her to begin being pleasant toward me. Could it be Yangchen's acceptance of me,

223

or perhaps Rinpoche's plan to include me in the *lhamo* project? Had Yangchen and Rinpoche asked her to change her attitude? Whatever the change, I was pleased and suddenly wanted to tell her what had happened to me here even though I'd vowed never to tell anyone. I thought she would understand, as I'm sure Jiachen would have.

'On my way down to the festival, I stopped here. I, ah, I had an unusual experience.'

'Oh?' Dechen was intrigued, 'what sort of experience?'

'I don't know,' I shrugged. I couldn't easily find words for it. I'm sure she saw tears welling in my eyes as I recalled the beauty and goodness of the experience.

'Everything was so, what can I say, so clear, so bright and, and alive! I felt so right and, ah, connected with everything!'

Dechen's face brightened with an amused sparkle in her eyes.

'How's it possible?' she playfully mocked me. 'And to you, a rational communist! How could you be brought to tears by beauty, truth, and goodness? Hard to believe!'

'What do you mean?' I didn't know what to make of Dechen's reaction.

'You had an awakening, a spiritual experience, a crack in that thick shell of your rational self. A glimpse of reality!' She laughed long and hard, 'how will you ever live with yourself now that you've had a mystical experience?'

'No! That's not what it was,' I blurted in denial, 'I was merely feeling exhilarated. Excited to be here. I was enjoying the scenery!'

Dechen abruptly turned Little White to the trail and shouted over her shoulder.

'I would be more open-minded if I were you. I guess you can't help being blind! First your upbringing, and then the communists kept you in the dark and fed you bullshit—like a mushroom! Ha, ha, ha!'

I hurried after her. She let me catch up. The trail was wide enough for us to ride side by side and talk.

'I'm glad we finally have a chance to talk,' Dechen surprised me with a reversal of her demeanour.

'Well, me too,' I responded lamely. 'You do remind me of Jiachen, you know.'

She ignored my comment.

'You speak English, don't you?' she asked in English, 'I have some ideas for you that might best be understood in Western terms.'

'Huh? Oh, yes, I speak English,' I replied in the language of my childhood at schools in Shanghai. Our accents were quite different but we could easily understand one another.

'The reason Jiachen reminds you of me,' Dechen said, 'is because we are identical twins. In fact we are more entangled than most twins.'

'Entangled?'

I knew she was Jiachen's identical twin but what did she mean by 'entangled'?

'Surely, you are familiar with the concept. You had a Western education just like I did, so you must have studied some physics, quantum physics, to be precise.'

'Yes, I was educated in the elite English school system in Shanghai. And I was taught mostly by nuns and Jesuits,' I announced proudly.

'Me, too, in Darjeeling, India,' she said.

In response to her observation about her twin sister, I asked, 'You said "entangled"! What do you mean?'

'Yes, while she was alive, I didn't know I had a twin but I always felt something was missing. Twins that are separated at birth often have this feeling. Now that Jiachen has gone beyond and I've awakened my own spiritual awareness, we are very much connected. Just as she is connected to you.'

'To me?' Her insight took me by surprise.

'Yes, Yangchen told me about your experience when Jiachen died. So actually, Wei Ming, at one level I know you already. I've been struggling to reconcile Jiachen's connection with you, and understand the kind of relationship you and I will have.'

I was stupefied. She was implying that she knew me through Jiachen, or perhaps, as if she were Jiachen and even so, she and I would have a relationship.

'Is that why,' I began, trying to find a way to put my emotions into words, 'you've been so angry, so dismissive?'

'I have been cantankerous for a reason,' she said pointedly. 'I am not Jiachen! You must not confuse the two of us. In this body, I am Dechen and always will be. Jiachen is in another dimension. But she is watching. As you must know.'

She looked at me and burst out laughing.

'She would be very jealous of me talking with you,' she continued with an amused expression. 'But, fortunately, she is beyond that now!'

I'm sure I looked confused.

'You and Yangchen have both said that Jiachen is connected to me but I'm having trouble understanding how.'

She looked at me as if to say I should know by now.

We rode on.

The clop-clopping of our horses' hooves on the stony ground slowly faded because I was now high in the sky, watching two people riding side by side on the trail. I was feeling, seeing, knowing what each of them was experiencing; together, simultaneously, and I knew I was again in Jiachen's all-embracing presence.

'Oh!' I said to Dechen when I was back on my horse. 'I had the most incredible... what do you call it, ah... vision. I was... I was looking down on the two of us riding side by side. She was... Jiachen was connecting me with everything. Just like the other day!'

'See what I mean? She's a *Dakini*, a sky dancer. She's right here!' Dechen pointed up to a spot above our heads.

'You mean, like Kwan Yin, the Chinese goddess of compassion,' I said, recalling my experience of her the other day, 'is that who she is?'

'Yes, that's a good way to see her. Each culture has its own way. Being Chinese, you'd see Kwan Yin. A Catholic would see Mother Mary, perhaps. Here in Tibet, we see the mother goddess as a *Dakini*, a female enlightened being who guides and empowers our yearning for enlightenment.'

I tried but realized I couldn't initiate a repeat of my connection with Jiachen. The connection could only be activated by Jiachen, or perhaps Dechen, but not I. Dechen had called Jiachen a *Dakini*, a sky dancer. I liked that. I imagined Jiachen dancing and filling the entire sky above us.

'We can't be seen together,' Dechen said suddenly, switching to Tibetan. 'It would give Tenzin the wrong idea, and fuel for his delusions. You'd better ride ahead and catch up to

227

the others. Don't worry about me. I can take care of myself. After all, I have Jiachen with me. Always. But then, so do you!'

'With me?'

'Yes.'

'Then why can't I feel her presence more often?'

'That's something you can work on. Rinpoche and I will be glad to help. You'll need to make some major changes.'

Again, she laughed and slapped Chestnut's rump to get her going.

I caught up with the group. No one had noticed my absence. They all rode in silence.

I took the opportunity to ponder the sudden chaos of my life. What was going on? I went downstream to a summer horse racing festival, and to determine if Mola township was a suitable place to form another cooperative. What actually happened was far more exciting.

Could life get any more complicated?

I was about to find out.

Betrayal

I accompanied Nawang to Lithang but declined his offer to stay with him. I preferred the tavern where Rabten welcomed me and let me have my old room. It felt like returning home; it was familiar and I knew the routines.

In the morning while having my usual butter tea with *tsampa*, a smartly-dressed PLA soldier came to the tavern and asked for me. When directed to my table, he was puzzled to see someone in local dress eating the local food.

'Excuse me,' he asked in disbelief, 'are you Comrade Chuang Wei Ming?'

'Yes,' I replied, noting his confusion, 'I'm Chuang.'

'Oh,' he paused, looking at my clothing and the food in front of me, perplexed that I could really be the man he was looking for. 'I have a message for you from Commander Deng Li Peng, you have to report to him at 10:00 this morning.'

'Very well,' I replied, trying to hide my amusement over his confusion, 'where will I find him?'

The question befuddled the messenger again, 'At his office in the permanent building.'

'And where is this permanent building?' I asked, continuing to seek clarification. He was apparently too bewildered to be clear about where this meeting was to be held.

'At our, ah... in the PLA encampment,' he managed to say.

'Very well,' I agreed, and with a hint of humour, asked, 'do you think it might be a good idea if I changed into, ah... more appropriate clothing?'

His nod was brief. Embarrassed, he left in a hurry.

After he left, I had a good chuckle with Rabten.

After bathing, I dressed in my worn-out Party uniform, and hid my long hair in a Russian-style hat with ear flaps that had become part of the uniform for cold climates. I walked into the encampment toward the lone stone building. A soldier stood guard by the door, and a Khampa leaned casually against the wall, holding the reins of a horse. The guard opened the door for me after I gave him my name. He said the commander was expecting me.

Commander Deng was a large-bellied military man in his mid-50s. He looked up from a crude wooden desk. His round face was covered with large black moles, and the fingers on both hands had the appearance of being webbed; the result, perhaps, of severe burns. A bold nameplate on the desk read 'Deng Li Ping, Commander, Peoples Liberation Army'.

'You must be Comrade Chuang Wei Ming!' he said as he stood up and came around the desk to shake my hand. I could see he was noting my well-worn clothing and tried, perhaps, to guess what was under my hat. He wore the same style hat so I was not obliged to remove my hat, and didn't.

'Yes, Comrade Deng,' I replied, accepting his disfigured hand, 'pleased to meet you!'

'I'm so glad you've come! Please, have a seat.'

'Welcome to Lithang,' I said, to establish who should be welcoming whom. After all, I'd been in the area four years already. I sat down on the opposite side of his desk, noting the crudely-made chair, identical to the commander's.

'I've heard of your exemplary work from several quarters!' he responded to my intimation, 'so, of course, I'm thrilled you've come to see me.'

'Thank you, commander.' I made a point of calling him 'commander' rather than 'comrade.' Officers were expected to respect Party members, and in my case, I hoped he would respect my opinions about the situation here.

'Your supervisor, Comrade Li in Chengdu, kindly shared your reports with me. I was very impressed! I believe you have achieved something we can only hope to emulate as our work here proceeds.'

'Just doing my job,' I acknowledged, taking note that he chose his words with care.

'I understand your cooperative's been running profitably for three years, and that its fourth production season is already looking very good. Commendable!'

'Yes, it's doing well,' I agreed, 'but it is not my cooperative. It belongs to the people of Gyawa. They came to mutual agreement about the use of their production base, and have worked hard. They are happy with the arrangement. Happy people work hard and enjoy life.'

'So you've stated in your report,' Deng acknowledged politely. 'It is commendable that you were able to persuade an aristocratic landlord to donate his land. An excellent example for other landowners!'

Deng smiled briefly, and quickly moved on. It was clear he had an agenda.

'Comrade Chuang, I've been instructed to make certain changes. Though our District Commissioner Tsering Nawang is a Party member and has some training, he requires our

231

supervision. As a wealthy merchant rather than a nobleman like his predecessor, we feel he is limited when it comes to dealing with the more privileged classes. Therefore, I've been asked to assume supervisory duties. I have not only assumed responsibilities here as commander of the PLA Forces but I'm also the local Communist Party Representative.'

None of this was news to me.

'You will, therefore, regard me as your local supervisor. Your reports will come to me rather than to Comrade Li in Chengdu. In this way, we can coordinate our efforts for the continuing liberation of Lithang district.'

I nodded in acknowledgement but I was worried how this would impact my mission. I much preferred the autonomy I had under Comrade Li's remote supervision. I hoped Deng would not be difficult to work with.

'The Party feels social reform needs to be implemented faster,' Deng resumed. 'They prefer a clean slate. It is best to start from scratch by revising or removing cultural impediments. As we have done in the heartland, we can and will do at the fringes of the Motherland.'

I'd dreaded this development! This was the hard-line approach Phuntso had warned me was likely to take shape. It shocked me to realize it was ready to manifest from the office of Commander Deng.

'That's sure to...' I started to warn him of the local reaction. But Deng suddenly got up from his chair and cut me off with a smile when he registered my negative reaction. He came around the table to put his hand on my shoulder; a comradely gesture.

'We must get better acquainted,' Deng said, trying to be friendly. 'One needs true camaraderie to survive in hell holes like this!'

'That would be good, commander.' I was about to say that I don't find this place so unbearable, but Deng said: 'No, you needn't "commander" me. Deng will do, Chuang. See me as your friend rather than as a military officer or Party comrade.'

'Of course, Deng, I will regard you as my friend and equal just as I have Comrade Li. He impressed upon me before I came here that my reports were a matter of courtesy between us; I was not to think I was reporting to him as my superior. He honoured my opinions and insights. I received nothing but good feedback and encouragement. I trust you will do the same.'

After an intense, curious look, Deng resumed his friendly overture.

'I find it extremely remarkable how you have created a cooperative in this wild place, among these...' Deng shook his head, disregarding my comment about our equality. 'It can't have been easy.'

Commander Deng returned to his side of the desk and I stood up to leave, but he waved his hand indicating I should sit back down. He picked up a packet of cigarettes, turned his back to me and went to open the window. He opened the package and lit a cigarette. He took several deep puffs, blowing smoke out the window. A cool breeze blew it back into the room, and he pulled his heavy wool overcoat tighter round his neck.

'Actually,' I ventured cautiously while watching Deng smoke, 'many people have seen the benefits of our cooperative, and some are quite eager to reorganize their own communities.'

Deng appeared more intent on the pleasure of smoking than on what I'd said. He changed the subject.

'Oh, there's another change that I feel must be made. The young man you mentored...'

'Tsering Tenzin? He's returned and already in Gyawa.'

'Yes, he's a good lad but like his father, he'll need continuing supervision. I know you have new responsibilities, so I am assigning Major Gan to the Gyawa Cooperative.'

'I see,' I said in acknowledgement but alarmed by the authoritarian one-sidedness of the decision. 'I think the cooperative can continue to do quite well, with or without Tenzin's help. There's no need for supervision. The cooperative is fully established and has been running very well. That's why I felt confident about expanding my activities to other areas.'

'That's right,' Deng disregarded my observation about Tenzin and Major Gan's dispensability, and focused on my role. 'Your expanded activities include preparing other communities for communism. I'm sure you already have new areas in mind?'

'Yes, actually, I do. I've been in touch with opinion leaders in the southern part of the district,' I said, 'things look quite promising.'

'Good. Shift your focus there. Let Tenzin and Major Gan handle Gyawa Cooperative.'

'I will need your assurance that there will be no interference in the villages south of Gyawa while I, ah, "prepare them for communism".'

'Interference?' Deng frowned at me.

'I know the people. They will be reluctant to listen to me if PLA troops and Party officials move into the area.'

Deng flicked the butt outside, closed the window and turned abruptly to face me with renewed interest.

'Fine!' he agreed abruptly, 'my resources are thinly stretched already in the rest of the area. Do what you can in the southern part of the Lithang district.'

I nodded to acknowledge his agreement.

He seemed distracted.

'That reminds me,' he said suddenly, 'I was just informed about a lama in that area who is a potential troublemaker.'

'You must be referring to one of my contacts, Palden Rinpoche.'

We looked at one another intently a moment, each of us trying to outguess the other.

'There is significant pressure from the community to limit this man's influence.'

The 'significant pressure', I suspected, came from Nawang who would have already debriefed the commander about Palden Rinpoche's arrival and influence in the area.

'I'm sure there is,' I responded, as if to agree with him. 'You need to understand that this observation is, ah, motivated by jealousy between various factions of Khampa society. I'm sure you are aware of these factions. Be assured, however, I know what I'm doing,' I tried to explain, 'once this lama and those associated with him clearly understand the benefits of our way of life, he will be a driving force in promoting the revolution.'

'He's been accused of recruiting and training resistance fighters. Unfortunately, the warrant for his arrest can't be rescinded.'

'Arrest?' I blurted out hoping it didn't sound like I was objecting. I was alarmed but quite sure the accusation was false. I covered up by saying, 'Oh well, it would certainly make my job easier with him out of the way.'

There was a knock on the door. Rather abruptly, Deng turned to open the door and noticed the Khampa horseman standing impatiently.

'You'll have to excuse me now. I have to finish a report. The courier is impatient to get on the road to Dartsendo.'

I hesitated a moment but the subject was closed; there would be no further discussion. He nodded and I walked briskly out of the room. As I left, he called out.

'See that you get fresh clothes. Go to the quartermaster's tent and say you want to collect the winter outfits Comrade Li sent you.'

I had to suppress outright laughter but I went to get my new uniform.

I returned to Gyawa Cooperative instead of going to Mola. I wanted to warn Thupten and Pema about the possible arrival of Major Gan. Besides that, I wanted to take a look at areas other than Mola township. It would have been an obvious focal area, but Samphel had been non-receptive, and I decided not to complicate my delicate position with Commander Deng by pursuing a relationship with Palden Rinpoche because of the suspicion that he was training a militia. With the transfer of my supervision from Comrade Li to Commander Deng, I felt I was being closely watched and my presence here could easily be jeopardized by any perceived misstep.

Pema and Thupten were happy to have me back but I did my best to stay out of Tenzin's way, though it rankled me how he strutted around the village in his Party uniform. He had taken up smoking and spread the foul stink of cigarettes everywhere he went. I wondered if his behaviour would change once Major Gan arrived. I didn't tell him this was immanent.

I also kept away from Dawa and Thampa's house because I didn't want to run into Dechen and fuel Tenzin's jealously. How Dechen was handling Tenzin, I did not know. Unconsciously, I longed to catch a glimpse of Dechen. Perhaps that was the main reason I returned to Gyawa.

From my base in Gyawa, I headed off in different directions each day. Often, the people I met did not know who I was or had not heard about the Chinese Khampa from Gyawa. When they realized I was not really a Khampa, conversations quickly ended. If they knew me, they would welcome me but were not really interested in talking about social or economic changes even though they understood the benefits it had brought to Gyawa.

After a few weeks of this, I grew discouraged. I was getting nowhere.

'Why don't people want to listen to me anymore, Thupten?' I asked one evening, after a long day.

'It's not you, Wei Ming!' he assured me. 'People are suspicious. They know these new ideas have to do with the soldiers they see so often these days.'

'What can I do to change their perceptions, to help them understand what we've achieved and what we have to offer?'

Thupten shrugged. 'Keep trying,' he said. 'Talk about our achievements here.'

'I do!' I appreciated Thupten's encouragement, but my frustration and impatience were not relieved.

The next morning, Tenzin called a special meeting with a group of community leaders he had organized, and called it the Cooperative Management Committee. I remembered that Phuntso had used this name. It came to be—along with

237

its authoritarian tone. Thupten insisted I attend the meeting with him; he wanted a witness, he said, though he didn't explain why.

We entered Thampa's courtyard and proceeded to the large room on the first floor. Tenzin was already seated at the front of the room. Thupten took a seat among the row of seats opposite Tenzin. Tenzin saw me and frowned. I sat down in the back corner, trying to be inconspicuous. Thampa, Dawa, and Pema entered and found seats. A few others who I knew to be strong supporters of the cooperative such as Sonam and Dorje also entered, but there were several members who would very likely support Tenzin.

'There are new directives I am authorized to carry out,' he said, getting bluntly to the point without calling the meeting to order. 'We are required to centralize collection of all produce in Lithang for district-wide redistribution.'

A low, uneasy murmur rose and Thupten fully comprehended the new directive.

'I see no reason for this!' he said in an attempt to intimidate Tenzin, 'why should we send our produce to Lithang?'

Thupten looked around for support.

'That's right!' Dorje took up the objection, 'how do we know what will really happen to our produce? Will we get back enough to feed ourselves?'

Members were beginning to understand the implications of the new directive.

'We must control our own affairs!' Sonam added strongly, 'management of all produce and resources must be local.'

There was vigorous head nodding in agreement.

Dorje stood up again to make another point. 'What you're saying means we are no longer a cooperative. So what are we, part of a larger collective?'

Tenzin looked toward the door as if someone was standing just outside the room, and nodded. Major Gan and several armed soldiers entered the room.

Dorje turned to see them and slowly, quietly sat down.

'Yes, that is the case,' Tenzin said decisively. 'All villages, once liberated and reformed into socialist communes, will be part of a larger collective with centralized collection and redistribution of the worker's production.'

The room suddenly felt chilly. Committee members fully understood the new directive; control of what the cooperative produced was out of their hands. Their ability to prosper was threatened.

I understood now why Thupten wanted me there. In challenging Tenzin's 'new directive', he was testing their position. Once Major Gan stepped into the room, it became clear; resistance would be dealt with harshly.

I was thinking how wrong this was; imposing reforms without the people's consent was clearly in violation of my idea of communism. By forcing people into communes, they would become workers for the state rather than liberated members of their own cooperatives. All that I'd been promoting—the very idea of local cooperation, equal voice, and equal share of the resources—was suddenly discounted and overruled. The people I had befriended, who had trusted me, were now becoming slaves of the state! I'd been betrayed by the Party.

If my reports had been received, as Deng acknowledged they had been, it was clear my work no longer fit the current

239

Party line. I would be regarded as a 'revisionist', though in reality it was the Party who was revising the purity of communist philosophy. I could hardly point this out without facing 're-education'.

Tenzin's new policies brought considerable distress to everyone in the village. His veiled threat of violence had shaken the community. Thupten and Pema consoled worried visitors in their house late into the night. I offered what support I could but spent a restless night trying to find a way we could modify, if not reverse, this new development.

At first light, not having slept at all, I went out for an early morning walk. Mist rose from the river. Sparrows called to each other and fluttered from bush to frosty bush, not flying far. I saw someone through the mist coming out of the forest, a basket on her back. Her breath, as she sang, was visible in the crisp morning air of early autumn. I recognize the beautiful voice of Jiachen but knew it was Dechen. I hurried between the barley fields, thrilled by the chance to be with her!

'Here the earth maiden is beautiful indeed. Her virgin streams fill with garlands of bubbles as they laugh and dance over rocks and crags. Her meadows are laden with flowers, sweet grass and fruit. Rings of snow mountains, their peaks draped with white silken clouds, tower above. Crystal glaciers hang like tassels over her apron of blue-green forests.'

'What a lovely song!' I exclaimed when she finished singing it.

Dechen was startled by my sudden appearance.

'Why are you wandering around out here so early?' she demanded.

'Staying out of Tenzin's way.'

'Me too!' she laughed.

'Why so early?'

'Ama-la isn't feeling well. I'm collecting medicinal herbs.'

I peered into the basket but she twisted it away and walked faster. I kept pace with her.

'Do you have any medicine to fix the idiocy being forced on our cooperative?'

Dechen frowned a moment and then began to laugh. 'Ba-la told me. It's a shame, isn't it? All you've tried to accomplish destroyed in the blink of an eye!'

It shocked me how flippant she was. Then she looked at me as if she realized she'd said something hurtful. 'I'm, sorry. That came out badly! I didn't mean to trivialize your efforts. I meant how thoughtlessly the Party has destroyed such a good thing.'

We walked in silence.

'Dechen-la,' I began after a while. 'I need some advice. I've realized people are reluctant to listen to me anymore. They'll be even more reluctant once news of what's happened in Gyawa gets out. What do you suggest I do?'

She stopped walking suddenly. A thicket obscured us from the village.

'Everything you've done so far has been good. And the changes you've made—adopting our dress, speaking our language, adopting our customs and habits—all of it has helped people believe what you say but, in the end, you'll still be seen as that Chinese communist who wants to be one of us.'

241

'Pema suggests I'll be accepted if I marry a Khampa girl.'

'No, even that is all external and people will know it's superficial!'

'Superficial? What if I marry you? They respect and love you.'

She glared at me and was about to respond angrily but thought better of it. She changed the subject.

'There is another way,' she said, 'we like to call it the Middle Way.'

'Are you suggesting I become a Buddhist?'

'Of course!'

'How can I do that? I'm a communist, an atheist, a rational materialist. No, that's too much of a stretch for me!'

'Well, if you really want to become one of us and help us assimilate communism to our way of life, you'll have to first see the world through our eyes. That's the reason things aren't working for you! You need to fully participate in our view of the world.'

She regarded me thoughtfully, then added, 'We can't help you as long as we are here in Gyawa. You need to go see Yangchen and Rinpoche. They can help you.'

'Rinpoche? I can't do that. There's a warrant for his arrest. Under false pretences, probably, but just the same I'm not at liberty to be seen with him.'

Dechen chuckled. 'Well, that puts us in an awkward place. I can't help you here in Gyawa because of Tenzin's jealousy, and you can't seek Rinpoche's help because of your legalistic scruples. I guess your position is beyond hope!'

I gave a brief smile as I tried to see the humour she was injecting into the situation.

'With Rinpoche in hiding, what are your plans? How will you continue to sing the Gesar story?'

'Hiding?' Dechen laughed again, 'he's not hiding, and don't worry about our plan. I'm free to sing where I please.'

'What if I joined you? Oh. I mean, not as Gesar, but if I help you with your performances.' I'd suddenly seen a new possibility that could accomplish both our objectives. 'We could work together to bring about a truly enlightened society. We can spread the revolution by teaching the people how to achieve a liberated and enlightened society through your performances!'

I was enthused by my bright idea but I could see that Dechen was not!

'Wei Ming! Listen to me. There is more you need to understand,' she was quick to pour cold water on my idea.

'Your idea of an enlightened society and what Gesar extols are poles apart. We can't possibly work together until you understand what we mean when we talk about enlightenment. And don't for a second think I'm going to get on stage to extol the benefits of rational materialism for you. I will not help you twist the minds of our people!'

'All right! I get it,,' I said putting my hands up in a gesture suggesting she back off. But she wasn't finished.

'If we work together at all,' she said with a look meant to silence me, 'you are going to help us tell people what real liberation is and what a real enlightened society can be.'

She brushed past me to get out into the open again but without thinking, I grabbed her arm.

'Listen to me, Dechen.' I shouldn't have done that and realized it immediately and released her. 'I'm sorry. I'm not... Forgive me.'

243

Our eyes met. I thought I was looking at Jiachen looking through Dechen's eyes, piercing my heart with recognition and remembrance. Perhaps it was the touch that reminded me how much I missed the intensity of our conversations and the warmth of our bodies together.

'You look as if you've seen a ghost,' Dechen said.

'I have. I saw Jiachen for a moment.'

'I'm sorry. I warned you. She's likely to appear from time to time.'

'What I was about to say was,' I interrupted, and then took a moment to regain my composure, 'there are aspects of your old Tibetan way of life that are holding you back from social and economic progress. Chairman Mao's kind of enlightened society is also important!'

'To whom? And don't call Mao's corruption 'enlightened', nor is it liberating. Just look at Tenzin's new policy. Do you think we want so-called classless equanimity that reduces everyone to a nameless and numbered slave of the state? I'm not a stupid village girl! I know a thing or two about the world.'

'Oh, I know that! We're not so different; we both came here as outsiders!'

Dechen stepped right up to me to look at me, eye to eye.

'That may be true,' she said softly but forcefully, 'but I returned to my roots to discover true wisdom. You, however, have been infected by the communist lie! I see how this so-called People's Revolution is going. It destroys the traditional class structure only to set up a new one. It replaces one set of repressive overlords with another! Do you honestly believe those in power will not feel superior to the rest?' she asked, and continued, 'don't you see what's going on right here in this village? Already, the Party has replaced the people. The Party is not interested in an enlightened society. Not even the kind you dream about creating. Ask yourself, is true communism happening? Does Tenzin operate as a consultant? Does anyone else have a say?'

'Oh, I see all right!' I blurted defensively, 'I agree with you. I'm deeply distressed with the way things are going. But your society, stretching all the way back to Gesar's kingdom, is feudalistic, autocratic, and totalitarian. Don't you think you need to get past patriarchy and establish a true communal democracy?'

I had to throw in English words because I couldn't think of Tibetan words for 'patriarchy', 'autocratic', or 'totalitarian'. Dechen had done the same for 'classless equanimity'. We thought nothing of supplementing English words when we came up against a limitation in our Tibetan vocabulary; these were concepts much more easily expressed in English.

'Tell me, Dechen, do you respect Jiachen's involvement with communism?'

'Yangchen said she was level-headed and knew what she was doing. She served a purpose. She...'

Dechen stopped abruptly. Tears welled in her eyes. 'Yes, I respect Jiachen's position. I think she understood, as you do, that communism is a good social tool, but I also know that, at the end, she had a very deep understanding of the nature of reality. Yangchen told me how she shared it with you.'

I was moved by Dechen's emotional recollection; it was as if Jiachen herself had spoken of the gift she'd given me as she died.

'This is what I mean, Wei Ming,' Dechen continued, very much herself again, 'you need to understand the deeper side of life, not just the superficial.'

'You keep saying that! I don't need to become a Buddhist!'

'There you go again!' She said with a look of utter exasperation, 'your misunderstandings; your preconceived ideas! Really! Go see Palden Rinpoche.'

'It wouldn't be right for me to see him. I mean, I'd be questioned about not turning him in. I can't go there.'

'Are you such a fake?' Dechen was livid, 'of course you can! If you believe this warrant for Rinpoche's arrest is wrong, stand up to Commander Deng! Just go to Mola and up the western horse grazing mountain. You'll reach the hermitage by nightfall if you leave this morning. Find out what he's doing! He can help you.'

I was so stunned over Dechen's dismissiveness of the warrant and her exasperation with me that I just stood there and watched her go.

What she said was true. I was playing Deng's game. He would expect me to be his spy. I'd already decided I wouldn't report Rinpoche, but had chosen to do it by remaining ignorant of his whereabouts and activities. So what was the difference? Even if I went to see him, I had no reason to report him.

Dechen was still in sight and I called out to her.

'Dechen! Wait,' I had to shout.

She turned around and waited for me to catch up. 'I'll go,' I said when I was near enough to speak without yelling, 'it's important that Rinpoche and I come to an understanding.'

Dechen smiled at the thought and shook her head. 'You won't come to an understanding the way you think you will. He will not help you set up a cooperative in Mola like this one in

Gyawa unless you understand Buddha dharma first. And then it will be a different kind of cooperative.'

'You're not listening to me. I want to find a way to integrate communism and Buddha dharma.'

'Exactly my point. You still don't see what I mean. How do you plan to integrate communism and Buddha dharma? That sounds like an extremely tedious process to me. Rinpoche will not be open to it. Actually, you need to see Rinpoche about something else. You need to tell him what happened to you by the river.'

'What? About that? No! I don't think so. I shouldn't have told you.'

'No, Wei Ming, I'm serious. You must tell him!'

'That I hallucinated?'

'Experiences like that mean you are trying to discover your true nature, who you really are.'

'That's ridiculous! I know who I am!'

'Ha, ha!' Dechen laughed, 'no, I'm talking about your true Buddha nature. Let Rinpoche explain.'

'Is Rinpoche ready to learn about communism?'

Disgusted with my thick-headedness, Dechen turned around and walked away.

I returned to Thupten and Pema's house. They were just getting started with the day; Pema was about to pour hot tea in the butter churn. Thupten was putting *tsampa* in bowls. When he saw me, he got another bowl ready.

'Thupten-la,' I began, 'I've just seen Dechen. She insists I go see Rinpoche.'

'Yes, you should,' Thupten agreed.

'Dechen said he's still at the hermitage.'

'That's right,' Thupten agreed. He put a bowl of *tsampa* in front of me. 'You thought he was in hiding?'

'Isn't it our duty to report his whereabouts?'

'Why? I'm sure they know very well where Rinpoche is living. Everyone does.'

'Then why hasn't he been arrested?'

'Ha, ha! Not a chance!' Thupten found this amusing. 'You go there and see if it's possible.'

I had no idea what Thupten meant. 'Why is it impossible for soldiers to arrest a lama in a mountain hermitage?'

'His hermitage is a training camp for Khampa warriors!' Thupten replied as if it should have been obvious to me. 'There are scores of young men in training there. Remember the young men who rode horses with you at the festival? And the ones you showed how to shoot arrows in the ancient style? Many of them were inspired to learn the ancient warrior arts and asked Rinpoche to set up a training camp. He has some skills in that area himself.'

I was dumbfounded! The warrant for Rinpoche's arrest was justified! What was Rinpoche up to? As a proponent of non-violent Buddha dharma, how could he be training warriors? Did Rinpoche want to drive the PLA out of Kham? If so, he was no better than Lobsang!

'Is he helping Lobsang, that warlord from the Chengtreng?'

'Oh, I'm sure he'd love to have Lobsang's support, but so far I don't think so.'

I pushed my bowl aside, stood up and staggered out of the house.

I'd been so naive!

How many warriors was Rinpoche training at his hermitage? Fifty? A hundred? A small army?

Dark Night

I wanted nothing to do with Palden Rinpoche! If this is what he was really up to, I'd been deceived. All his talk about King Gesar's peaceful kingdom and warriors who fight demons rather than engage in killing men! Lies! Deception!

Clearly, it would be dangerous to make contact with Rinpoche. He had already said he would not help me establish a cooperative in Mola. He had other ideas. He wanted to raise an army and drive the PLA out of Kham. Why were Dechen and Thupten encouraging me to go see him? Were they hoping I'd go along with Rinpoche's scheme of training men for armed revolt? Is that why he was interested in me? Did he think I'd teach all those young men the martial arts skills I knew so they would be better prepared as warriors?

No! I'd had enough.

I would leave Tibet altogether.

I had done what was in my power to do; my time was up. The Party wasn't interested in my methods and the people no longer listened to me. I'd go back to Chengdu, and put my energies into something else; back to Shanghai and work among the factory workers again.

These gloomy thoughts tumbled through my troubled mind as I walked away from Gyawa with no destination in mind. I needed to clear my head and calm my anger.

I was heading down river toward Mola and Rinpoche's hermitage but that was the last place I wanted to go. When

I realized this, I deliberately headed north toward Lithang. I'd go there but I wouldn't tell Commander Deng I was leaving. I'd keep going! What difference would it make?

Pushing my way through thickets of juniper bushes, I began climbing the heavily-forested hillside, looking for a path. The physical exertion forced me to deal with what was immediately before me. Covered with scratches, my skin ripped and bloodied, I was now high above the valley where a mist blanketed the ridge. In the wet cloud, I had no idea which way to go nor which way I'd come up. After walking one way, self-doubt turned me to the opposite direction. Giving up, I sat down to wait for the mist to clear.

My predicament encouraged me to have second thoughts, at least about my hasty escape. Perhaps I should return to Gyawa and confront Thupten about Rinpoche's true intentions. Perhaps I'd jumped to a conclusion that might not be completely true. There must be a reasonable explanation. Even if my suspicions were accurate, I wasn't prepared for the long journey to Chengdu; I should get Chestnut and some of my things from Thupten's house.

The sun broke through the cloud. It was low in the sky so I knew it would soon be dark. Every valley below me, however, was filled with mist; it was impossible to know which valley held Gyawa.

Through the mist, a column of smoke began to rise. It came from the flank of a mountain ridge in the direction I hoped was Gyawa. The column rose to the level of my mountaintop and began drifting in my direction. As the smoke and fragrance of a sacred juniper bonfire neared me, I heard singing.

'Shambhala is and is not real; this joy does and does not fill the world; this moment is and is not everlasting; each being does and does not share one Buddha nature.'

The words of the song were clear, and I recognized it as one of those perplexing spiritual teaching songs I'd heard from time to time.

'If you don't see this, you stumble in confusion and sorrow. When you realize where you come from, and who you are, you become tolerant, kind-hearted, and joyful.'

The column of smoke, taking the shape of a white stallion, galloped toward me.

'When I see that no one knows this, my heart breaks in mourning sadness.'

The song ended, the horse-shaped cloud spread and vanished with the wind. Only then did I realize the voice sounded like Jiachen's. Had I heard it with my physical ears? That seemed unlikely over such a distance. I suddenly realized with an unexpected heartache, it had been an inner communication again.

Darkness was coming quickly; I walked in the direction the smoke had come from and soon came upon a trail. The sky was clear; there was no moon but the stars were bright enough for me to follow the ribbon of a path stretching out before me and winding down the mountainside into the mist below.

I hadn't had anything to drink all day so when I heard the sound of running water, I left the trail to find it. My thirst was stronger than my common sense! I stumbled through the thick underbrush in darkness, found the stream and drank deeply from it. Feeling refreshed, I tried to find the path again in the darkness and mist. Lost, exhausted, and discouraged,

I lay down in a small clearing by the stream. My sheepskin chuba, high boots and fox fur hat were thick and protected me from the cold earth beneath and the frigid mist around me, and I fell into a deep sleep.

Water laps on a pebbled shore. Stars reflect beneath the even surface. Distant mountains form dark shapes that separate the stars above from their reflections below. Against this faint light, a young woman sits in meditation on a rock surrounded by water. There's a sudden brightness and she lifts her head. She watches a meteor explode in white light at the lake's surface, and sink into the depths where it continues to glow. The young woman slides from the rock into the water. She wades in until she can gather the light in her arms, and lifts the glowing orb out of the water.

The vivid dream stirred me; I wanted to slip into those warm waters to be enfolded in the gentle arms of Kwan Yin, the Mother Goddess; protected, loved, connected.

Waking more, I smiled. I imagined the woman as Jiachen.

Or Dechen.

Suddenly, tears welled in my eyes as images, and feelings from deep mythic realms gave way to ordinary, self-centred desires and mental chatter. Beauty and goodness were swept away by anger and fear.

The impact of my current situation hit me hard. I still felt like leaving Kham but thoughts of Dechen reminded me I was about to leave my close friends—Thupten, Pema, Thampa, Dawa, Yangchen. I had no other friends. None who mattered to me more. They were more like family than my own family had ever been. Could I really leave? I would be alone.

A phrase from that mysteriously-heard song came to mind. I understood its sentiment: **'When I see that no one knows this, my heart breaks in mourning sadness.'**

That's how I felt about the Gyawa experiment. No one knows what I know to be true. And my heart was breaking. If left to pursue its own course, the cooperative would continue to prosper and become an example for the rest of Tibet to follow. Why couldn't the Party see how this was the direction the revolution should take in Tibet?

I no longer trusted the Party; it was veering in the wrong direction. Would I have the courage to point this out? Could I go to Lithang, or to Chengdu, and confront the Party? I'd be turned over to the re-education squad as a counter-revolutionary.

On the other hand, did I have the courage to confront Rinpoche and ask what he was really up to? How could I tell him what I knew to be true? That our aims were not so different?

Here I lay, lost in a wilderness: literally and figuratively. Trapped between the people I thought I knew and the Party I was beginning to distrust. I had no idea where I was, nor to whom I should return.

The thought of Jiachen's voice saying 'Awaken my people' distressed me more than ever. Her people were a stubborn lot. I came to liberate her Khampa people by bringing the revolution but I realize she had actually said *awaken*. Dechen hinted Jiachen meant something entirely different from what I presumed.

I admitted defeat.

Desperate for a drink of water and something to fill my empty stomach, I struggled to stand. I felt weak. It had been more than 24 hours since I'd eaten anything.

I drank deeply from the stream and followed it downstream into the valley, as the first streaks of light appeared in the East. The stream joined another one but it was not the familiar Lithang River. It was no river; only a larger stream.

I found another trail and let my stomach make the decision. If I followed it upstream, it might take me north to Lithang and less likely to a village. Instead, I might chance on some nomads who might be less willing to help me. I decided to go downstream, hoping I would eventually reach the river and perhaps a village.

I came to a crossing and thought it best to wait for more daylight. As I found a place to rest, the silence of the night was shattered by the bellow of a distressed yak from the opposite bank. My instinct was to run back the way I'd come. I didn't trust yak; a startled yak could be unpredictable. Once I felt a safe distance away, I looked downstream and, in the early morning gloom, I could make out the yak sniffing the breeze and bellowing several times as if calling to others.

Now I was going upstream. A yak had intervened and turned me toward Lithang instead of Gyawa. I continued walking until, at a bend in the valley, I heard noises in dark shadows ahead. Cautiously, I crept forward until the unmistakeable growls and snapping barks of wolves brought me to a standstill. I'd come upon a pack of wolves devouring a recent kill. The kill was a calf; perhaps belonging to the bellowing yak downstream.

I concealed myself behind a thicket and watched in wonder. Like a dance, these beautifully terrifying creatures fought over choice parts of the kill. The frightful beauty of animal need overwhelmed me. They could have found me! It could have been my bloody flesh reflected in those eyes, ripped apart by sharp teeth and devoured. I thanked the young yak for taking part in this deadly dance instead of me!

A big tree in the thicket looked climbable. Quietly, I scaled high enough to be safe from snapping jaws, and settled in for a long wait. Eventually, the wolf pack would have their fill and move on; hopefully without noticing me.

As the light increased, I noticed that the more dominant wolves were sated and napping. Others were eating the leftovers. By the time the sun crested the eastern ridge, all had had their fill and the napping ones roused themselves. The pack trotted to the stream to slack their thirst and crossed over. They disappeared into the forest but I continued to wait until I was sure they had gone.

From time to time, the bellowing of the distressed yak continued to echo up the valley. Around noon, I watched a herd, led by the she-yak, cautiously approach. The smell of wolves gone, she approached the carcass. Sniffing it, she moaned in recognition. The others, fire in their eyes, sniffed the air in the direction the wolves had gone. Several of them bellowed long and hard in that direction, venting outrage.

Still wary of the yak herd, I remained in my uncomfortable perch until a woman and a young girl came downstream. Examining the devoured carcass, they raised their own voices in anger along with the bellowing yak. The woman lovingly embraced her yak cow, joining in her sorrow. I was touched by the deep connection she demonstrated toward the animal.

I climbed down from my perch in the tree and emerged from the thicket.

'*Tashi delek, tashi delek,*' I said smilingly, with partial but respectful bows.

They were clearly surprised and curious.

'I'm sorry for your loss,' I said, attempting to connect with them. 'Is the herd yours?'

'Yes, the wolves must have chased them down here, and the little one was singled out.'

The woman looked up the tree I had been in to see, perhaps, if someone else was around.

'I'm alone,' I explained, 'this morning I had to hide from the wolves.'

'No horse?' she asked, clearly surprised and suspicious.

'No, I'm on foot.'

'This is a dangerous place. People travel this way on horseback, and only during the day. Are you crazy or running away from someone?'

That sounded appropriate. I'd been asking myself the same questions.

'I'm Chuang Wei Ming, from Shanghai, China,' I said, hoping to appeal to her basic goodness by addressing her curiosity with the truth. 'I have been in Gyawa for the last three years.'

'Oh, the Chinese Khampa!' she said, 'yes, I've seen you before at the horse festival in Mola.'

Having placed me, she still regarded me warily. I was, after all, Chinese, even though I wore a *chuba* and had been publicly recognized as friendly at the festival.

The young girl , presumably her daughter, stood behind her. 'Isn't this the one who won all the contests?' she asked.

'It is,' the older woman said coldly.

'He's okay, then,' the girl replied with a smile for me, 'Rinpoche and that beautiful singer, Dechen-la, like him.'

Encouraged, I began to explain my situation.

'I was out walking yesterday and got lost in the heavy mist,' I explained.

'You must be hungry,' the older woman sounded concerned again. 'Dolma, give him one of our *tsampa* balls.'

The girl willingly produced the food from the folds of her *chuba* and handed it to me. I eagerly took it, and she watched with amusement as I immediately bit into it.

'Thank you, oh, thank you!' I said through a mouthful of food.

The women laughed. She produced a small flask of tea and I immediately took my drinking bowl from the folds of my *chuba*. The woman poured me some tea that she kept warm with her body heat.

'Which way is it to Gyawa?' I asked after finishing the tsampa and tea.

'Gyawa? It's too far. You're too weak to get there today. You'll have to come with us. Help us drive these animals back to our camp, and I'll feed you a good meal.'

Though she offered me food and drink, I began to worry what would happen once I got to her camp. I trusted her but didn't know if I could trust any men at her camp. From past experiences, I knew it was dangerous to arrive at a nomadic camp unless invited by the chieftain. The fact that I was very hungry helped me ignore this anxiety.

We drove the herd upstream toward open grasslands. I found myself envying the woman and her daughter; their life was so down to earth. They lived close to the elements, harsh though they were sometimes. Losing a young animal to a pack of wolves in the night was distressing and yet, here they were, singing as they leisurely followed their herd. They laughed, told jokes; they even teased me when my inexperience with herding became obvious.

We passed a pile of *mani* stones, stones inscribed with the mantra '*Om Mani Padme Hum*'. Keeping it to their right, the woman took time to completely circumnavigate the pile, repeating the mantra as she did. I couldn't understand why these nomads put so much faith in these ancient symbols, though I could always appreciated how the environment encouraged their spirituality.

As we neared their camp, I heard excited voices. Several men mounted on horseback were milling about impatiently to get going somewhere. One man was saddling a horse. He saw us coming and shouted out, 'We're off to the Chengtreng to see Lobsang.'

When he saw me, he stopped what he was doing and came toward us.

'Who's that?' he demanded bluntly.

'Why are you going to see Lobsang?' the woman shouted back, 'what happened?'

'I asked you, who's with you?' he demanded.

'I'm Chuang, from the Gyawa Cooperative,' I said before the woman could respond, 'I lost my way on the mountain yesterday. This kind woman offered me food and drink if I helped gather and herd her yak after the wolves chased them.'

'Gyawa? That Chinese Khampa?' he quickly drew his sword and yelled to his friends. Several of them galloped over, and seeing their friend confronting me with his drawn sword, likewise drew their own.

Action before reason, I thought to myself and wondered if I could protect myself if it came to that.

'He's that *gyame* from Gyawa!' my opponent yelled, he's responsible for what they did to Sonam's tribe! Let's take him to Lobsang!'

'Jigme-la!' the woman yelled, 'leave him alone!'

I had to assume Jigme was the woman's husband. He was displeased, to say the least; for his wife to order him about in front of the rest of the men in his tribe was an affront. Angry, he took it out on me. He raised his sword and my instincts took over; avoiding the swing, I grabbed his sword arm at his wrist. He landed on his back at my feet, the wind knocked out of him. I picked up his sword and glanced up to see that the others were too astonished to move. I switched the sword in my left hand and offered my right to help Jigme up.

One of the men, putting his sword away, came toward me.

'Impressive,' he said as he withdrew a pistol from the folds of his chuba and pointed it at me. He looked me over carefully, and ordered his men to tie me up. I didn't resist.

'We'll take him with us.'

That raised a stir among the men. They liked the idea.

'Good idea, Gyaltsen-la!' one of the men shouted out, 'let Lobsang decide what to do with this *gyame* spy!'

My arrival delayed the men's departure enough that they decided to stay the night. Though I was tied to a post, I persisted in asking questions. Gyaltsen eventually responded by explaining how they were on their way to see Lobsang because a nomadic tribe had been forced to settle in Gyawa.

259

Yesterday, the day I'd left Gyawa, PLA troops brought a whole nomadic clan, some thirty people and their vast herd, from the Lithang grasslands down to Gyawa. The nomads were told they would be joining the collective and would have to live in permanent houses.

This new development in Gyawa was more outrageous than Tenzin's new policies. What was Deng up to? I felt I had to confront him and sort things out. How could I leave Kham now? The nomads needed to live free on the open grasslands. I needed to protect their way of life.

If these men dragged me all the way out to the Chengtreng, as they proposed to do, who knows what they or Lobsang would do to me? I needed to escape, go to Gyawa, find out just what was going on, and then confront Deng. As subtly as I could I, tried to free my hands from the rope securing me to a post in the middle of the camp. It proved to be a useless activity under the watchful eye of an armed guard.

My only hope was Karma, the woman who brought me here. She ignored the men's hostility toward me and graciously brought me food and drink. She fed me bite size amounts of *tsampa* mixed with tea, and put a bowl of *chang* to my mouth so I could drink.

'You eat like a Khampa, a true *tsampa*-eater,' she said.

'I'm honoured,' I replied, knowing how much pride all Tibetan's took in being *tsampa*-eaters. I had at least one friend among my captors, despite what I'd done to her husband.

'How's your husband?' I asked, 'I hope I didn't hurt him.'

'Oh, he's okay. Sulking somewhere, I guess. Only his pride is hurt. He's too quick to act and doesn't stop to think. Sometimes I wish I could do what you did to him.'

I smiled to acknowledge her sense of humour.

'I must get to Gyawa right away,' I said, hoping for her support. 'I need to find out what's going on there. Please believe me. What's happening in Gyawa is not the way I want things to be. You nomadic people must be allowed to live as you have always lived, free to roam the grasslands and highlands with your herds. It is a beautiful way of life!'

'You're a good man, Chinese Khampa,' she said, and added with a big smile, 'I remember how you surprised everyone with your excellent riding and shooting skills. I also remember how Manene chose you. What a lovely young woman. So beautiful! A living *Dakini*!'

Karma looked at me seriously for a moment, as if coming to a decision. With sudden resolve she got up, gathered the bowls.

'Please,' I pleaded before she walked away, 'tell the men I need to go to Gyawa. Tell them I want to go from there to Lithang to convince Commander Deng, the Communist Party leader, that he's making a big mistake. I am on your side, and will do all I can to help you keep your way of life.'

Karma walked away but I thought I saw her nod her head. After putting things away in her tent, she emerged and hurried to another tent. A few minutes later, two women came out of that tent and hurried to another.

I chuckled; I knew what the women were doing. I let myself relax and tried to lie down on the ground, even though my feet were shackled and my hands tied behind by back. Weary after a cold, restless night combined with a full belly, I was drowsy but unable to sleep. My mind continued to churn out thought after thought.

I saw clearly that I would not be returning to Chengdu; I would not be asking Comrade Li for a transfer. There was more to do here, more to fight for. I had no idea how, but I knew I had to defend the nomads, the villages, all the people of Kham against the blind sweep of Party policy and bureaucracy, with or without Rinpoche's help.

My decision was based on a visceral feeling that the Khampa way of life was right for them. Communism could offer some improvements but I knew the nomads must be allowed to continue to live in harmony within their natural and spiritual environment, as they have been doing for centuries.

'Get up, *gyame!*' The kick was hard enough to knock the breath out of me but not enough to break a rib.

It was morning. Jigme saw me as an enemy of Buddha dharma. Putting a disparaging name to an enemy, I knew, made it easier to generate hatred and stir up nationalistic pride.

My guard intervened before a second kick was delivered. He hauled me up roughly, untied the rope that secured me to the post, and shoved me toward the horse my assailant had brought. The guard untied my legs and ordered me to get on the horse. He steadied me when he realized it was quite a challenging activity with my hands tied behind my back. When he got me on the horse, he tied my ankles together under the horse's belly. It was uncomfortable and, I thought, dangerous. I protested saying it was enough that my hands were tied; I wouldn't run away. Jigme and my guard ignored me, and led me toward the milling crowd of eager horsemen.

Discouraged, I resigned myself to an uncomfortable journey, the outcome of which was far from certain. Alone among frenzied men of a nomadic tribe eager for Chinese blood, I imagined my chance of survival were slim.

Things looked bleak.

Several horsemen, Jigme included, shouted to different men around the camp. They were impatient to get going.

Several women approached. Gyaltsen was with them. He ordered my guard to untie my legs and get me off the horse. Several horsemen began to object but Gyaltsen silenced them with a harsh rebuke.

'Get back!' he shouted, to be heard by everyone. 'This man is not like the other *gyame*! Do you remember the Mola horse festival last summer? This is the man who won all the contests. I watched as he rode in the target contest. He put two arrows in the centre of each target while everyone else had trouble finding the target. I saw Palden Rinpoche give him his best white horse to ride and he was first to reach the sacred peak with Rinpoche's banner. No, this man is not *gyame*!'

Several men rode closer to take a better look at me.

'But he's from Gyawa,' another objected, 'he's responsible for making Sonam's tribe settle like farmers!'

I noticed the women, including Karma, standing behind Gyaltsen. Their appearance cooled the belligerence of the riders; it was obvious where this new perspective was coming from. Gyaltsen stepped a little to the side to allow his wife to stand beside him.

'No,' Gyaltsen said, 'since the time of the festival that traitor Tsering Nawang's son, Tenzin, has been running the cooperative in Gyawa. This man had nothing to do with what happened to Sonam's tribe.'

He looked around at several unsatisfied faces, challenging them to contradict him.

'What do you have to say?' Gyaltsen asked me suddenly.

First, I bowed to the chieftain and his wife. Then I looked at all the Khampa riders surrounding me. One of them could easily use a pistol to finish me off, but they waited. They respected their chief enough to let me have my say.

'As Gyaltsen-la has said,' I began, 'I have not been in Gyawa for a long time. I did not know that Commander Deng in Lithang had ordered his soldiers to move Sonam's tribe to Gyawa where Major Gan and Tenzin are in charge.'

'I say we ride to Gyawa and free Sonam's tribe!' an agitated tribesman shouted, 'we'll capture that traitor Tenzin!'

Several raised a cry in agreement.

'Stop this!' the chief bellowed. 'We will first consult Lobsang. Besides, we would be outnumbered. There are 20 or 30 armed soldiers in Gyawa now. How many guns do we have? Maybe 15, if they all work.'

'That's right,' someone in support of the chief added, 'keep to our plan to go see Lobsang. With greater numbers, we will drive the *gyame* out—starting with Gyawa, and then Lithang.'

The prevailing attitude was a knee-jerk call to take up arms. Didn't they know their forces would surely be wiped out by an overwhelmingly violent response from the PLA? Armed with modern weapons, including aircraft, the PLA would hunt down and decimate any rag-tag Khampa militia. I shuddered at the thought.

Was Rinpoche really encouraging this option? Surely not!

'Please listen a moment!' I raised my voice, 'I beg you to talk to Palden Rinpoche before you go to see Lobsang. His advice right now is good for you and for all of Kham.'

I'm not sure why I said that. It must have occurred to me that I might be mistaken to assume Rinpoche was training young men to fight. Perhaps he was training young men to use non-violent techniques of self-defence and intervention, the way I'd disarmed Jigme and the man at the tavern. Rinpoche said King Gesar's battles were against evil forces. He and Dechen admired Mahatma Gandhi's non-violent resistance movement.

How stupid I felt to have doubted Rinpoche!

The women moved to encourage the chief's wife to speak. 'Listen to the Chinese Khampa,' she said. 'What he says is right. Go see Palden Rinpoche first. He is our spiritual leader. We have always followed the advice of lamas in times of crisis before making drastic decisions. It is no different now.'

'How do you know we can trust this *gyame*?' one of them shouted, repeating the original opinion.

'Palden Rinpoche recognized this man as someone he could trust!' Gyaltsen replied emphatically, 'that's good enough for me.'

Recruited

When we reached the Lithang River, Gyaltsen had another shouting match with Jigme, and a few others who insisted on taking me with them to Lobsang's camp. Gyaltsen argued that I would be more useful trying to secure the release of Sonam's tribe. He set me free with a stern warning that if I was unsuccessful, he would hunt me down and kill me.

Exhausted and stiff from being tied on the horse, I made my way slowly on foot along the river trail to Gyawa. I hoped Gyaltsen would take my advice and visit Palden Rinpoche's hermitage on their way into Chengtreng, but I felt he would be overruled. He undoubtedly compromised a visit with Palden Rinpoche when he let me go.

Something big was going on when I arrived in Gyawa. The entire cooperative had gathered at our usual community meeting place. Tenzin and Major Gan stood on a newly-built raised platform. Several armed soldiers stood on either side of the platform. At the front stood a cluster of nomadic men, surrounded by the original cooperative membership. A couple dozen more soldiers flanked the gathered villagers and nomads.

Thupten and Pema stood at the back of the crowd, where I joined them. Intent on following the proceedings they hardly noticed me, or if they did, they were too upset to notice my bedraggled condition.

I, too, put aside my discomfort when I understood what was going on; I began to seethe along with Thupten and Pema.

Major Gan held several sheets of paper in his hand. Beside him, Tenzin shouted at everyone, 'As your name is called, come forward and receive the deed to your land. As promised, this land is yours to settle. Permanent houses will be built for you and you will be part of this collective.'

In a garbled attempt to use Tibetan, Major Gan called a name and handed the paper to Tenzin. Tenzin repeated the name correctly, and a self-conscious nomad shuffled forward to receive a piece of paper. He glanced at the paper covered with Chinese characters and frowned. It was clear he knew enough to recognize Chinese characters when he saw them.

One by one, nomads received their papers from Tenzin while a few strategically placed stooges clapped their hands and tried to enthuse the crowd. A photographer shouted at each of them to hold up the paper and smile while he took a picture.

Thupten whispered at my shoulder.

'The Chinese call these papers 'deeds' but they are really orders requiring each nomad family to settle here in the village. They tell the nomads they must help the cooperative—sorry, new name—help the collective grow crops on land that is only useful for grazing. What a farce! Have you ever heard of nomads farming?'

Pema looked around anxiously and elbowed Thupten in the ribs.

'Watch what you're saying.'

I glanced at Pema and Thupten. They still did not appear to notice my scruffy condition. I looked around for Dechen; she wasn't at this gathering and it crossed my mind that Tenzin would be annoyed if he noticed her absence. That thought made me smile. I knew she took advantage of Tenzin's soft spot for her. Tenzin had too much to lose if he bullied her around like he did everyone else.

'Our reforms,' Tenzin was saying with practiced emotion, 'guarantee that food, clothing, and shelter will be equally shared by all; nomad and farmer alike. Collectives will eliminate poverty. Everyone will have a place to live, food to eat, and clothing to wear and work to do.'

Cheers and clapping by the same stooges interrupted his flow, but also inspired him to be even more eloquent.

'A truly classless society is being created throughout Kham. Everyone will live as equal contributing members. The People's Liberation Army devotes itself to our heroic struggle for liberation and justice. Long live the invincible leadership of the Communist Party and Chairman Mao!'

During one of Tenzin's strategic pauses filled with the applause of his few supporters, Thupten urged me away from the assembly. We ducked and moved behind the crowd toward a narrow alley, where we could converse.

'I've heard,' Thupten began urgently, 'that in many parts of Kham, soldiers are collecting produce and property from every house. Guns are confiscated and people are told it is against the law to own guns of any kind. Nomads are told they won't need guns for hunting because they will be resettled in collectives. All their needs will be provided; everyone gets a place to sleep, food to eat, clothing to wear but everyone works as they are told. Everyone goes where they are told to go.'

I listened attentively. What he was saying corroborated what Karma and Gyaltsen had told me. The Party seemed determined to eliminate nomadic life and settle everyone in communes.

'PLA soldiers from Lithang forced the nomads here yesterday, and today they are promising them land and houses!'

'Where are their herds?' I asked.

'In corrals down by the river.'

'How is this supposed to work? How can you feed the extra animals and people this winter?'

'How do I know? Of course, I objected. Tenzin said he had orders from Lithang to accept the nomads. We have to feed them, cultivate more land, and manage their animals. We were told we have to build houses for the families, too.'

'I don't get it. Land, houses?'

'Like I said, it's a farce!'

'How are the nomads reacting?'

'You saw the looks on their faces! They don't want or need land! But what could they do when armed soldiers forced them to march here? In other places, people are resisting. It's a natural reaction to being robbed of property and freedom. Resistance is dealt with swiftly and violently!'

Thupten was worked up. Stopping a moment to catch his breath, he continued, 'Some are shot immediately, others are taken to labour camps and forced to work on the roads. Sonam's clan could have resisted and faced harsh treatment but fortunately they did not.'

Thupten nodded his head indicating he approved of Sonam's decision.

'I asked Sonam,' he continued, 'why they hadn't resisted. He said they decided joining Gyawa Cooperative might be beneficial for them. At least they would give it a try. They didn't know how things have changed here since Tenzin's been in charge.'

Tenzin, with the support of Major Gan and his soldiers, was already moving ahead to implement the Party's agenda. Would Deng honour my request to hold off implementing reforms in the southern parts of Lithang district?

'Things have changed,' Thupten was saying when I turned my attention back to him. 'Ever since Commander Deng came to Lithang, Tenzin has been dancing to Deng's tune like a puppet on a string. On the outside it looks like Major Gan and his soldiers do whatever Tenzin says, but in reality, it is the other way around. Major Gan is here to see that Tenzin complies with Deng's directives.'

Thupten was worked up and, pointing in the direction of the assembly, continued his verbal rampage.

'The people are fed up. It won't be long before the soldiers start using force here, too. Can't you do something?'

'What can I do, Thupten? Now, I have been removed from authority.'

'I'm afraid to speak up here,' Thupten admitted. 'Even Thampa keeps his mouth shut.'

Thupten's anger, worry, and fear showed in his tightened shoulders, his stiff back. The change in his bearing saddened me. Gone was the energetic, positive leader; diminished by heavy handed authorities who were far removed from the people here.

The implications of these new policies consumed me to the point where I started thinking that an organized militia like Lobsang's might actually be justified. Although I was angry enough to fight, I had the common sense to see that outright battle with the PLA would have disastrous consequences. I had to make that clear to Rinpoche, and to Lobsang, if possible.

'I must get back to the assembly,' Thupten said quickly. He looked me over a moment, and a hint of his old self showed up.

'You look terrible! What happened to you? Go to my house! There's hot tea, and help yourself to *tsampa*. You know where it is. Pema and I will come home once this song and dance is over, and we've organized the day's work.'

I realized how hungry I was. Just mentioning tea and *tsampa* made my mouth water! I hurried to his house, entered the courtyard and caught a glimpse of Jiachen, no, Dechen, in the upstairs window just as someone said my name. I turned. My immediate thought was that one of Major Gan's soldiers was there to confront me. Perhaps I'd been seen.

It wasn't a soldier. It was a young man with a long pole and he was charging! He swung at my head. In an instant he was on the ground, his weapon in my hand ready for the end to be thrust into his chest if he moved.

Behind me, someone emerged from the house.

'There!' said a voice tinged with annoyance. I immediately recognized the voice as Rinpoche's, and imagined his anger with me; wanting to confront and thrash me for my distrust. Overnight I'd become everyone's enemy: the nomads', Major Gan's if he discovered me here, and now Rinpoche's!

Overcome with exhaustion, I dropped the pole and released my attacker.

'Why are you attacking me?' I blurted angrily.

Rinpoche's face softened, 'We're not here to harm you, Wei Ming! I merely want to demonstrate to you why you should come to the hermitage.'

'How is attacking me supposed to encourage that?' I demanded, more confused than ever.

271

Instead of responding to me, Palden Rinpoche held out his hand to help the young man stand up. 'This is Wangdu, my training assistant.'

I didn't bow or apologize to the young man. I turned my back on him and faced Rinpoche.

'Look at yourself,' Rinpoche remarked. 'Crazed, angry, confused, starving!'

I agreed; I looked a mess.

'We met the gentlemen who brought you out of the wilderness,' Rinpoche explained. 'Quite a tale of wolves and captivity! I do not really know what Lobsang would have done with you.'

When I remained silent, he continued, 'How did you get lost?'

'I was angry and left Gyawa with the idea of going back to China. I wasn't thinking.'

'Angry? Why?'

'Are you training warriors and preparing for an armed revolt?' I asked with hostility.

'Oh, is that what you think?' Rinpoche replied with a sigh. 'Well, it's not your fault that you misunderstood what we are doing at the hermitage. Indeed, I am training men to be warriors. Do you remember what I had told you about Gesar's warriors earlier?'

'Yes,' I said, 'I found myself having second thoughts once I remembered what you'd said about non-violent methods to overcome evil forces rather than actually killing one's enemy.'

'We call them windhorse warriors,' Wangdu contributed. 'Warriors who are courageous enough to harness the power of basic goodness.'

I turned to Wangdu. He seemed intelligent, as well as strong and skilful. He showed a newly acquired respect for me, I thought.

'Listen,' Rinpoche said moving closer, 'we both know you are not like other Chinese Communist Party members. Nor are you like a soldier in the Red Army. You have taken time and shown interest in getting to know us. Who else has done that?'

Rinpoche looked intently in one eye of my eyes, then the other, while saying, 'And then there is the evidence of what you did at the festival. You excelled in our ancient warrior skills and carried a banner with honour to the sacred peak. No, you are no ordinary Chinese by any means.'

Rinpoche glanced at Wangdu, then back to me and, to my embarrassment, continued extolling me. 'Do you realize you were trained by the greatest master in all of Asia? I know this because Master Tashi of Mongolia is also my teacher. I must consider you my brother because of our mutual mentor,' Rinpoche concluded. 'He taught you well. He taught you skills I do not have, but there are a few things Master Tashi was unable to teach you.'

I was astonished that Master Tashi was Rinpoche's teacher. My mind was suddenly filled with many questions, but Palden did not pause.

'Mindfulness requires the greatest courage. Are you brave enough to master your own mind? To know where you stand on this earth? To truly experience being alive? Do you have the courage to completely empty yourself into pure presence? That's the kind of courage a windhorse warrior needs.'

Palden watched my reaction.

'Palden Rinpoche is right,' Wangdu said, 'you are a true windhorse warrior. You easily disarmed me despite my determination to succeed in my attack. How did you do that? You must teach me. Please, come to the hermitage. Train us.'

This request took me by surprise. I looked from Wangdu to Palden, and back again. This was why they wanted me!

'A spiritual, non-violent warrior,' Rinpoche declared emphatically, 'has greater courage than one who relies on eliminating an enemy by killing. The violent man fights out of fear; the non-violent warrior acts with compassion. If force is directed toward him, he knows how to redirect that force and keep it from hurting himself and his opponent.'

'Jujutsu,' I said. 'You want me to teach your warriors the art of jujutsu.'

'Yes!' Wangdu said enthusiastically, with a glance at Rinpoche.

I shook my head but I wasn't declining the offer. I was overwhelmed. I held up my hands in exasperation.

'How is it you came here today, anyway?' I demanded.

'When you didn't come on your own to the hermitage, we decided it was time to persuade you. We had no idea you'd disappeared until we met the nomads who found you in their territory.'

Rinpoche scrutinized me. 'Would you have returned if you hadn't been captured?'

'I don't know,' I replied truthfully, 'I felt useless here because I wasn't making any headway toward forming another cooperative. And when I suspected you were training a militia, I was disgusted and wanted to get as far away as I could. And then, of course, what the Party is doing here completely discourages me. It is not right! Yes, I was angry, upset, not thinking clearly! I ran away!'

Rinpoche looked at me with kindness but waited while I composed myself.

'I got lost, ran into a pack of wolves, and was saved by a kind nomad woman. When I got to her camp, her husband assaulted me. Gyaltsen, their chief, prevented others from joining in but I was tied up. They wanted to take me to Lobsang.' I took a moment to breathe. 'Fortunately, the women of the tribe recognized me from the summer horse racing festival, and convinced Gyaltsen that I was okay because you trusted me. When we got to the river, Gyaltsen convinced the more determined ones that I should be given a chance to set Sonam's tribe free. If I couldn't, they'd come after me and kill me.'

Rinpoche laughed. 'Quite an adventure!'

'Yes,' I responded without humour.

'But wild animals and wild women intervened!' Rinpoche chuckled, a sparkle of humour in his eyes. 'Now here you are. Have you changed your mind?'

'Well, yes, I have.'

'That's good!' Rinpoche suddenly gave me a big hug. 'Come, younger brother, you look hungry and tired. Come inside. Dechen has the kettle on.'

My heart skipped a beat when Rinpoche mentioned Dechen. It was her in the window upstairs! I made my way inside quickly, eager to see her again. She welcomed me graciously, and I went off to wash up and change into the fresh clothing I'd left here. Rinpoche, Wangdu, and Dechen were in quiet conversation when I returned. Dechen got up to serve us tea and gave me a hearty meal. When I'd had my fill, it was Dechen who spoke first.

'Rinpoche, Yangchen, Wangdu, and I are planning,' she began, 'a strong cultural defines against the heartless policies being thrust upon us. From the beginning, Rinpoche encouraged Thupten and my parents to work with you to set up this cooperative. We wanted to test your ideas. You see, Yangchen knew you through Jiachen, my sister. She knew Jiachen embraced the highest communist ideals, which she managed to instil in you. We have nothing against real communism as long as it actually corresponds with the principles of Buddhist compassion: selflessly working to relieve the suffering of all people, and to establish an enlightened society in which all can be happy. If communism can help us do that, we will use it as a means to our ends.'

I nodded. I remembered Jiachen's passionate elaborations about the benefits of communism.

'You see, Wei Ming,' Dechen said, 'you were part of our plan even before you were chosen by the goddess Manene. You've been working toward this all your life. Yangchen found you through Master Tashi, who you've already heard is Rinpoche's teacher.'

I prickled. This kind of talk was outrageous, pure hocus pocus! I began to feel like a pawn in some kind of game.

'So,' I responded out of my growing sense of confusion and anger, 'I've been set up, have I?'

'Not set up,' Rinpoche interjected calmly, 'identified. Yangchen told us about you long ago. In her heart, she knew you would come.'

'What utter bullshit! It's all coincidence! My orders to come here came from the Chinese Communist Party. I never asked to be sent here. I never knew Jiachen's family lived here.'

'Wasn't it Comrade Li's idea?' Dechen added to support Rinpoche. 'Have you ever wondered why he was familiar with

Tibet? He became father's friend when he served in Lithang with the nationalists long ago.'

This web was very sticky. Thampa and Comrade Li were friends? Now I really knew I'd been set up. While I seethed, Dechen continued talking but I heard only the last part, '...you've met all the criteria.'

'Criteria? What the hell for?' I was in no mood for this! I was battered and bruised, weak with exhaustion, and at my wit's end.

They remained silent.

'Come to the hermitage,' Rinpoche implored after a moment, 'you'll understand soon, I promise.'

'No!' I said adamantly. 'I must do something about the settlement of the nomads in Gyawa. I'm going to give Deng a piece of my mind. What they're doing is completely wrong. An economic disaster if they keep this up. The Party must finally recognize they cannot implement the same policies here as in the lowlands, I said angrily, adding, 'Besides, Lobsang will be organizing for war. If Gyaltsen and his men convince him, Lobsang will attack Gyawa to wipe out Major Gan's men, including Tenzin, and then go on to attack the garrison in Lithang. I need to do whatever I can to reverse the decision to settle Sonam's tribe here.'

'Okay,' Rinpoche agreed with a nod of his head, 'do what you must. Ask Thupten to arrange a meeting with Sonam. Tell him what you've told us. Then go see Deng. But be careful! Every time you go there, I hold my breath thinking they'll kick your ass all the way to some prison in China. How you manage to charm Deng, I have no idea. I just hope things continue to work in your favour.'

'He's PLA, I'm Party. That makes me at least his equal and since I've been here longer, he's obliged to listen to my opinions. Besides, Party leadership thinks I'm a revolutionary icon. I've had that to rely on so far.'

Thupten and Pema came in. They were pleased to see us making ourselves at home.

'Thupten-la,' Rinpoche said, 'our friend Chuang-la would like to speak with Chieftain Sonam-la. Can you arrange that in secret? He has news that Lobsang may organize an attack. We'd like to avoid that, if possible.'

'Of course, Rinpoche-la,' Thupten replied deferentially.

'We must be on our way, Wangdu,' Rinpoche announced as he got to his feet. He turned to Thupten, 'Is it safe to leave now?'

'Oh yes, I think so. Major Gan and his men are busy. They are showing the nomads where they are to begin farming. The nomads are not happy about it, of course.'

'But what can they do now? Winter is already here!' Wangdu observed.

'They want them to clear the land of bushes and trees,' Pema put in.

As the others carried on about how ridiculous it all was, Rinpoche and Dechen took me aside.

'After you've done what you can here and in Lithang,' Rinpoche said with his arm on my shoulder, 'you must come to the hermitage. Promise!'

'Okay, I promise,' I said without hesitation, 'I apologize for my anger. I... I'm very confused about the things you're saying... about the purpose of my life.'

'Don't say anything more,' Rinpoche cut me off, 'your confusion is understandable. Things happen as they should,

I've learned. Now things are moving forward faster than we expected.'

He gave me a hug and walked out the door, leaving me wondering what he meant.

Thupten and Pema left to see them off safely. Dechen began clearing the bowls and dishes. She noticed the rope burns on my wrists but didn't make any remarks.

I met her eye briefly then, and caught a glimpse of Jiachen looking back at me. Did Dechen do that deliberately? Did she want to remind me of Jiachen or was it really Jiachen looking through those beautiful eyes? Was Dechen offering me a glimpse of Jiachen as a gift or was she trying to attract me to her? Maybe I wanted Dechen to be Jiachen! Maybe I was deluding myself; I was too confused to deal with it in my exhaustion.

'Rest now,' Dechen said, acknowledging my state of mind and body. It was an order. I nodded, and obediently went upstairs to my room and collapsed on the bed.

Confronting the Commander

The PLA camp was already larger than it was a month ago. Several permanent buildings were being built. Soldiers stood with guns in their hands watching Tibetans break and carry stones, saw timbers into planks and frames, mix mud for mortar, among other tasks. A large part of the camp was sectioned off with a high wire fence. I suspected the secured area was for the incarceration of this forced labour pool.

I'd taken pains to dress for this encounter. I looked sharp, well-groomed; a Party man. But, as before, I hid my long hair under my winter hat.

I heard Commander Deng's curt 'Enter' command, and found him pacing his office. He was less than pleased to see me. His brow was creased, his face red. Anger was heavy on his shoulders, in his heavy steps.

'What do you want, Comrade Chuang?' he growled.

I was angry too. Commander Deng was not my superior; if he could growl at me I could yell at him. So I did.

'I thought we had an agreement to delay reforms in the southern part of the district,' I began defiantly. 'That includes Gyawa! Instead I find your goons overrunning the cooperative!'

Deng ignored my outburst.

'My experiment worked!' I shouted again, 'you know that, Party leadership knows that. Gyawa has been self-sufficient and prosperous. The members fully understand communist principles and live together harmoniously. Now your stooges are making the people disgruntled, shattering their trust in communism. Do you even realize how much effort it takes to build trust? To encourage people to voluntarily live according to communist principles?'

Deng continued pacing; his face reddening more, but he was listening.

'Centralizing all produce here in Lithang? Really, comrade! Don't you see how that affects people? Do you think they wouldn't see right through this scheme? They know you are making sure your soldiers are fed first.'

I glared at him, took a deep breath and continued.

'That is not the communist way!' I spat out.

Deng held his tongue but I could see his fury building.

'I have just come from Gyawa. I don't have to tell you what is going on there. It was on your orders that nomads from nearby grasslands were forced to settle in Gyawa! How do you expect the cooperative to cope with more mouths to feed when you've taken away all their produce?'

I paused to give him a chance to respond. He continued to stew and pace, but said nothing.

'You've forced a nomadic tribe off their ancestral lands,' I continued. 'Do you realize what a dangerous move that is? As we speak, a warlord of Chengtreng is mobilizing to attack Gyawa and rescue that tribe. They are likely to come here next. Do you understand what that means? Obviously you don't. It's time you listened to me and not to those bureaucrats in Chengdu and Beijing.'

Deng looked at me as if about to reply but turned away abruptly and continued pacing.

'What about Mola?' I went on softening my tone. 'Given time, we can start another, larger cooperative. This one could include nomads from the surrounding grasslands.'

I hoped to give him the broader picture, the positive possibilities if the politicians would stop meddling.

'I've already talked to landowners and nomad leaders,' I stretched the truth a bit. 'Workers are putting pressure on landlords to turn over their lands and herds voluntarily to the people. What you don't seem to realize is that these heavy-handed tactics are turning people against communism, ruining the possibility of acceptance. Given time and non-interference, the people will choose to make changes if we...'

Commander Deng stopped pacing abruptly and pounded his desk with his fist. His nameplate jumped, rattled and fell over, face down.

'Time? There's a rebellion going on!' Deng shouted in my face. 'I know about Lobsang in Chengtreng. He's not the only one! There are others north of here, west of here too.'

'So listen to me!' I shouted back at him. 'Ask yourself; why are the people rebelling? You have to help me shout at those desk idiots in Chengdu and Beijing. We're the ones up here who know the situation. Hold off you reforms for a while longer!'

'No more time, Comrade Chuang. I'm telling you, time has run out. It's Beijing. The people at the top have lost patience. You failed to make changes fast enough. Comrade Li told me Party officials greatly appreciate your efforts, but said your results are too little, too late.'

Commander Deng actually looked a little apologetic. His tone softened and he sat in his chair to speak frankly with me, after resetting his toppled nameplate in an effort to affirm his authority.

'I have my orders, comrade. By the end of next year all property—holdings of monasteries included—will be confiscated and redistributed. Herds are to be gathered and managed in collectives. Villages will be organized into communes. Voluntarily or not, like it or not, there is no way to stop this.'

'That spells disaster!' I said in shock.

Commander Deng poked his finger at me across the desk. 'You question the Party?'

I ignored Deng's aggressive suggestion of non-compliance. But, yes, I did question the Party. Creative, contextual thinking was not happening anymore, as Mao promoted in 'On Practice'. He should know that transferring a solution from one place to another does not work!

'The climate, the potential of the land to produce, and local experience must be considered. Imposing the same structures here as in the lowlands is a grave mistake. These people have been successful here for centuries. Their way of life is vastly different from ours,' I tried to reason, 'their economy depends on large herds of yak that range freely on the high grasslands and on village farms in the valleys. If you corral herds down in the villages, the yak will not produce and people will starve.'

The commander shrugged as if this meant nothing to him. 'My job, our job, is to implement the will of the Party.'

'The will of the Party reflects the will of the People,' I threw a familiar slogan back at him, 'the will of the local people must be considered and implemented. I don't see that happening. The people here have their own way of life and their way of life has been good for them.'

My boldness continued to alarm Commander Deng, and our eyes locked in a battle of wills. He studied me thoughtfully and then, as if reconsidering his stance, leaned back in his chair.

'I am curious, Comrade Chuang. What would happen if we had more time?'

'As I've already said, and demonstrated in Gyawa, given time, the locals will come to accept communism willingly. We must educate and persuade more communities to voluntarily establish their own cooperatives. People need time to understand what our system can do for them, and how it fits their Buddhist lifestyle,' I offered. 'Through this approach, people will meet the goals of the Party without being forced to comply. Confiscating property for redistribution, resettling nomads, confining herds, and creating communes will enrage the people. They have seen how Gyawa worked. That's what they want. Why not let them form cooperatives voluntarily? Why force communes on them? This move reveals the Party's weakness, not the strength of communism!'

I thought I'd gone too far with that last statement but Commander Deng was listening intently. I leaned toward him and lowered my voice. I wanted to reach him on a personal level, if I could.

'These people recognize the need for change in their society. The common people want social justice and economic reforms. They understand that! They know their system is far from perfect and they are open to changes. Give them a chance. Give me a chance to complete my mission here. Let the people meet your goals without the use of force.'

'Well,' Deng responded calmly after a thoughtful pause, 'that road sounds like a very long one, Comrade Chuang. As I've already said, they think you've run along that road too slowly.'

Commander Deng got up, went to the window, lit a cigarette, and turned his back on me. He looked out the window toward the monastery. It was his way of saying, I'd lost.

'That's truly unfortunate,' I said sadly, 'I have spoken with many Tibetans who fully understand the benefits of communism but...'

'But what?' Deng prodded.

'For one thing, our arrogance puts them off. They do not want a group of people far away in Beijing imposing decisions on them without consultation, and without the consent of the local people. Secondly, the Party shows an obvious lack of understanding of Tibet's rich cultural heritage and sophisticated philosophy, to say nothing of its historical independence. Mutual understanding and respect for each other's cultural heritage is what they want.'

An idea struck me as I said this: Rinpoche and Dechen had already told me how communism and Buddhism could support each other.

'They see communism as a good way to live outwardly in the world,' I said after absorbing my insight, 'but Buddhism must continue to inform the inner life. And the people in China can clearly benefit from Tibetan Buddhist wisdom.'

The Commander turned around swiftly, looking at me accusingly.

'You sound too sympathetic, comrade!' Deng said, 'and is it true what they say? That you dress like them!'

Deng walked over to glare at me inches from my face. I held his eyes without flinching.

'Yes,' I responded evenly, 'it's my job to identify with the people as much as possible. By speaking their language,

285

adopting their dress, participating in their work and lives, I have learned much about them. The Khampas trust me because I have taken time to understand and identify with them. My job is information transfer. I do what I can to explain the benefits of our system to the local people, and I have been trying to tell you what I've learned! As a Party member, it is my duty to know and represent the People, these people. I transfer information both ways.'

'Just the same, what are your true personal feelings in this regard?'

'It is my duty to encourage social transformation. I believe we have an opening here. We must continue working with those who understand the benefits of communism and encourage them to embrace it voluntarily.'

Deng dropped his steely gaze and returned to the window. He remained quiet while sparrows chirped in the eaves of the building and a raven's claws scratched on the tin roof, underscoring my malaise. I waited.

Finally, with tired resignation, Deng turned to face me.

'Comrade Chuang,' he said with a hint of respect, 'everything you tell me indicates that I should recommend reassignment after some, ah, re-education. However, I won't do that just yet. Because you can speak to the people, you can still be useful here. Your job now is to make your local friends understand that they must adjust to the current policies.'

The commander went to his desk and stood as tall as he could before adding, 'What has been set in motion cannot change. The train has left the station and there is one track ahead of it. Do you understand? Reforms will be made. Your way, good as it has been, does not achieve the desired results quickly enough. Your friends must accept the authority of the Party! As must you, Comrade Chuang.'

'This approach,' I responded out of disappointment and anger, 'can only end badly. For everyone! I am not in need of re-education. I am here to spread true communism. I smell tyranny of the Party, not the will of the People.'

'Comrade Chuang!' Deng was red with rage, 'you are driving me closer to reporting you for your treasonous attitude.'

I got up to leave his office. I'd had enough.

'One more thing,' Deng said and gestured for me to sit down, 'I've been informed that you know the whereabouts of that renegade lama.'

'That's true,' I said as I sat down and leaned back in the chair. 'He's at his hermitage, as always.'

'Why haven't you reported this to Major Gan?'

'What harm can that lama do?' I found myself defending Rinpoche, 'he is not training an armed militia.'

'Then what are his intentions?'

'He's not a warlord, he's a Buddhist teacher. He believes in non-violence.'

'Of course!' Deng appeared to have a flash of insight, 'a truly dangerous man. He spent time in India, if I'm not mistaken. Perhaps he wants to be like Mahatma Gandhi who ended Britain's hold over India. Is that his intention?'

'He has an idea to use the story of an ancient Tibetan King, Gesar of Ling, as a means of rousing the spirit of the Tibetan people. Apparently, this ancient Buddhist kingdom established equality among all its citizens, very much along the lines of modern communism.'

'Interesting,' Deng noted unenthusiastically.

'I am exploring this connection, myself. I've learned quite a bit about the people from this story.'

Deng regarded me thoughtfully again. Presently, as if making up his mind, he stood up, and reached across the table to shake my hand. I stood and accepted his brief handshake.

'Carry on, then, Comrade Chuang! Personally, I admire your work,' Deng said in a friendly manner. 'I will continue to support you if you return to Mola township and keep an eye on that renegade lama for me. Work with him and influence him to accept the situation as it is. Encourage him to use his popularity among the people to generate a non-violent acceptance of Party authority—not to demonstrate against us. Do I make myself clear?'

Before Deng's friendliness became more hollow and disingenuous, I said, 'Commander Deng, I understand that you must obey orders but I hope that you want a positive outcome for the people here. If you believe in what I'm trying to do, give me your word that reforms will not be forced upon southern Lithang district until the end of next year.'

His friendliness disappeared and was replaced with a more cautious tone.

'I will observe your progress,' he said. I realized he could not officially make this promise but he seemed willing to give me a chance. 'If it looks like you are accomplishing the goals set by the Party, I will leave that area alone.'

'And what about the nomads forced to settle in Gyawa? Can that be reversed? Will you allow them to leave?'

'I will give it some thought.'

I wanted to hear him say that if the nomads were to leave, he would not stop them or force them back. But that was wishful thinking.

'What about the warrant for the arrest of Palden Rinpoche?'

'I know the warrant, as you said, is based on a private vindictiveness accusation and I have ignored it. I will continue to do so if you make use of this lama to stop rebellion in the district.'

That reminded Deng of another thorn in his flesh. 'Regarding the mounting rebellion,' he asked, 'do you know this Lobsang, the warlord of Chengtreng?'

'Yes, I ran afoul of him during my first few months here. One of his men drew a sword and attacked me but Lobsang put a stop to it. I think he wanted to avoid trouble while he was in town. Haven't seen him since.'

'Well, if you meet him again, use your charm on him, too,' Deng suggested.

'Letting the nomads in Gyawa go would pre-empt Lobsang's threat. Remove Major Gan and his men from Gyawa and reverse the order to centralize the cooperative's produce to Lithang. Those moves will defuse the situation in the southern part of the district. Lobsang and his warriors will have no reason to rebel, and I will have enough good will to create cooperatives more quickly.'

'I see what you mean,' Deng considered thoughtfully.

I nodded, got up, walked to the door, and stepped out of the office into fresh, cold air. The sunshine was warm. I walked away with a lighter step; I'd had my say and remained in control of my mission. Deng had listened to me and seemed willing to give me a chance to continue implementing a revolution by the people and for the people. I might get away with telling Sonam's group they could leave when they got a chance.

I returned to my room at the tavern where I quickly changed back into my accustomed attire, the common sheepskin *chuba* worn in colder weather. I wanted to rid myself of anything that connected me with the Party! I removed the hat and glanced in a small mirror. My hair was now long enough that I braided it with red tassels and wrapped it around my head like every other Khampa man.

I went out into the street. Many people recognized me and greeted me with genuine, friendly remarks. Some of the boys who had joined me on my walks before, now grown older, gathered around me and suggested we go up the hill above the town just as we used to do. Up there, they felt free to talk about the growing and bustling PLA encampment visible below us.

'The Reds are not like you,' one of them pointed out, 'you have learned our language and our ways. Those bastards want us to learn their language and be like them.'

I nodded in agreement, 'That is the Chinese way, unfortunately. We do not call our country 'the middle kingdom' for nothing. The world revolves around China and we assume all people would rather be Chinese.'

'What should we do?' one of them asked, 'should we take up arms and fight? It is not our Buddhist way but sometimes it is necessary to protect our way of life.'

'Perhaps there is another way,' I replied as hopefully as I could sound.

As we stood on the hillside, a monk came toward us from the monastery. I recognized him as the one who had shown me around on my first visit inside the temple. I reminded him of his kindness and he was pleased I'd remembered.

'I've come to invite you inside once again,' he said, 'the *khenpo* would like to see you. Will you come with me?'

'Of course,' I replied. The abbott wanted to see me? He was a very powerful clergyman.

The boys who had come with me bowed with respect and returned to town. I walked with the young monk who introduced himself again as Nima, and we exchanged pleasantries about the weather. Then he told me that many, but not all, of the monks at the monastery were supportive of my efforts in Gyawa. There were other factions at the monastery; a few monks who openly worked with the new communist regime and supported Tsering Nawang, but another faction was in favour of armed resistance against the Chinese communists.

'And what about you?' I had to ask.

'I'm first of all a Buddhist and secondly a Khampa. I'm supportive of social reforms that will bring happiness and a good life to all of us. This is the bodhisattva way.'

'Bodhisattva?' I asked. I'd heard the term but wanted him to explain it.

'Yes, one who sees that one's own happiness depends on the happiness of others and devotes himself to this purpose.'

'Ah, so we are not so different,' I pointed out, 'my mission is for the well-being of others, too. I use communist terminology while you use Buddhist; but I think we want the same thing.'

'Almost,' Nima said, 'communism focuses on the external world. That is good and important, but we focus on changing the external world by first changing the inner world.'

I wanted to follow up but we had reached the monastery and entered the huge courtyard. It was mostly empty except for a group of monks in one corner whose loud voices indicated they were arguing. Nima noticed my inquisitive look.

'It's a form of philosophical debate,' he said, 'the gestures and shouting are ways to drive a point home. It's stimulating and exciting. We enjoy it.'

Nima led me across the courtyard to a doorway on the right. We climbed a series of steep, dark stairs. Nima pushed open a door, stood aside and ushered me in after I removed my felt boots. He closed the door behind me, leaving me to wait alone.

I was looking at the *thanka*s and murals on the walls when the door opened again. To my surprise, Palden Rinpoche and an elderly, though impressively big monk entered, followed by Wangdu and Nima. I bowed respectfully to the elder monk who I assumed was the abbot. The *khenpo* responded by touching my head. I bowed to Palden Rinpoche, too. He touched my head gently as if to say all was forgiven between us.

'Your Reverence,' Rinpoche said, 'this is Chuang Wei Ming, the young man from Shanghai I told you about. And Wei Ming, this is Kunchen, the *khenpo* of Lithang Monastery.'

'Pleased to meet you,' I said sincerely.

The *khenpo* indicated we all sit on cushions around a low table. It was an informal meeting room. Though his cushion was at the same level as the rest of ours, he sat taller; even Palden Rinpoche's charismatic presence was overshadowed by this man, at ease with himself as a ruler of men in spiritual and political realms of life.

'Welcome to Lithang Monastery,' Kunchen Khenpo began once we were seated comfortably. His voice was deep and booming, trained by a lifetime of chanting.

The *khenpo* watched me closely, measuring me up against rumour and what Palden had probably already told him about me.

'You get around,' I said quietly to Palden.

'Yes,' Palden agreed, 'you keep me busy.'

'How so?'

'I'm organizing forces to create an alternative that we Khampa can live with. As you know, we appreciate your approach but oppose what is actually happening. I'm hoping Khenpo-la will agree to our proposal.'

'I have just been with Commander Deng and voiced my objections to the Party's current policies.'

'And you are still here?'

'I'm still here. He won't be sending me back to Chengdu for "re-education"; not yet, at least. It helps that I'm still a "revolutionary hero". I asked Commander Deng to give us time to implement reforms on our own terms in the southern part of Lithang district.' I paused for a moment. 'If it works, he will claim success and let us get on with it. If it doesn't, he will go ahead and implement reforms in our area as the Party dictates. The deadline for universal compliance all over Kham is the end of next year.'

Palden nodded thoughtfully for a moment, then, as if recalling where he was, turned to the elderly monk, a bit embarrassed that we'd conversed privately in his presence.

The abbot ignored the slight and said to me, 'I've heard many things about you.'

'I hope you've heard a few good things,' I responded with a smile.

'Of course, all good. For example, I've heard that you want to find a way to integrate communism with our way of life without disrupting our religion.'

'Yes, something like that,' I agreed.

'Communism, as I understand it, does not recognize the need for, nor even the existence of, spiritual knowledge.

293

This material world that can be manipulated through physical labour, technology, and scientific ideas is all that matters. In fact, I have heard that you communists believe that thoughts and emotions arise from the chemistry of the brain. Once the body dies, that's the end.'

'True. Many people in the rest of the world subscribe to this point of view.'

'We believe the opposite,' the khenpo explained. 'The physical body is given life because, first of all, spirit or consciousness acts upon the material body. These human bodies are designed to hold consciousness and, indeed, are the place where consciousness can be fully aware of itself. Only in the human form can the universe fully experience itself.'

'Yes, I've, ah... been introduced to this point of view,'

I said, recalling my experience in the meadow.

'Good,' the *khenpo* acknowledged approvingly. 'Now, Palden Rinpoche-la tells me the circumstances of your arrival here are auspicious. He says that in one respect, the two of you are brothers, and in another respect, you were nearly related by marriage.'

'Palden Rinpoche exaggerates,' I said, trying to gracefully overcome my discomfort with this topic. 'By chance, I was trained in horse riding and archery by a man from Mongolia, who had once been Rinpoche's teacher. A coincidence, that is all. And as for being related; it never happened because the young woman I was in love with was killed by the nationalists. She happened to be Palden Rinpoche's sister's granddaughter, his grandniece.'

'But circumstances brought you to Lithang, the very place where your riding teacher's former disciple and your lover's family come from. Astonishing!'

'I did not ask to be assigned here nor did I know the name of this place. It was purely by chance.'

'There is no such thing,' the *khenpo* declared, 'it was meant to be and I'm looking forward to understanding why.'

I bowed respectfully again, and just hoped for the topic to change.

It did.

'The reason we are here is to explore ways to deal with the Chinese occupation of Kham,' Palden began. 'Previous Chinese so-called "ownership" of Kham always allowed us to live according to our own ways. These communists are different; they want to change everything. They want to make us just like themselves. Because of this, there are forces preparing to strike the PLA.'

I noticed that the khenpo nodded in acknowledgement that this was so.

'That's an approach sure to intensify Chinese resolve. They already perceive us to be rebellious, and are prepared to respond with increasing force. It is the way of fear and power. We must not give them a reason to be afraid of us,' Palden continued, 'That's why we need a way to restrain forces that want to wage war. Not just Lobsang, but there are several other warlords raising armies with the intention of driving the PLA all the way back to Chengdu. That can only happen if they are able to cooperate.'

'War should not be dismissed,' Kunchen Khenpo objected, 'we face a monstrous threat to Buddha dharma. We must consider the use of armed force against them if necessary.'

'No, Your Reverence,' Rinpoche responded, 'let's consider other options as long as possible. We must not lower ourselves by emulating an enemy's depravity.'

'We are prepared to support Lobsang, and the other warlords, if it comes to that,' Kunchen declared emphatically.

'May I say something?' I asked. Palden was on the verge of exasperation, so he welcomed my interruption. 'Perhaps we should talk to Lobsang.'

'Believe me,' Rinpoche said, 'I've tried.'

'I know the man. I had an unfortunate encounter with one of his men. Lobsang was impressed with the way I defended myself. Perhaps he'll listen to me.'

Wangdu, who'd been sitting quietly beside me, leaned close to me and said, 'If you're willing to risk a ride into Chengtreng, I'll take you to him.'

'Yes, of course, I'll go,' I laughed, 'I nearly ended up there a few days ago, tied on the back of a horse! Riding there of my own free will would be so much better; it would certainly surprise and impress Lobsang.'

I'd heard about the wild and mysterious Chengtreng, an area full of bandits and dangerous beasts. It was a high altitude plateau with Arctic-like weather conditions, southwest of Gyawa and Mola. Even in the summer, sudden blizzards could blind the unsuspecting traveller. Mammoth boulders, frigid lakes, glaciers, and treacherous ravines made it an inhospitable place and ideal terrain for outlaws.

'Now,' the *khenpo* interrupted my train of thought, 'there is the matter of Tsering Nawang and his son, Tenzin, in Gyawa. Their traitorous behaviour needs to be challenged. We need to find a way to remove them from their positions of power.'

'So long as Commander Deng and his troops are allowed to go wherever and do whatever they like, the Tserings will keep their positions of authority,' Palden Rinpoche said. 'If the Tserings are removed, Deng will replace them with other stooges from our community or do away with the charade altogether. We all know who controls them.'

'Deng needs the troops in Gyawa to prop up Tenzin,' I agreed.

'Is Deng willing to retract policies he authorized in Gyawa?'

'I asked him to release the nomads, remove his troops, and reverse the centralization of produce,' I announced. 'He said he'd think about it, and I got the impression he might not consult Chengdu about it. He agreed not to implement changes in the southern parts of Lithang district if I could form a large cooperative quickly.'

'It is unlikely they'll retract an order at this point,' Kunchen observed.

'He cannot retract an order, but he doesn't have to enforce it either. Just like the arrest warrant for you, Rinpoche. Deng admitted Nawang and Tenzin put him up to it, but he never carried through with it.'

Both Palden and Kunchen nodded in agreement but remained thoughtful.

'Meanwhile,' I continued, 'the people in Gyawa, both the villagers and the nomads, face a difficult situation. The centralization policy already emptied their stores. The grain went to feed the growing number of PLA troops here in Lithang. Now, the cooperative will have to buy grain and other items to feed not only themselves, but all of Sonam's tribe, too.'

'I fear it will be a bleak winter for the people of Gyawa,' the *khenpo* observed. 'These thoughtless policies must be corrected and prevented in the future.'

297

'We need to mobilize all the people to protest peacefully,' Palden suggested, 'perhaps we can rid Tibet of the Chinese like the Indians rid their country of the British.'

The *khenpo* looked surprised. He frowned as if this idea hadn't occurred to him.

'Like Gandhi?' he questioned. He knew immediately what Palden was calling for. 'Do you think that will work? The Chinese communists haven't got even a pinch of goodness compared to the British. And, I'm afraid, we are far too independent to work together on the scale this would require. We have no sense of community beyond the immediate family or clan. We are nomadic at heart, even the village folk.'

'Even so, we must give it a try,' Palden insisted. 'Surely with your support, it could be done. People will listen to you. What do you think, Wei Ming?'

Distracted by my own train of thoughts, I didn't respond. Deng had immediately linked Palden with Gandhi, too. I tried to imagine protest marches, sit-ins, and other mass gatherings that might be used to convince the PLA and the Party to let Tibetans voluntarily implement a form of communism acceptable to their own way of life—including religious freedom. I liked the idea but realized the *khenpo* was right, the Chinese were not the British.

'Oh,' I said when I noticed Palden was waiting for my response, 'non-violent protest would certainly get the attention of the Party. It is worth considering, of course.'

'But you have reservations,' Palden noticed.

'Well, the scale would need to be massive. Refusal to work in labour camps, refusal to turn over surplus to the PLA, refusal to surrender household possessions of any kind, refusal to send children to China for education, mass marches and sit-ins at PLA encampments, blocking roads, refusal to loan animals for their caravans. The ways to protest are endless, but will the people cooperate? And the response will surely be violent. Will the people remain non-violent?'

Silence followed my observations. It was clear to me why Palden had asked for this meeting with the *khenpo*; he was hoping for his support in this immense undertaking. The *khenpo*'s influence over the people would be crucial; therefore he must be convinced it was the best approach.

'Your Reverence,' Palden said after we'd been immersed in our own thoughts on the matter, 'this is the Buddhist way. We must take the middle way between submission and violence. I agree that if all else fails there might come a time to use arms against the enemies of the Buddha dharma, but now is not the time.'

The *khenpo* listened thoughtfully, nodding every now and then with understanding.

'I'll summon Lobsang and the other warlords,' the *khenpo* finally said, 'we will talk.'

Kunchen turned to me to say, 'I see why Rinpoche has included you in our discussion. The local people respect you and you are able to stand up to Commander Deng! You are in a unique position between the Party and our people. Your insights are helpful. Thank you.'

He turned to Rinpoche and said, 'Now, if you'll excuse me. I must attend to monastery business.'

We stood and bowed respectfully as the *khenpo* left the room. With a subtle hand gesture, the *khenpo* instructed Nima to stay with us. I looked at the young man and realized he was the *khenpo*'s trusted aide.

We sat down again immediately to discuss our situation. Palden and Wangdu would return to Mola. I would stay until Samphel arrived. Together, Samphel and I would meet with Nawang Tsering and, hopefully, with Deng again to outline the terms of a new cooperative in Mola township that would include several nomadic tribes. Samphel would need me as a translator since he could not trust Nawang to translate adequately for Commander Deng.

As Rinpoche had said, things were moving quickly. I was pleasantly surprised that the Mola cooperative was about to form.

Warriors of Another Kind

While I waited for Samphel's arrival, I engaged in conversations with several old acquaintances in town. I heard comments that revealed the growing resentment of the reforms. Tensions were rising; people were angry. News from communities to the north, the east, and the west was disturbing. The PLA responded to any level of resistance, more frequently, with indiscriminate arrests and shootings. Members of the wealthy, privileged class were their primary targets for persecution, arrest, and execution. Labour camps were growing in size and number.

The morning after Samphel arrived, I accompanied him to see Nawang.

'Welcome, Gyatotsang Samphel, and you, too, Comrade Chuang,' Nawang said nervously. It was obvious he was making an effort to be magnanimous. 'Such a pleasure... yes, yes, do come in. Come in. Have a seat, drink tea with me. Or would you prefer *chang*, even at this early hour? Ha, ha!'

We spent an hour or so going over our proposal to create a cooperative that would include all the villages along a stretch of the Lithang River Valley, traditionally considered Mola township. We wanted to reach out to nomadic tribes in the surrounding areas both east and west of the valley—tribes economically connected to Mola. Nawang's response was, as expected, noncommittal. When we suggested a visit with Commander Deng, Nawang reluctantly agreed.

This time when I entered Deng's office dressed in my *chuba* and with my long hair exposed, he did not recognize me immediately. But when he did, he stared for a moment before acknowledging me with a frown. The four of us, Nawang, Samphel, Deng, and I, sat around his wooden table for the rest of the day, going over details of the new cooperative. I did the translating as well as offer my own suggestions to both sides of the negotiations.

'What we need,' Samphel emphasized through me, 'is your guarantee that we can pursue this plan without pressure from any of your troops while we implement reforms to meet your deadlines.'

It was hard for Deng to guarantee non-intervention. I understood his position, which I later attempted to explain to an unsympathetic Samphel. 'Deng is a middle man,' I said unconvincingly, 'he obeys orders from Chengdu.'

Samphel huffed his annoyance.

'At least Deng had listened,' I told Samphel, 'for the foreseeable future, we should proceed with our plan. If troops arrive to apply pressure, we will make decisions about what to do. In the meantime, let's proceed in good faith.'

'Okay,' Samphel finally agreed, 'but only because there is no other option.'

Samphel suggested we take the direct trail from Lithang to Mola that bypasses Gyawa. The trail started on the ridge behind the monastery. It provided a commanding view of the vast Lithang grassland and the endless ridge tops stretching eastward. The impressive scale of the landscape confirmed my insight that this rugged landscape moulded and defined Khampa character; their culture blossomed out of the very spirit of this place. I knew for sure now that my allegiance lay with the land and people of Kham; my allegiance to the ideals of communism were secondary. My time among the Khampa had changed me. I recognized a need to speak up for them, to defend their right to live in harmony with this land and their herds—as they had done for centuries.

I also knew it was the right decision to return to the hermitage, and submit to whatever Rinpoche had in mind for me. I wanted to find out what Manene had called a 'sacred mission to create an enlightened society, a people of goodness, courage, and dignity'. Perhaps that idea of an 'enlightened society' was closer to what I really wanted.

Samphel was a silent travelling companion, but his few comments helped me see that I'd made the right decision.

'It looks like your plan of forming a large cooperative is falling into place,' Samphel began, 'I have agreed to release my property, and I think I can persuade other land holders to do the same. I agreed with Rinpoche that by including the adjacent nomadic tribes, the Mola Cooperative may well be the key to establishing an "enlightened society".' He seemed deep in thought, before continuing, 'Rinpoche explained to me that our cooperative would be a re-formation of current Tibetan society. At the same time, it would not resemble Chinese communism as currently promoted by the Party. He envisions a new kind of society that enhances our collective harmony in our material and spiritual environment.'

I began to appreciate Rinpoche's influence and vision a great deal. But I knew full well it was not only Rinpoche who had prompted the people of Mola; Yangchen had probably influenced Zema and many other women. Just as in Gyawa,

303

where it had been the women who convinced their husbands to accept the idea of forming the cooperative.

'It is important at this time,' Rinpoche later told me, 'for yang to submit to the grounding intelligence of yin. Women set the tone in the home, in the community, and for the culture. In all areas of life, women are far more empathetic; they see the goodness in initiatives that will meet everyone's needs and give us all opportunities to thrive. While the men are ready to go to war, women are much more level-headed. They see the human costs of war. Women are better Buddhists than men.'

It was Jiachen leading the protests in Shanghai that had stirred my imagination about the possibilities of the communist revolution: feminine energy, feminine intelligence. Since joining the Party, I'd noticed that all the Party leaders were men who lacked vision and enthusiasm for the peaceful possibilities of establishing a harmonious society. Instead, they exerted their power through policies of control and backed these up by instilling fear through threats and frequent use of violence. These men created division instead of community, separation instead of wholeness.

Tenzin fit this profile exactly. He brought division where there had been community. Lacking imagination, he had no vision; lacking intelligence, he obeyed his superiors. The new political machine in China was filled with men like these.

The trail brought us near Karma's camp, and we found it soonafter. Karma was happy to see me. She invited us to share her mid-morning meal, and we exchanged news. She told us they had not heard from the men of the camp for several days.

Samphel and I told her it was important to let Sonam know that if his tribe had an opportunity, they should leave Gyawa. Commander Deng could not release them but if they should manage to get away from the soldiers, they would not be forced back to Gyawa again.

'You have done well, Chinese Khampa!' Karma said, 'I will send your message. Thank you! You're a good man.'

Samphel suggested to Karma that she also send a message, if she could, to Lobsang that the *khenpo* wanted to see him at Lithang Monastery.

'We don't want armed rebellion,' I said, 'we have a little more than one year to find the middle way. Rinpoche-la and I met with the *khenpo*. A few days, later Samphel-la and I met with Tsering Nawang and Commander Deng. We have proposed a larger cooperative in Mola, and we will invite your tribe, and others nearby, to join us in a loose community for our mutual benefit.' I continued with as much clarity as I could, 'You will hear more about it soon. You will not have to settle in Mola, I promise! That will never be part of any agreement. What we are looking for is a closer connection for trade and prosperity for all groups in the area. Hopefully, this new cooperative will include all the groups who attended last summer's horse festival in Lithang.'

'That's a large group,' Karma observed with surprise.

'It is,' I agreed, 'and it is the women who will make this happen. That's why I'm telling all this to you first.'

'You speak the truth,' Karma observed. She laughed and gave Samphel a sceptical glance before continuing boldly. 'It is us women who know what is good for our people.'

'I completely agree,' Samphel acknowledged with a grin, 'it was my wife who persuaded me to listen to Rinpoche and our Chinese friend here.'

'I'll talk to other women,' Karma said, 'and we'll do what we can to encourage our tribes to cooperate.'

After we left Karma's camp, we followed the ridge to a viewpoint overlooking the entire Mola township. Now, in early fall, the few deciduous trees had changed colours. The fields were bare, pastures were turning brown. In a few weeks, snow would turn the valley white. People would huddle close to the kitchen hearth to meet and talk, to sing and dance together, throughout the winter. I looked forward to what would be accomplished around hearth fires; the new cooperative would take shape there.

'We have a long history in this place,' Samphel said when I stopped my horse next to his. There was a hint of pride in his voice as he pointed things out.

The trail was visible all the way to the festival grounds under the sacred mount that terminated the valley. Samphel looked proud surveying the valley he called home.

There was, nevertheless, also a hint of worry on his brow.

The sound of bells announced a caravan making its way down the trail. Caravan drivers motivated their animals with sharp whistles and crude curses.

'The trail is a trading route to the Yi, Yolo, and Naxi lands in the mountain forests south of here. Horse caravans bring tea from the hills of southern Sichuan and Yunnan. This is where the transition from lowland horses to highland yak takes place.'

'Just like in Dartsendo,' I suggested.

'That's right...except there is much less trade here, of course,' Samphel pointed out. 'That group there will return the yaks they borrowed from us months ago. They will take back their horses for the journey down to tea plantations in the foothills. Our villages manage this transfer. We feed and care for their horses while they travel higher and farther into Tibet. We lease our yaks to them for the onward journey. It is a profitable business for us.'

'You'd better be looking for another way to do business,' I suggested.

'What do you mean?'

'Once motor roads are built, who's going to use this trail? It will be easier and quicker to transport tea and other things by truck through Dartsendo. One truck can carry a whole caravan worth of goods. The days of horse caravans are over!'

Samphel was thoughtful a moment. 'I hadn't considered that yet.'

'It's inevitable,' I explained, 'things will change. Mola will need to change in many ways to remain prosperous.'

'Will a road come through here?'

'Not likely, not for a long time. Roads are costly and difficult to build in these mountains.'

Samphel straightened in his saddle, elevating his stature.

'All the more reason to celebrate our horse racing festival in honour of King Gesar. We can keep our heritage alive while we face new situations. We are warriors called to defend our way of life and Buddha dharma!'

I nodded to acknowledge Samphel's mention of 'warriors'. I decided to be a bit mischievous even though I understood that Rinpoche and Wangdu were training non-violent windhorse warriors. I wanted Samphel's perspective.

'Warriors?' I questioned, 'I thought your religion forbids killing. Why would you pride yourself as a warrior?'

'We are warriors of another kind,' he said proudly, 'do you know what *lungta* is?'

'Windhorse,' I said.

'Yes, *lung* is wind and *ta* is horse. We put a windhorse on prayer flags as a symbol of the energy of basic goodness. When we call ourselves warriors, we mean windhorse warriors. With courage and dignity, we accept the challenge to resist evil and establish basic goodness for all!'

'Hmm... I like that. But what if PLA soldiers attacked Mola? Would you defend yourselves?'

'Of course! Living in the world often means defending families, our herds, our fields, and homes!'

He suddenly smiled. I think he knew Rinpoche had explained all this to me. 'Hopefully, you'll teach us how to defend ourselves as non-violently as possible. Rinpoche-la and my nephew Wangdu are counting on you. They hope you will teach us the skills you learned from Master Tashi.'

'Oh! So the onus is on me now?'

We both laughed. Samphel and I had connected. It would be good to work with him as we established the Mola Cooperative.

Our trail down the hillside joined the main caravan trail along the river. Samphel was eager to get home, and urged his horse to quicken its pace. Not in much hurry and a bit travel weary, I let Chestnut set a more leisurely pace. As usual, I was preoccupied with my own thoughts and Chestnut took advantage of my lack of attention. When we reached the meadow she turned off the trail and helped herself to some grass, as she had in the summer. I smiled to myself when I recognized what had happened.

I took Chestnut's hint that we needed a rest. Once on the ground, I walked around a bush to a place that looked inviting and had a good view.

'Am I in your way, Chinese Khampa?'

Dechen mocked me as I nearly walked into her; reminding me of the time I'd blocked her path in this very place.

'Dechen! What are you doing here?'

'Annoying you, obviously,' she laughed.

'I'm not annoyed. I'm delighted!'

'Of course you are. But which aspect of the *Dakini* delights you more. Your out-of-reach Jiachen or me?'

'Ah, what do you mean?' I didn't know how to respond.

'There's only one *Dakini*.' She noticed my confusion. 'Oh, never mind, I'll explain later. You need to take me to Rinpoche's hermitage. I've had enough of Tenzin's games. I just told Samphel not to expect you in Mola. We are taking the direct way to the hermitage from here.'

I accepted her request willingly, and wondered why she'd stayed so long in Gyawa with Tenzin panting to have her.

'Where's Little White?' I asked.

'Wangdu took him to the hermitage. He didn't like it in Gyawa either.'

'The horse? How do you know that?'

'He said so!'

Of course, if the horse said so! Dechen liked to say incomprehensible things.

'Do you remember our conversation at this place before?' Dechen asked while looking into my eyes intently.

'Of course, I do,' I was thinking of how delighted I'd been to talk with her for a few minutes.

'If you'll recall, you mentioned your experience a few days earlier.'

'Yes, I did.' It bothered me that she brought it up again.

'Do you remember what I said about it?'

'Yes, you called it an awakening, a mystical experience.'

'That's exactly what it was!' Dechen thrust her finger in my chest, challenging me to deny it.

'Okay,' I admitted, 'I've accepted that it was some kind of extraordinary experience.'

'Then lucky for you that we meet again at the very spot, because Rinpoche and I are going to teach you how to turn awakening into enlightenment.'

Unable to speak, I stood and watched Dechen go toward Chestnut and take hold of the reins. She brought Chestnut toward me as I processed what she'd said. Was she saying it was possible to repeat and sustain an experience like I'd had here? It would be wonderful but I wondered... Wouldn't the visceral intensity of it make it impossible to carry on like an ordinary rational person?

'When?' I demanded. Despite reservations, I wanted what Dechen and Rinpoche were offering me. I didn't care if I was ever 'rational' again if I could experience things like that!

'Be patient. It takes time but I'm sure it will happen to you. Right now, we need to go to the hermitage.'

Once I was mounted, Dechen took hold of my forearm and gracefully leaped onto Chestnut behind me. She put her arms around my middle, her thighs pressed against mine, and her head rested against my back appreciatively. Not being able to see her, I imagined Jiachen's presence with me again. It was enough to bring a lump to my throat. Dechen moved so she could see my face.

'Enough!' she said sternly, 'stop feeling sorry for yourself! How many times must I tell you, Jiachen and I are not separate anymore?'

'What the hell are you talking about?' I demanded.

'I'm talking about your *Dakini*; your teacher, protector, and partner.'

We crossed a wooden bridge over the river and followed a trail up the hillside. It was too steep to ride, so we walked until the mountain path levelled along the flank of the mountain. We rode again until we reached a stream with a small patch of green grass.

'Stop here,' Dechen ordered. Both of us admired the view and found a place to sit near the stream. The grass was so very soft and inviting.

'Wei Ming,' Dechen said my name while holding my eyes firmly in her gaze like she couldn't resist telling me what was on her mind. 'It's time for you to understand and practice Buddha dharma.'

'Practice? Why?'

'There is no Buddha dharma without practice and no understanding without awakening. We use a practice called mindfulness to encourage awakening.'

'I've heard Rinpoche, and even Master Tashi, talk about mindfulness.' I wanted to sound as if I knew all about it.

Dechen smiled. She was sitting on the ground directly in front of me with her legs crossed like Buddha.

'Mindfulness begins with learning how to be fully present here and now. Most of the time we are not present, are we?'

'I was noticing that when Chestnut wandered onto the meadow,' I observed. 'It's happened to me twice at the same place. I was somewhere else and had no idea that Chestnut had left the trail!'

'We call it monkey mind because our thoughts jump around unpredictably. Sometimes we recall—with happiness or regret—things in the past, and our mind gets caught up in these thoughts and feelings; or we anticipate, hope for, or fear things in the future, and let our thoughts and emotions get wrapped up about things that haven't happened or don't even exist. Seldom are we right here, right now; seldom are we present enough to experience each moment as we live our lives. Seldom are we present enough to fully appreciate this moment, and the interdependence we share with all other beings.'

Her words sounded true.

'Here!' Dechen said, suddenly coming to a decision. 'Let's give that monkey a job to do. Sit like this. Back straight, chin tucked in a bit, hands on your knees or in your lap. Let your attention follow your breath, in and out. Use the flow of breath to train yourself to concentrate on one thing.'

'Like shooting an arrow,' I observed. I knew about presence, and aiming at a target.

'Exactly. What do you think about when you shoot an arrow?'

'Nothing,' I replied suddenly, getting her analogy. 'I'm fully concentrated on the target; I'm not worried about how I'm holding the bow or how hard I'm pulling. It comes naturally.'

'Right! It's effortless. Let go of thoughts as easily as you let go of an arrow. Master Tashi showed you how to concentrate and be fully present for that task effortlessly. Practice naturally leads to transforming everything you do into effortless play.'

I sat with my back straight, attempting to imitate her posture. My legs were not as limber as hers, but I managed to sit cross-legged. With my eyes closed, I focused my attention on each breath, in and out, a couple times. Every few breaths, I caught myself thinking of something that crossed my mind; 'how long will we sit here', 'my knees ache', 'it will get dark before we reach the hermitage', 'why am I letting her do this', 'how can concentration lead to awakening?'.

'Just sit and watch your breath,' she encouraged. 'Notice that the moment you start each in-breath you can feel a subtle change in your belly, and as you continue breathing in, an energy rises up to your head. Then, as you breathe out, the energy settles down in your belly again. Feel this energy circulate from the bowl of your pelvis to the crown of your head.'

I sat. I watched.

Soon I felt energy circulate, and my entire body was alive with awareness.

I sat a while more until Dechen said I could open my eyes.

'Wow! That was great,' I said, sincerely. 'I feel exhilarated.'

'Good. You'll be doing much more of it at the hermitage.'

We stood up and I looked at our surroundings. A hint of peaceful connection and vividness flowed in and through everything around us. I found myself paying attention to the circular flow of energy tied to my breath, even though I was not sitting in meditation. I could watch this subtle energy circle within me anytime, anywhere.

My chest was bursting with joy. I stretched my arms toward the surrounding peaks and an involuntary shout of joy exploded from me.

'*Ki! Ki! So! So! Lha Gyalo!*'

313

Dechen, standing close to me, joined me.

'*Ki! Ki! So! So! Lha Gyalo!*'

'*Ki! Ki! So! So! Lha Gyalo!*'

I retrieved Chestnut but instead of riding, we walked quickly. The path was wide enough for us to walk side by side, with Chestnut following behind. We fell into a conversation as the shadows of evening fell across the valley below.

'Tell me,' I began, 'the philosophy behind what we just did. Is that how you have been practicing Buddha dharma?'

'That's it—awareness, mindfulness, the joy of compassion and insightful wisdom; understanding the philosophy of mindfulness is as important as the practice. It is like this walking on this path...we need a little light to keep from falling off.'

'True,' I noted. I recalled how lost I was in the wilderness without a path. 'Up until now, you would probably rather spend your waking hours being so busy you didn't really let yourself become self-reflective enough to ask the question: "Who am I?". Our education systems and society traps us into believing we are the story we tell ourselves, and that our life is all about what's going on outside and around us.'

We were conversing in English again; this came naturally to us.

'We learn to see ourselves and everything else,' Dechen continued, 'as separate objects: things to be measured, quantified, controlled, and used. We are taught to function in a dualistic world of this and that, mine and yours, us and them.'

'This rational, scientific, and materialistic worldview assumes that we live in a four-dimensional universe; three dimensions of space plus the dimension of time. Three dimensions give an object shape while time gives an object the ability to move and change, the possibility of an event taking place. But we actually live in five dimensions. The fifth dimension is hard to describe because, like time, it can't be seen. It can only be experienced,' Dechen explained.

'So what is it?' I asked, my curiosity roused.

'It's the "inside" of everything; the subjective experience, the awareness or consciousness of living things, and perhaps even of non-living things. It is spirit or soul. The modern world, both the capitalist and communist worlds, denies this fifth dimension. Like fish denying the existence of water, the modern mindset denies the unitive reality of our inner being. We would rather occupy ourselves with doing than experiencing that we are all really immersed in a subtle awareness and energy that permeates everything.'

Dechen paused and waited as I took in what she was saying.

'We are connected in this fifth dimension through the heart,' she continued. 'I don't mean your physical heart, I mean your whole inner being. Through mindfulness, we learn to connect our head with our heart, our intellect with awareness of our actual experience. Through regular practice, we learn to quiet the ceaseless mental chatter of the monkey mind that takes place in the rational part of the mind. Then the more intuitive, creative, and experiential part of us can make an appearance and allow us to experience our immersion in the fifth dimension, the Spirit.'

We walked awhile as I absorbed these ideas. I was elated listening to Dechen. These were beautiful ideas that sounded good and true.

'Our goal as human beings is to become fully integrated; head reconnected with the heart so the whole body is invigorated by Spirit. Or perhaps you could say, to fully manifest divinity in our physical being. In this sense, like Jesus, each one of us is a potential son or daughter of God. Of course, we Buddhists say that this fifth dimension is our Buddha nature and we are all potential Buddhas.'

I stopped walking. Dechen did, too, and we faced each other.

'It's possible,' she said with deliberateness, 'to live in the present moment fully experiencing our own centre of awareness while fully connected with every other centre of awareness through the spiritual dimension.'

I may have appeared confused, so she found another way of putting what she'd just said.

'It is as if there is one person in a room looking out of many different windows. Each window has its own view. In the fourth dimension we are the windows, but in the fifth dimension we are the person looking out through all the windows.'

Dechen held up her hand and wiggled her fingers.

'Or how about this: we could see ourselves as separate as these fingers or we can say, "but look, we're all connected to the palm".'

She was having fun and we shared a laugh.

'So when we ask "Who am I?",' she continued on a more serious note, 'the answer is ultimately this larger experience of being, not the ego self of my thinking mind—not the window but the observer. My four dimensional self, my ego self, is created by my thoughts and emotions. It is an illusion compared to the firm reality of the all-knowing, all-loving being-ness of the spiritual dimension.'

Dechen was glowing with excitement as she recognized how excited I was with everything she was telling me. We walked on again for a while in silence. The clop-clopping of Chestnut's hooves rhythmically accompanied out thoughts.

'While we live here in our physical bodies,' she said, breaking the silence with new insights, 'while we remain in the four dimensions, we need our individuality. Through spiritual practices, we learn to build a bridge between the dimensions. While we live with the separations of "this from that" and "me from you", we discover the sacred third force, or middle way, that makes it possible to live in both realities and overcome all separations.' After a deep breath, she continued, 'Our individual sense of self is raised to its highest potential and is infused with that most mysterious force in the cosmos—love. Finding it is enlightenment. Living it is true liberation.'

Dechen stopped walking first this time.

'Do you see now how Mao's liberation and enlightenment differs from this?'

In the fading light, I looked directly into Dechen's eyes. Hidden beneath my joy and excitement, she could see that I still had questions, doubts, and fears.

'Just keep in mind,' Dechen said, 'Jiachen and I are here. I've already told you, your *Dakini* will be supporting you as you practice Buddha dharma, and as you fulfil your mission.'

'My mission? You mean what Manene said?'

'Yes,' Dechen agreed.

'What's my mission?'

'We'll discover that together. Come, Rinpoche is waiting. We have to step up our pace if we are going to reach the hermitage before it gets pitch dark.'

Taking Refuge

Rinpoche, Yangchen, and Wangdu welcomed us with joyful hugs after touching our foreheads with their own, and draped our necks with *khata*. It felt like arriving home!

'Welcome, Wei Ming,' Palden said with affection. 'We are ready for you, and I believe you are ready for us. Am I right Dechen?'

'He's ready, Rinpoche-la,' Dechen said with a glowing smile, 'he learns quickly, as if he knows everything already.'

'As we expected,' Yangchen acknowledged, and gave me another hug.

'Good,' Rinpoche said. 'Wei Ming, this is the deal. You will train Wangdu and Dechen in the things Master Tashi taught you. In exchange, Dechen and I will teach you what Master Tashi was unable to do. Is that fair?'

I was about to open my mouth but Palden made a gesture to clear away my objections.

'And yes,' he added, 'we will create the Mola Cooperative; but first things first.'

In the quarters Rinpoche shared with Yangchen, watching Yangchen set out small bowls of steaming yak butter tea and large bowls of *thukpa* made me realize how hungry I was. Dechen and I ate like starved animals while Palden, Yangchen, and Wangdu, eating with more dignity, enjoyed watching us. Yangchen filled our bowls several times, laughing as she did so.

Once our bellies were full, we settled comfortably against the wall.

'Where are all the young men you are supposed to be training?' I asked.

'It's only the five of us now,' Wangdu answered. 'The warriors will come back when we are ready for them. First, you will train Dechen and me so we can train more women and men.'

'Yes, women!' Dechen responded with indignation to the look of surprise on my face. 'Why not women windhorse warriors, too?'

'I'm not objecting. I'm pleased women want to be trained.'

'Don't forget that you will also be in training,' Rinpoche interjected. 'When you're not training, you will be learning and practicing Buddha dharma. After Wangdu and Dechen are proficient enough to be trainers and after you have progressed sufficiently with your spiritual training, we will invite others to come for training.'

Wangdu got up to clear the bowls and took them out to wash. I watched and noted his willingness to serve.

'Let's talk about our Chinese communist friends,' Palden said with a sigh that indicated we needed to discuss more troubling matters. 'We must love our enemy without falling under any illusion that your comrades are as selfless and open-minded as you are, Wei Ming. They are not listening to local people, and deliberately introducing changes that are disrupting the existing system as a way to place themselves in control. The Communist Party has become an authoritarian system that has strayed from its intended purpose.'

'I agree and I've registered my complaints,' I said. 'Nevertheless, Rinpoche, whether we like it or not we are part of Sichuan Province, and part of the People's Republic of China. We are not part of Tibet.'

'True, that's something we don't like much, but it appears to be the situation,' Palden conceded.

'Commander Deng suggested that the cooperative in Gyawa is going in the right direction, but going too slowly. What they really want are communes that look just like communes in China.'

'Yes, they may speak of cultural diversity and religious freedom, but they actually want uniformity.'

'True,' I agreed, 'uniformity is a defect in our system, in our Chinese character, I'm afraid.'

'From our point of view, the cooperative in Gyawa had no intention of becoming an enlightened society. Do you understand what I mean?'

'Yes,' I said, looking at Dechen, 'I think I understand now.'

At that point, the door opened and Wangdu came in with the clean bowls.

'Wangdu, come sit with us,' Rinpoche indicated at a seat beside him. 'I want to properly introduce you.'

Rinpoche turned to me and said, 'Wangdu's father, Akong, was Samphel's brother. Akong and I had a lifetime of adventures together all over Asia. That's how we met Master Tashi in Mongolia. We both became his students in our younger days. Years later, Akong was killed by the Bolsheviks in Mongolia when we went to rescue sacred Buddhist scriptures and images.' After a moment's pause, he continued, 'Master Tashi was one of the treasures we rescued. He did not return here when I brought sacred texts and images out of Mongolia. He insisted on going to Shanghai because he had heard about a Japanese master of martial arts training capable students.'

I was intrigued by the layers of relationships going on between us. Now, Wangdu seemed part of the web connected to Master Tashi!

'The two of you,' Rinpoche continued, 'will be a good match for each other. Wangdu will work with you to remind your sleeping body and mind just how strong and aware you can be. Then you will begin training Wangdu in skills he has not yet mastered. Understood?'

'Yes,' I said with a slight bow of my head to Rinpoche, and then to Wangdu.

'Good,' Rinpoche said with finality.

'One more thing,' Dechen offered, 'you forgot to mention that Wangdu is my cousin and your great-nephew. He was visiting us in Kalimpong from Lhasa for a short time, and organized our travel back here before returning to Lhasa.'

It was late. I was ready to go right to sleep when Wangdu showed me to a room. I would occupy it alone, it appeared. I was pleased about that. Soon I was settled and asleep.

Before dawn, Wangdu came to wake me.

'When you're ready,' he said, 'come to the meditation room. It's the large hall next to Rinpoche-la and Yangchen-la's room.'

Dechen greeted me with a smile and invited me in. Palden, Wangdu, and Yangchen were waiting. I sat on a cushion facing Rinpoche and Dechen, between Yangchen and Wangdu.

'Dechen tells me,' Palden Rinpoche began abruptly, 'she has already given you some preliminary training in mindfulness along with some teaching.'

'Yes, and I'm grateful,' I said looking at Dechen.

'She also told me you have had a moment of awakening. Tell us about it.'

I glanced at Dechen to remind her I'd wanted her to keep it to herself. But it didn't matter now.

'I thought I was hallucinating at the time. Things began to look different. I could see right through things. Nothing had solidity. Colours were brighter. At the same time there was joy and a wonderful freedom from daily cares and problems.'

Rinpoche showed interest, and smiled encouragingly. I continued.

'There was also a knowing that I was connected to everything I looked at.'

I looked at Yangchen. She was nodding.

'It was an exhilarating experience,' I concluded.

'Good,' Rinpoche said without further comment or acknowledgement. 'I want you to close your eyes a moment. Straighten your back and sit quietly. Breathe slowly, deeply, and focus on the joy you experienced when you saw the luminous inside of things.'

To my surprise, it worked. I focused single-pointedly on my breath and felt an energetic joy fill me to bursting.

'Now, slowly open your eyes,' Rinpoche said. We were alone. I must have been in that state for quite a while because I had no idea when the others had left.

Rinpoche opened the curtain and I saw the forests and pastures around the hermitage alive with life already. I heard the sound of the mountain stream, the songs of the birds, and felt inwardly connected to it all.

'Rinpoche,' I said when tears of joy came to my eyes, 'when Jiachen died, she raised me to a place of shared knowing.

We hovered above the street where the soldiers had murdered her. I saw with her eyes and shared her deep compassion.'

'Yangchen told me,' Rinpoche said, 'that's how she knew you were connected to us. Jiachen planted the seed of spiritual yearning in you.'

My expanded awareness was focused entirely on Rinpoche as he spoke.

'This sense of knowing, of compassionate union, is a rare and wonderful gift,' Rinpoche continued, 'it is *bodhicitta*, the enlightened mind striving toward empathy for all living beings. Enlightenment is awakened wisdom tempered with compassion. We say the mantra "Om Mani Padme Hum" to help us remember and invoke it. You've been blessed with these experiences to remind you that there is much more to life than the objects and situations presented to us through our senses, and interactions in the tangible world. Our thoughts and feelings are temporary, fleeting, and unreal compared to the true nature of being.'

Rinpoche watched me for a moment, holding my gaze.

'I understand,' I said, once I realized Rinpoche was waiting for a response. 'Dechen explained how we find ourselves trapped in this material existence, while we are actually immersed in a much larger, more real existence.'

'She explained it well, I'm sure. She's very good at that. And did she explain liberation?'

'Yes, liberation is escaping the entrapment of our limited existence and awakening to our true being.'

'Excellent!' Rinpoche smiled very broadly. 'Wangdu will be annoyed I kept you so long. Go!'

I got up and left the meditation hall. Wangdu was waiting for me in the courtyard. While he proceeded to take me through one vigorous activity after the next, I recall feeling very much alive while remaining detached. It was as if I watched my body and mind thus engaged from somewhere above and outside myself, similar to the experience Jiachen had given me when I was with her above the street. The training was more like play than hard work.

Over the next several days, we repeated this pattern of morning stillness and vigorous daily activity. The clarity of mind generated through meditation continued through every activity as if I was still meditating. After a mid-morning meal, I worked with Wangdu and Dechen to explore the limits of our physical and mindfulness skills while passing on jujutsu techniques I learned from Master Tashi. It was important to explain the philosophy behind it as we trained. The version Master Tashi preferred was aiki-jujutsu or aikido, 'the combining of forces'. It emphasized redirecting an opponent's force while preventing harm to either contestant. It is based on the spiritual principles of compassion for those who seek to do harm.

One morning a week later, when Yangchen, Dechen, and Wangdu got up to leave the meditation hall, Rinpoche asked me to stay. He pointed to a *thanka* on the wall of a bodhisattva, holding a flaming sword and a flower.

'That's a *thanka* of Manjushri, the bodhisattva we honour at our training centre. It reminds windhorse warriors that the weapon in their right hand is the blazing sword of truth. But with the left hand, they must hold the enemy close to their heart with compassion.'

Rinpoche looked intently at the *thanka* as he spoke.

'We believe Gesar was an incarnation of Manjushri. That's another reason Manjushri is important for us. The flaming sword in his right hand cuts through ignorance and duality. In his left he holds a blossom, representing compassion, which supports a sacred text proclaiming: "form is emptiness, emptiness is form".' Smiling gently at me, he proceeded, 'There is ultimately no separation of manifest creation from spiritual reality. Spirit and matter are inseparably interdependent. The enlightened being sees form as emptiness, emptiness as form; matter infused with spirit, spirit manifesting in tangible matter.'

I fully understood what Rinpoche was saying.

'Imagine yourself as Manjushri,' Rinpoche said earnestly. 'Use the flaming sword of truth while seeing the goodness and beauty of all with your heart!'

One evening, another week or so later, Rinpoche gathered us all in the meditation hall. He invited me to sit at a low table opposite him. Dechen, Yangchen, and Wangdu sat behind me.

'Are you prepared to open your heart and mind to journey within?' Rinpoche asked me.

'Yes!' I said solemnly but emphatically.

'Good!' Rinpoche responded, and explained the procedure for becoming a follower of Buddha dharma. 'Following Buddha dharma is both easy and very hard. All you have to do is continue striving for your heart's desire. In this simple little ceremony, I will ask you to take refuge in the Buddha, the Dharma, and the Sangha. That means you will regard the Buddha as your teacher and guide, you will study his teachings and commit yourself to the community of people who have also dedicated themselves to this path. All of us in this room are your Dharma friends, your Sangha. Do you understand?'

'Yes.'

'Are you ready to become a Buddhist?'

'Yes, I'm ready.'

'I will give you a new name and take a tiny clipping of your hair. May I?'

'Yes.'

'Repeat after me.'

'I, Chodak, take refuge in the Buddha,' I repeated after him. 'I, Chodak, take refuge in the Dharma. I, Chodak, take refuge in the Sangha.'

Rinpoche then took a pair of scissors and cut a pinch of hair from the top of my head. With a gesture of blessing, a light touch on my head, he marked the moment of my symbolic transformation.

'Now that you have taken refuge, you are a Buddhist. But all it really means is that you are someone who is committed to discovering your own true nature.'

'I understand.'

'From now on, your name is going to be "Chodak". In Tibetan, it means "Dharma spreader".'

'Oh, I like that,' I said immediately, with a smile.

Palden Rinpoche leaned toward me and touched his forehead to mine, saying 'Chodak-la'.

I turned so that Dechen, Yangchen, and Wangdu could each touch foreheads with me, too, as they repeated my new name. It was a moving experience for me, sweeping me with an emotion of connection and belonging to these people in a deeper way.

'I will teach you an 18-syllable *mantra*,' Rinpoche said, pointing to the *thanka* of Manjushri on the wall. 'It is from the *Heart Sutra*, part of the text balanced on the lotus blossom Manjushri holds. It describes our journey into Buddhahood, and is translated in several ways. The meaning I like is 'Om. Going, going, going beyond, going always beyond, Buddha nature awakened!' It means going beyond form into emptiness, and in emptiness, awakening to the sacred fullness of form!'

'*Om gate para gate parasam gate bodhi svaha!*' we all chanted.

'*Om gate para gate parasam gate bodhi svaha!*'
'*Om gate gate para gate parasam gate bodhi svaha!*'

Too soon, we stopped chanting.

'Can you remember that mantra?' he asked me.

'Yes, of course.'

'Good. Remember it, repeat it as often as you can. Say it to yourself when you ride your horse, when you walk, when you are not talking. Say it on the practice floor. Say it everywhere. It will help you unlearn bad mental habits and deceiving habits of the heart. Think of the meaning as you say it.'

Samphel often came to report on progress with the villages and tribes. Discussions were going on, plans were being made but handing over property was still not happening. Reports of violent suppression and coercion from other places in Lithang district and other parts of Kham reached our people. They were disturbed by the ever-increasing presence of Red Troops, and the demands the Chinese were putting on villages elsewhere. Samphel tried to assure them that Mola would be left alone if we formed a cooperative within a year. People were not convinced, and said we'd end up being controlled like Gyawa. We couldn't dispute their fears, nor could we fault them for their reticence.

One piece of good news, however, was the successful departure of Sonam's tribe from Gyawa. Apparently, Sonam had been able to distract Major Gan, Tenzin, and the soldiers by hosting a drinking party for them in a tent on the opposite side of the village from the corralled yak herd. The tribe slipped away during the night while Tenzin and his friends were blind drunk.

I wanted to visit Mola with Samphel but both Rinpoche and Dechen said I was still too unstable in my practice to embroil myself in my previous affairs. They said it would be too easy for me to return to the mental and emotional habits I was trying to break; if I wasn't careful, I could revert to being 'a fish denying the existence of water'! They indicated I needed more time to establish myself on the path.

It was Rinpoche and Yangchen who went with Samphel. Rinpoche hoped to help clarify the nature and purpose of our cooperative while Yangchen encouraged the women. Although supportive of how I had organized the cooperative in Gyawa, Rinpoche and Yangchen wanted this new one to be firmly established according to Buddhist principles. I was beginning to appreciate their vision.

Meanwhile, Wangdu, Dechen, and I opened our training program to others. A growing number of young men, and several young women, turned up—wanting to be trained in the ways of non-violent resistance. Wangdu, Dechen, and I rotated groups and put them through different activities. Wangdu built up their physical strength and reaction times. Dechen taught them to apply mindfulness to every activity we taught them. I passed on the skills of aikido and the Japanese art of archery Master Tashi taught me called kyujutsu.

Archery was perhaps the most popular training activity. Coordinating eye, hand, body posture, and mind with breath enabled the archer to be totally present. I started with simple standing archery, close to the targets. Once the warriors internalized the importance of mindfulness in archery, their confidence allowed them to succeed at more difficult targets, and eventually, to attempt hitting targets from horseback.

I greatly enjoyed this interaction with the young warriors and emphasized that the use of weapons such as bow and arrows were a last resort, and if used, must not be used to kill.

Naturally, all the warriors were in awe of Dechen. She was an accomplished practitioner of all of our training activities, including shooting arrows from horseback. She even repeated my '12- arrows' feat by riding Little White past six targets. This elevated her high in their esteem and they began to regard her as a goddess, like Manene herself, rather than a flesh and blood human being. I had noticed that even Rinpoche deferred to her with reverence. This reverence for her came from the inspiration she gave all of us to follow the path of Buddha dharma.

'Dechen is continuously connected to the divine,' Wangdu explained to me during an afternoon break. 'She embodies and manifests Buddha nature for us to behold. Because she lives fully aware of both this world and the divine realm, we regard her as an enlightened being. Enlightened beings might as well be gods or goddesses. compared to us in our ordinary, ignorant mindset.'

My own feelings toward Dechen were complicated. I understood what Wangdu said about embodying and manifesting Buddha nature. I had no doubt she was enlightened.

329

I agreed with the male trainees that she was indeed a goddess and, like most of them, I had amorous yearnings for her. But, for the sake of our relationship and my own sanity, it was safest to see her as my enlightened meditation teacher even though she insisted on referring to herself, when we found ourselves alone with each other, as my *Dakini*.

'I am your muse!' Dechen declared, using the English word, when I asked her again what she meant when she called herself a *Dakini*. 'The inspiration to follow the path to spiritual transformation.'

'Of course!' I replied apologetically, though I'd actually hoped for it to mean more than that.

'The purpose of human life,' Dechen said as if needing to remind me, 'is to become a fully enlightened being, to become divine—the Greeks called it *"theosis"*. What other purpose is there? Why else do we have these physical bodies that are so capable of action, of thought, of feeling, of awareness? The human form is ideally designed for awareness of the fact that we share one consciousness. This liberates us from the illusion that we are separate beings in a four-dimensional world.'

'Okay,' I began to object, 'but you made a leap there that most people would not make. How would they know we share one consciousness?'

'You're right, most people don't see that,' she agreed. 'It's not a subject taught in schools and universities, so most people have never heard of it. Some lucky people, like you, get a glimpse of the spiritual dimension that surrounds us. Others intuit it's there through the experiences, writings, or teachings of others.'

'So, for most, it's a matter of faith.'

'Yes, faith that such an experience is possible, but it should lead to yearning for a personal experience.'

'I understand all that,' I said.

'You understand with your head but you don't know it yet in your gut, with your belly, in your heart!'

She looked at me as if she could see right through me.

'This ego existence we call the "self" needs to get out of the way so Buddha nature, the divine, can manifest. The small self must die if the larger Self is to be resurrected in you, as you. This is what we mean by enlightenment. An enlightened being is one who is consciously connected to the divine yet fully participates in the world as it is.'

Dechen's look changed to compassion.

'You've come a long way, Chodak-la,' she said lovingly. 'Don't be discouraged. You must continue struggling with your mind to limit conceptual thinking. Become aware of what is always, already present for you; the naked experience of consciousness. You've learned to still your mind, to be mindful in activities...now learn to rest in the present moment without examining, identifying, categorizing, or analysing whatsoever. As your mind rests in this non-conceptual state, the power of love, compassion, and wisdom naturally increases. Resting the thinking mind allows the feeling and being self to fully blossom.'

This was inspiring though obviously difficult to achieve.

'The miracle of enlightenment happens often,' Dechen continued, 'but not often enough. There have been great masters, yogis, teachers, and saints all over the world, beings who prove we can be fully human and fully divine. There have been many, but never enough!'

'Are you one of them?'

Dechen didn't answer but the more I learned, the more I saw her in action, the more I came to agree with Wangdu and the warriors that she was indeed an enlightened being.

Dechen did not encourage a closer relationship and I respected the boundary she drew. Like all the trainees around me, I was in awe of her; she was skilled, beautiful, and fully present!

We were all in love with her.

Rinpoche and Yangchen had been back a few days. Their visit to Mola had been helpful but not entirely successful. There was more work to be done; many people still had to be informed. We needed to proceed with our program of teaching everyone mindfulness, Yangchen insisted. Only then would they understand what was at stake.

I sensed, though, that this was not why Yangchen and Rinpoche had asked Dechen and me to join them on their usual walk after our morning meditation. The four of us went along the narrow mountain trail that led from the hermitage to the cliff overlooking the gap, where the Lithang River plunged between the sacred mountain above Mola's festival ground and our hillside.

We came to a stream. and Rinpoche and Yangchen made themselves comfortable on a rock and invited us to sit with them. Yangchen produced a bowl from the fold of her *chuba*, broke through a film of ice on the surface of the stream, scooped up some cold water and passed the bowl around so we could each have a drink.

'When I was a young man,' Rinpoche said after taking his drink, 'in my mid-30s, I was in the desert with Akong on one of our trips to Mongolia. We met a very interesting man alone out there. He was a French scientist, but he said he was also a Catholic priest, a Jesuit. His name, if I remember correctly, was Pierre. He invited us to join him at his campsite and late into the evening, we had the most interesting discussion in Chinese—the only language we shared in common.' Taking a sip from the bowl, he continued, 'He was studying bones in the ground, from very ancient times; our oldest ancestors, he called them. The discussion came around to the purpose of man, and our ultimate destination. Pierre's firm convictions were founded on an unshakable knowledge that matter is infused with spirit.'

Rinpoche sat quietly, reflecting and remembering that great man and his words out in the Gobi Desert under the canopy of stars.

'One thing he said that I have never forgotten,' Rinpoche continued, 'is that he described divine presence in the universe as a radiant energy pervading the evolving cosmos. The direction of the process of evolution, he said, is toward complete matter-spirit integration—to the point when all matter is self-aware. Our purpose, indeed our deepest impulse, is to raise consciousness across the physical universe, across the entire cosmos.'

Rinpoche paused briefly, deep in thought.

'The vast scale of Pierre's vision spanned time from the fiery beginnings of the universe billions of years ago to ultimate consummation in fully enlightened matter billions of years in the future. He envisioned humanity evolving mentally, socially, and spiritually toward a Great Perfection. This gave me a new

333

perspective on the bodhisattva vow.' After a lingering smile, he continued, 'As bodhisattvas, we participate in this process of transforming, or infusing our world with divine presence, so we and others can strive to become fully enlightened. Immersed in divine presence, we experience an outpouring of divine love that sets us on fire. When we are on fire, we inspire and set others on fire. He said we are called to set the world alight with this kind of passion, this Great Perfection.'

Rinpoche's face glowed. He looked at me with teary eyes brimming with joy and love. It was a side of him I hadn't seen before, and it was infectious.

I thought I knew what 'being on fire' was as a communist. But what he described was so far beyond that transient, worldly, righteous zeal; beyond anything connected with temporary social justice. The fire he described was timeless, eternal. It came from a deeper, higher sphere. It was the place Dechen had called the fifth dimension. It was that place in the story of King Gesar called Shambhala. And I remembered from my school days, it was what Jesus called the Kingdom of God. It is neither separate nor visible to us here; it is intangible, but more real.

I remembered lines from the song I heard when I was running away from Gyawa.

'Shambhala is and is not real,' I said aloud and looked at Dechen, knowing she was the singer I'd heard. 'This joy does and does not fill the world; this moment is and is not everlasting; each being does and does not share one Buddha nature.'

Dechen nodded her head, 'Now you understand.'

'Yes, that translucent place shimmering just beyond the surface of our material world is real but intangible.'

What would the cosmos be like when all matter is completely translated into spirit-matter? A shining emptiness filled with goodness, beauty and truth... Being itself!

'Is this my purpose, Rinpoche-la?' I began hesitantly. I was in awe of the magnitude of our task. 'I mean, as a bodhisattva or a windhorse warrior, isn't it our purpose to help others become fully human, fully alive? Aren't we called to help transform human beings and this complex society into the likeness of Shambhala?'

'Yes, Chodak-la,' Rinpoche agreed with a wide grin, 'but you mustn't doubt. Look at what you've accomplished already when you were not aware of these things. Once on fire, you can draw on the very source of wisdom and compassion.'

I was beginning to understand the magnitude of the plan Yangchen and Rinpoche had set in motion.

'I brought you out here to discuss our plan,' Rinpoche continued. 'Yangchen, Dechen, and I have been very pleased with your progress. We think you are ready now to help us.'

'You mean to play King Gesar in the *lhamo* tours to educate the people?' I asked. 'I thought I was not to be involved in your public performances.'

'The *lhamo* tours were an early part of our plan but we don't have time for that now. Working to create the cooperative is part of our greater plan but to tell you the truth, we are still trying to understand the full extent of our purpose. It appears we need you to show us the next step. You've shown us that recreating our social structure is important, now, perhaps, you'll also lead us in rekindling our spiritual heritage.'

It surprised me to hear that they were waiting for me to help them fully understand and carry out their plan as if I was a missing piece!

Obviously Dechen, Yangchen, and Rinpoche were key players. I could see, too, that Thupten, Pema, Dawa, and Thampa—and even Wangdu, Samphel, and Zema—were involved. I had assumed they all knew the plan. It humbled me that this incredible group of good people brought me to where I was now. They believed in me; they encouraged, instructed, inspired me, and expanded my horizons. In fact, Yangchen and Master Tashi had been doing this since I was a little boy in Shanghai. I could no longer deny it. No, now I felt very grateful. I could see that their goal and my own were one and the same.

'I'm still a communist,' I remarked suddenly as the thought popped up, 'I can't turn my back on that.'

'Of course!' Rinpoche agreed, 'that's as it should be.'

'But now,' I added hastily, 'because I'm a communist I want to remove social injustice and the suffering it causes. And because I'm a Buddhist I understand the causes of suffering, and want to remove ignorance. I see no contradiction.'

'I agree,' Rinpoche said. 'Both can work together.'

'We have talked often about an enlightened society,' I said, 'let's find out what that might look like! I think we can create a society of spiritually transformed human beings that will outshine any communist or capitalist dream this world can envision today.'

Several days later, after further discussing our goals and setting plans, people began arriving at the hermitage from the valley below and the hills around. Rinpoche had invited them to hear Dechen perform; her performances were still an appropriate way to share our vision with the people. Along with her singing, we would talk about the economic and social benefits of forming the Mola Cooperative. The program would be designed to instil in their hearts a longing for spiritual transformation that would lead to an enlightened society like King Gesar's.

The trainees had set up a stage for Dechen, and were busy preparing a feast for mid-afternoon so that people could return to their homes before nightfall. Some of the visitors, however, would want to stay and participate in the dancing and celebrations with the young warriors in the evening. We anticipated people would also want to discuss the pros and cons of our vision.

The stage was a large tent, elaborately decorated with coloured veils hanging to conceal the stage area. Dechen insisted I take part.

'This is our own place,' she said when I objected that we were violating our pledge of not involving me in the *lhamo*. 'Besides, you won't be singing. It's not like you're a *babdrungpa*.'

Dechen had me sit in meditation, left of the stage, while Rinpoche stood at the centre of the stage and, backstage, Yangchen played the drum and blew the horn. We both remained concealed. Dechen told me to enter a deep meditation and focus on the words of the song, to see the picture she painted with her voice. From the moment Dechen began singing, I had no idea what the audience witnessed; I was in another reality.

'Into an empty sky, fragrant juniper smoke billows from burning coals into bright clouds.'

I entered empty sky, empty even of light except for a single point twinkling into existence and moving closer, rapidly closer.

337

'A bridge of longing joins heaven to earth for great Guru Rinpoche to descend. The clouds of brightness rise while rainbows cascade in a mighty waterfall.'

The light expanded into a bright cloud, billowing with radiant colours, as Guru Palden Rinpoche descended on the rainbow bridge.

'Singlen rules the Kingdom of Ling; he is old, secluded in retreat. Troubles caused by his brother Todong bring ignorance and bondage for all. For 17 years Todong has tried to slay the divine golden child who threatens his plans.'

Guru Rinpoche took his seat on the Guru's throne with a small table set with ceremonial objects between us. I found myself seated before Guru Rinpoche's throne as he began a ceremony.

'Guru Rinpoche awakens the future King of Ling, and reminds him of his strength and his destiny. He tells the young man to go and claim his throne.'

Attending to his every movement—my hands held together in supplication over my heart—I remained receptive as he rang a crystal clear bell, chanted from sacred texts and made offerings of butter, tsampa, and water. The ceremony concluded, I rose to my knees. Leaning forward, our foreheads touched; I physically felt my awareness drop from my head into my heart, and a warmth expand in my chest. This warmth spread from my chest toward everyone and everything around me, not because I willed it but because I could not stop its flow through me.

'Having completed the ceremony, the Great Guru re-ascended the rainbow bridge to Shambhala.'

I watched Guru Rinpoche ascend the bridge of blazing rainbow light until he merged with all-pervading spirit-matter, the source of the current of loving light coursing through my being.

'That same morning Gesar began his journey from the desolate cold wastes to his promised kingdom.'

Emerging gradually from meditation, I heard Palden Rinpoche speaking softly to rouse Dechen from her trance state. The beating of Yangchen's drum ended, and I emerged from meditation. Before I opened my eyes, I knew both Rinpoche and Dechen were emanating the same luminous current through their hearts.

'As you well know, dear Chodak-la, that was not just a regular performance,' Rinpoche said to me quietly. 'It was an empowerment ceremony. You are now empowered to begin your true mission.'

Part Three

Shambhala
Once and Future

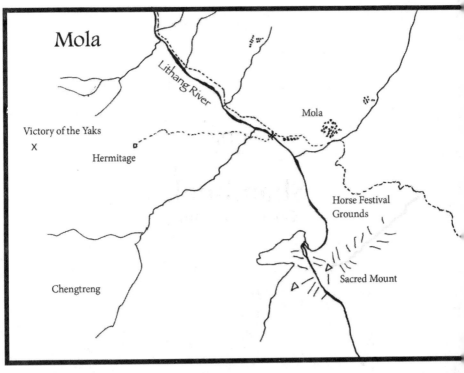

Mola

Lithang River

Victory of the Yaks
X

Hermitage

Mola

Horse Festival
Grounds

Chengtreng

Sacred Mount

Southern part of Mola Township Cooperative

Grain Tax

Dechen accompanied me down the mountainside, to Mola, to begin our work. She would teach mindfulness and help me build awareness of the full economic, political, and spiritual scope of our new cooperative.

We walked Chestnut and Little White because the trail was too steep for us to ride. Part way down, we stopped at a bluff that offered a good view of the township. Dechen raised her arms across the valley, as if she was blessing it. I tried to do the same but a wave of timidity swept through me; the immensity of what we were about to attempt overwhelmed me. Creating a cooperative among these people who were head-strong and independent was by far the easier of the tasks ahead of us. Setting them 'on fire' and creating an 'enlightened society' was truly the more monumental task.

'Don't give in to doubts, Chodak-la!' Dechen admonished suddenly. I knew she could always read me. 'Surrender; let the fire flow through you.'

She was right, of course. Habitual thought patterns were resurfacing, now that I'd left the security of the hermitage to face the challenges ahead. I slipped into seeing the problems and obstacles from my old narrow perspective and not, as Dechen reminded me, from an immersion in the fifth dimension.

I listened to the sounds rising from the valley below. The river provided a continuous undertone but over it, I could hear other sounds. There were ravens cawing nearby, and a young woman sang while herding a few yaks and sheep. It reminded me of my *Dakini* singing to me through the mist while I was lost. Sounds travelled far in the cold, clear air.

A different sound, the tramping of marching feet on the trail, alarmed me. I looked for the source.

'There! Look, Dechen-la!' I pointed out a troop of soldiers heading toward Samphel's village. 'Soldiers, armed. Do you think that's Major Gan riding beside Tenzin?'

'Yes, Gan and Tenzin,' Dechen agreed.

'I'd better get down there,' I said as I handed her my horse's reins. 'Go back up and take Chestnut with you. I'll be quicker on foot. Tell Rinpoche and Wangdu.'

I kept an eye on the troop's progress while hurrying downhill. I saw them leave the main trail and, sure enough, head for Samphel's village.

'Remember who you are, Chodak!' I heard Dechen shout as I hurried on. I acknowledged by raising my right arm as if holding a sword. I needed that reminder.

I crossed the river and ran up the hillside to the village. I guessed they would go to Samphel's house first. When I entered Samphel's courtyard, I found Major Gan and Tenzin with a troop of 20 or so—all armed. Tenzin was cocky, and looked like he enjoyed being in charge.

'What are you doing here with all these soldiers, Tenzin?' I asked pointedly.

'*Tashi delek!*' Tenzin shouted, making a mocking bow. When I didn't respond to his greeting, he shrugged his shoulders. 'How nice to see you, too, comrade! You look so holy!

I'm sure your time at the hermitage has been, ah, what should I say, uplifting? Ha, ha!'

Then Tenzin turned to Major Gan, pointed at me and shouted, 'Arrest him!'

Major Gan nodded to a couple of his soldiers. One pointed a rifle at me while another grabbed my arms. A short length of rope was produced and my hands were tied behind my back.

'Why are you arresting me?' I asked Major Gan, somewhat angry. I completely ignored Tenzin.

'There are several orders from Lithang,' Major Gan stated in Chinese. 'One of them is for your arrest, on charges of kidnapping.'

'Kidnapping?' I was astonished. Then I realized Tenzin blamed me for Dechen's sudden departure from Gyawa.

'You were seen with Andrutsang Dechen after she went missing from Gyawa!' Major Gan confirmed.

'That must have taken some convincing, if that order came from Commander Deng.' I said defiantly.

Gan shrugged to suggest he didn't care where it came from.

Strutting back and forth across the courtyard, Tenzin was unconsciously imitating Commander Deng's habit of pacing, I noted. His behaviour was laughable, really. It amused me to see how Major Gan played along.

'Orders from Lithang arrived and I acted immediately,' Tenzin boasted. 'Another order is the long-standing warrant for the arrest of Palden Rinpoche. We will find and arrest him.'

'He's up at the hermitage. Go, get him.'

I turned to Major Gan and switched languages. 'Once you start up the hill, he'll be gone. So what other business requires the use of armed soldiers?'

'Our concern here in Mola,' Tenzin announced pompously in Tibetan, 'is the insufficient payment of the grain tax. We're here to collect what's due. Every village, this one included, must do its part to support the services provided by the Party and the PLA. Oh, and while we are at it, we'll be conducting a house-by-house inventory of personal property.'

The real reason for the presence of the soldiers became crystal clear.

'I have an agreement with Commander Deng,' I said to Major Gan, 'Mola township is to be free of intervention for a year.'

Tenzin stiffened. 'How are we violating your agreement by conducting an inventory and collecting the grain taxes?'

'To me non-interference means non-interference,' I observed in as steely a voice as I could manage. 'Stay away from this township!'

Zema, who up to this point had been watching dispassionately, could no longer hold her tongue. Tenzin's arrogant authoritarianism set her off! She went and stood right in Tenzin's face, and challenged him forcefully.

'First of all,' Zema raised a finger to indicate her first point of objection, 'the procedure is to make an official request at our next village council meeting about a grain tax.'

Tenzin scoffed.

'Secondly,' Zema glared at Tenzin and raised a second finger, 'our taxes never provide us with any services, asked for or not! And thirdly, doing an inventory of our household goods is completely out of the question.'

Tenzin did his best to stand up to the infuriated woman, and responded by likewise holding up his fingers.

'Firstly, your village has failed to provide the grain tax required by all villages in Lithang district. Secondly, the PLA is here to implement reforms and build infrastructure necessary for economic and social development. And thirdly, a household inventory will be conducted to establish available resources in preparation for implementing collectivization!'

Zema raised a clenched fist in Tenzin's face.

'We care nothing for your collectives!'

Tenzin signalled Major Gan, who ordered his soldiers into action. One of them approached Zema and pushed her toward the storeroom, pointing his rifle at her.

'Open your storeroom!' Tenzin shouted.

Defying my supposed arrest, I hurried forward and shoved the rifle away from Zema as best I could with my body.

'That's no way to treat the woman of this house!' I shouted at Tenzin.

Then more quietly, I spoke to Zema. 'I'm sorry, Zema. We must adjust to this situation. I'll do my best to reach a compromise. Please don't resist. Leave it to me.'

'Restrain him!' Tenzin shouted at Major Gan and the soldiers in Chinese.

I was grabbed and pulled away from Zema, toward Major Gan. I spoke quietly with him while Tenzin was busy inside the storeroom supervising Zema and several soldiers.

'This is going too far,' I advised Gan, 'it borders on banditry. The woman is right. You should make a formal request for supplies. That's it, isn't it? Your supplies have disappeared because you had too many mouths to feed in Gyawa. So you thought you'd come here and just take what you need.'

347

'Yes, Sonam's tribe stole grains from us; we have very little left. Lithang is keeping all the grain we sent there earlier.'

'What's the problem,' I said, trying to keep the 'I told you so' tone out of my voice, 'are the policies backfiring?'

'Mind what you say, Comrade Chuang!' Major Gan tried to intimidate me, 'or should I call you Chuang-la, the Chinese Khampa?'

'You can't solve your problems in Gyawa by antagonizing people in Mola. Does Commander Deng really know what you are doing?'

'Mola refused to send anything to Lithang this fall,' Gan responded calmly, 'so we thought it necessary to put pressure on them.'

I knew Mola was providing some grain and supplies for our training program at the hermitage but the trainees were required to bring their own supplies as payment. The amount sent to the hermitage from Mola could not have been very much. They would probably have enough to pay the annual taxes to Lithang if they wanted to.

'I was unaware that Mola was behind in its taxes,' I admitted. 'In that case, take no more than the taxable amount.'

'Agreed,' Gan said.

'As for my arrest...' I started to say, but Major Gan put up his hand to stop me.

'There is a warrant, and Commander Deng is obliged to comply since it comes from the office of the district commissioner.'

'From Nawang? Tenzin's father?' I laughed. 'Another farce! Well, let's see if there's sufficient evidence.'

'The young woman will have to make a statement,' Gan informed me.

'She left Gyawa of her own free will. Truth be told, it was more like I was kidnapped! Instead of letting me go to Mola, she insisted I take her to the hermitage.' I imagined Dechen giving Nawang and other officials a piece of her mind while she was at it!

'I'll go with you without objection, if you will drop this idea of an inventory of every house. It's a cheap scare tactic and from what I know about you, you wouldn't really like it if people started to resist and you had to resort to violence. Besides, I am making progress toward creating a cooperative here.' After giving him a moment to soak in what I'd just said, I continued, 'Final negotiations are underway for the transfer of property from all the landlords in this township. It is a significant step and the idea of an inventory at this stage is highly counterproductive, if not irrelevant. All property will be collective by definition!'

'But...' Gan began to object.

'Who is really in charge here, you think?' I asked quickly. 'Commander Deng tells me you are Tenzin's superior. He's given me authority in regard to the incorporation of Mola township. As far as I'm concerned, you are conducting an illegal raid and making demands beyond your authority in my jurisdiction. I advise you to re-evaluate your orders from Lithang or I'll make an official complaint about your conduct. Surely you can bring Tenzin to his senses.'

A flash of anger crossed the major's face. I'd hit a nerve but I saw he was also relieved. He didn't want to create a scene in which people could get hurt. As far as I knew, he had been able to enforce policies in Gyawa without using violence. It helped that he had lived in the village among the people, and he knew them all by name. I wanted to encourage the best in him.

'You're a good man, Gan,' I told him just before Tenzin emerged with bags of grain.

For the rest of the day, I was tied to a post in Zema's storeroom. Major Gan ordered the soldiers to collect the 'grain tax' from every household in the village but abandon the inventory of private property. Tenzin's protest was loud but the soldiers did not listen to him.

Late that night, I heard Tenzin outside the walled courtyard calling for someone to let him in. It was obvious he was drunk. When someone let him in, he spoke in Chinese to whoever it was. He said he was having a good time teaching communist slogans in Chinese to people at the tavern down by the river.

It was Major Gan who met Tenzin; he said, 'Come in now, comrade. It's very late and everyone is sleeping.'

'Of course they're sleeping!' Tenzin blurted, 'these backward, ignorant fools go to sleep with the animals. So uncivilized!'

Tenzin began laughing and cursing in Tibetan.

'You damn fool! You let that Chinese Khampa talk you out of doing our duty.'

'That's enough, comrade!' Major Gan understood enough of what Tenzin blurted out in Tibetan. 'You're drunk and not thinking clearly. Come inside and sleep it off.'

'No!' Tenzin shouted, 'not until I give that fake a piece of my mind.'

I heard the storeroom door open, and sensed Tenzin stumbling toward me in the dark. He groped around until he tripped over my leg. When he got to his feet, he lit a match. Before the flame went out, he gave me a kick in the ribs that knocked the breath out of me. I suffered several more kicks to my face, ribs, and legs. He would have continued all night or until he'd killed me, except that Major Gan realized Tenzin was not talking to me, but beating me. He was about to deliver another kick when Gan pulled him out of the room and gave him more to drink.

Tenzin's rage was directed at me mostly because of his infatuation with Dechen; of that I was sure. But it was also because of his unpopular and lonely place among fellow Khampas. Like his father, he was an opportunist and had never really committed himself to communism. He had been at the right place at the right time to cash in with the new ruling power.

'Damn you, Gan!' he shouted, before falling into a manageable stupor. 'Why don't all you fucking Chinese go back to where you came from?'

I did my best not to harbour ill feelings toward Tenzin; he was a mere pawn in a much larger game. Confused and conflicted, he lashed out at those who were impeding what he'd imagined his life might have been like. He was suffering; and as a Buddhist, I had vowed to help elevate suffering— even Tenzin's.

Drifting in and out of consciousness that night, I tried to focus on my breathing to keep attention off my aches and pains. I have to admit it was a huge challenge; it was not at all easy to maintain my equilibrium. I felt that what I'd achieved at the hermitage during the past couple months had utterly disappeared. Rinpoche had been right; it was too soon. I should have gone into a three-year retreat. Instead, I had to do what I could to manage the deluge of change coming at us; the world we loved was in danger of being washed away.

I finally fell asleep alone, cold and in deep darkness; inner and outer.

⊕⊖

In the morning, after half-a-dozen pack animals had been loaded, we set off toward Gyawa. I staggered behind Major Gan's horse while Tenzin, obviously hung-over and angry, rode his tall black horse behind me. He had insisted on holding one end of the rope that bound my wrists at my back and, now and then, maliciously jerked it. This, to Tenzin's sadistic delight, pulled my arms agonizingly back and upward. My head swam from pain but I managed to keep the pace set by soldiers marching at the head of our group. Behind Tenzin came the pack animals and a couple of local men as minders, followed by a rear guard of soldiers.

As I had tried to do during the night, I focused on each breath, each step, while repeating the mantra: **om gate gate para gate parasum gate bodhi svaha.** I was better able now to clear my mind of worried thoughts.

The valley was unusually quiet when we marched toward a narrow part of the valley. Tenzin and Major Gan did not seem to notice the quietness and rode along unconcerned. The pack animals became skittish, and the soldiers grew nervous when we approached the bridge Dechen and I had crossed to reach the upper trail to the hermitage. Here, the forest came down to the river from both sides of the valley. I could see why the soldiers were getting nervous; it was an ideal spot for an ambush.

The moment I sensed their presence in hiding, the warriors sprang from above and below the trail, from behind trees and rocks—or they simply walked around the bend in the trail. We were surrounded. I recognized the men immediately, and knew I was among friends. I trusted they would put their training to good use.

I relaxed too soon. In a panic, Tenzin brought his horse beside me and gave me a vicious shove with his foot. I went over the edge of the trail.

Everything went dark.

Recovery

I was bouncing. Every jostle sent pain shooting through my shoulder. I struggled to open my eyes, and discovered a blindfold or bandage on my face. I moved a hand; it wasn't tied any more. With the good—or better—arm, I tried to lift what was covering my eyes. Someone called out and the bouncing stopped. I knew that voice.

'Chodak-la,' the voice said, 'gently, you're badly hurt.'

'Dechen?' I sought an explanation rather than doubting who she was.

'Easy,' she whispered. Her hands gently removed the bandage from my eyes.

The light was too much. I squinted until I got used to the glare, and Dechen came into focus. She was smiling with relief. Behind her, Palden Rinpoche was equally glad to see me.

I looked around and discovered I was on a makeshift stretcher. Four warriors carried me. Dechen told them to put it down, and the whole group stopped and gathered around me. Everyone was relieved.

'What happened?' I asked.

Several people started talking, all at once, to recount the events enthusiastically. I put my hands up and said, 'Wait! Only one of you, please!'

There was good-natured laughter, and Rinpoche-la began an account of the events I'd missed.

'Dechen and I watched from the hillside across the river while Wangdu and the warriors conducted a successful ambush at the bridge. We outnumbered them so it was easy enough to disarm them one-on-one. Unfortunately, Tenzin managed to shove you off the trail. He held onto the rope long enough to dislocate your left arm. You fell quite a distance. With all the cuts and bruises on your face, we couldn't tell if you'd hit your head in the fall or if those were done to you earlier. The caravan minders told us you were in a bad state this morning!'

I looked down at my arm. It was held tight in a sling. A wave of nausea swept over me when I tried to move it, and I nearly blacked out again.

'How long have I been unconscious?' I asked after a minute or two. My medical training began to raise alarms.

'Oh, not that long,' Dechen said and, to defuse my concern, added, 'You're back now with all your faculties intact, it seems!'

I did a spot check; eyes, yes, I can see; ears, yes, no problem hearing; I could talk; my mind was clearing.

'Yes, I'm alright,' I confirmed.

'When we heard you'd been arrested,' Palden recounted, 'and that the grain tax had been extracted from each house in Mola, we decided action was necessary. Using the upper trail, it was easy to get ahead of your captors and set up an ambush. I impressed on the warriors how important it was to put into practice all they had learned about preventing harm. They handled it superbly, except for Wangdu! He is sorrowfully apologetic, of course, for not getting to Tenzin in time to prevent that last vengeful action against you.'

'And what happened to them—to Tenzin, Major Gan, and the soldiers?'

'They're getting what they deserve!' Palden continued.

Several warriors chuckled.

'You should have seen them!' one of them said. 'They were so surprised we let them go!'

'Let them go?' I asked incredulously.

'Yes,' Palden said. 'Major Gan and his men will lose face when they arrive back in Gyawa without their boots, without their pants, without their guns, and without the grains they intended to bring back with them. We figured that would be punishment enough.'

'What about Tenzin?'

'That's a different story; we tied him like a sack on the back of his horse. We whipped his horse and sent it galloping up the trail toward Gyawa, with a couple of our warriors in pursuit to keep it moving. His arrival in Gyawa, strapped to an animal like a roll of yak hide, will be something he'll never live down! His punishment is uncomfortable, to be sure, but not dangerous or likely to cause serious injury. He can't fall off.'

Though I wanted to join in the laughter, I couldn't; doing so aggravated my aches and pains.

We returned to Mola with the rescued grains, though I heard Dechen and Palden discuss a plan to send grains to Gyawa later, so the village wouldn't starve this winter.

Zema was overcome with concern for me and put me in a room next to the kitchen, at the heart of her home.

After taking a nauseating look to examine my open wounds, I consulted with Dechen and Rinpoche about treatment. I had several deep cuts on my legs, arms, and head. A twisted ankle and banged up knees made it difficult to walk. Fortunately, no bones were broken; but my left shoulder was dislocated. It could have been both shoulders, since both arms were jerked in my fall.

A couple of strong men pulled hard to set the shoulder in place. Without modern painkillers, I was in unspeakable agony. Fortitude and imported whisky, that Zema kept on hand for this kind of occasion, somehow got me through the ordeal.

Zema brought in an elderly woman she introduced as Rinchen-la. She served the community as midwife, healer, and shaman because she was knowledgeable in the ancient arts of herbal medicines. Together, the three women—Zema, Rinchen, and Dechen—fussed over my cuts with poultices and gave me potions to drink. Yangchen came down from the hermitage and joined them as soon as she heard of my injuries.

Over the next few days, despite Yangchen's protests that I needed rest, Samphel brought in a steady stream of visitors to consult me about forming the cooperative. I was encouraged by the progress being made. Details of property transfer were being worked out. Contact had also been made with several nomadic tribes with favourable results. The Mola Cooperative was becoming a reality, and I expressed my gratitude to Samphel for the hard work he'd been doing.

When the four women weren't fussing over me and Samphel was out on business, Tashi—Zema's 10-year-old daughter, would pester me for stories about China or beg me to sing 'those silly communist' songs. She was right, they were silly. How could I ever have been moved by their sentimental patriotism? Instead, I tried to create songs about Gesar, since Rinpoche and Dechen had suggested I might also be a *babdrung*. Words came to me easily but it was clear, I was simply making up words from parts of the story I had heard. I wasn't singing from first-hand experience.

I mentioned this to Dechen one day but all she did was give my hand a quick, encouraging squeeze.

'It will happen!' she said.

I was seldom alone, even though Dechen and Rinpoche insisted I spend more time in meditation. I loved my daily meditation and knew it would help my body heal faster, too.

A few days later when Wangdu re-joined us, he was relieved to see that I was alive. All this time he thought I was dead. The last he knew, my condition was uncertain. Assuming the worst, he'd taken pains to impress on Tenzin that he'd killed me.

Wangdu told us Tenzin was in a terrible state when he arrived in Gyawa. Thupten had untied him, given him water and a meal. Early next morning—terrified and sore— Tenzin had gathered up a few belongings and fled to Lithang, abandoning Major Gan and his troops, who had staggered in throughout all hours of the night. The villagers and Wangdu's warriors treated the soldiers, including Major Gan, with kindness. They dressed wounds on their feet, gave them back their boots and pants, fed them, and looked after them as if they were members of the cooperative. When they were able to walk again, Major Gan marched his men back to Lithang.

What Commander Deng would do with the information that Tenzin had killed me, we didn't know. We could only assume my agreement with Deng to let Mola township pursue reforms its own way would not be upheld. It was inevitable that troops would move into the area, but we thought it likely it would not happen until spring. This gave us a window of time to proceed with our plan.

News that Lobsang and his militia were determined to run the PLA out of Lithang reached us through Samphel's contact with the various tribes. He had called off the raid on Gyawa when he learned that Sonam's group was able to leave. But the recent PLA incursion into Mola was too close to home for him. I reminded Palden that I still wanted to meet Lobsang, but he said it was out of the question. I was in no condition to travel, nor would I be for several weeks.

'Then ask Lobsang to come here!' I insisted.

'Ha! Why would he do that? He's preoccupied at the moment and couldn't be bothered to talk things over with us. However, I'll keep trying. There may be an opportunity to see him before long. So far, he's ignored Kunchen-la's summons. If he meets with the *khenpo*, I'll be there, too. Meanwhile, get your strength back!'

The next day, we heard that Deng had sent two hundred troops to Gyawa. They stayed the night, and were marching south. They appeared to be heading toward the hermitage but from the opposite side of the mountain, hoping, perhaps, to surprise Wangdu's warriors. We guessed Deng was determined to arrest Palden, wipe out his 'militia', and demolish his training centre.

Wangdu immediately dispatched warriors to track the progress of the PLA soldiers. We later learned that the soldiers made no effort to conceal their intentions, and had proceeded without a clear idea of the conditions ahead. They had relied on guides conscripted in Gyawa who, to their credit, cleverly rode the fine line between helping and misleading them. The troops traversed more difficult terrain than necessary while the warriors watching had a good laugh about the guides' cleverness.

By nightfall, the PLA troops were camped near the top of the mountain in bitter cold conditions. Wangdu took advantage of their predicament and, with access to a large herd of yak sheltered near the hermitage, prepared a surprise for them.

The warriors waited until the soldiers settled for the night. When all was quiet, they drove the herd over the hill and into the soldiers' camp. Terrorized lookouts screamed, and the yak reacted to the noise as expected. Chaos ensued. Tents caught fire as lamps were overturned or firebrands from campfires scattered. Fire frightened the yak even more. Soldiers were trampled, some in their beds. Others dropped everything and scattered into the darkness, fleeing the monsters intent on running them over.

By dawn, the warriors had disarmed and rounded up the soldiers without firing a single shot. Unfortunately, a few soldiers had died in the mayhem, and several suffered serious injuries. Wangdu got permission from the officer in charge to take the injured to the hermitage for treatment while the dead were prepared for sky burial; their bodies stripped and laid out on a rocky outcrop for vultures to consume. The soldiers watched in horrified silence. They would have been even more horrified if the warriors had taken the time to hack the bodies into pieces to make it easier for the birds.

Three injured yaks were killed and butchered. A good portion of the meat was sent to the hermitage with the injured soldiers. The rest was roasted over fire pits to feed the captives that morning. Several warriors tried to cheer up the sullen soldiers with *chang* and butter tea.

After the meal, Wangdu and his warriors escorted the able-bodied captives back to Lithang by way of Gyawa. When they got to Gyawa, Wangdu heard that Lobsang's militia was attacking the PLA camp in Lithang. Aware of the danger to his captives, Wangdu kept them in Gyawa to save them from Lobsang's wrath. After some discussion with the captives, Wangdu agreed to see them off toward Dartsendo, and back to China without going through Lithang. The people of Gyawa gave them some food and wished them luck. Wangdu told them to find other PLA camps or, since they were unarmed, rely on the goodwill of local people as they travelled east.

We were greatly dismayed to learn how many soldiers Lobsang's militia killed at the PLA encampment in Lithang. Lobsang's men had surprised them with an attack at dawn, and greatly outnumbered them. Mobile on horseback, they caught the soldiers in their beds. It was not unlike what the yaks had done near the hermitage, though Lobsang's warriors had no qualms about using their weapons to cause mortal harm.

A few days later, we heard from Kunchen Khenpo that Commander Deng had withdrawn all his remaining troops from the district and that Nawang, along with Tenzin, had fled to Chengdu with the PLA.

Rinpoche treated a dozen injured soldiers at the hermitage. When they were strong enough, they were transferred to Lithang. Because the PLA camp was empty, housing had to be found for them in town. A vow was extracted from each soldier to behave non-violently and to accept Khampa hospitality graciously. In turn, it was impressed upon each host family to treat their 'guests' as members of the family. Two soldiers were placed together with a family. For the most part, the soldiers behaved as grateful and respectful guests. One or two resented this help, and had to be sent off to try their luck reaching China in the winter.

I was pleased to learn that there had been little trouble between host families and Chinese guests. Like myself, these soldiers were soon speaking Tibetan—a few began to wear the *chuba*, and came to genuinely appreciate local culture.

With the PLA gone from Lithang, our situation greatly changed. The entire district heaved a collective sigh of relief. We would be free of military pressure until the spring, when the road over the high passes opened again. But no doubt, Commander Deng, or someone more ruthless, would be sent in with many more soldiers. We had four or five months to organize Mola Cooperative, and to encourage more cooperatives throughout the district.

Kunchen Khenpo assumed leadership of Lithang district. The people were delighted to have their well-respected *Khenpo* back in charge. They were fed up with the Reds and their puppet, Nawang Tsering. We hoped to work with Kunchen, Lobsang, and other leaders to mobilize a district-wide reorganization along the lines of the Gyawa and Mola Cooperatives.

Meanwhile, I languished in bed. My injuries were not healing well. On the contrary, some were infected and I was feverish. I could tell Dechen was worried.

Water lapped on the pebbled shore. Stars reflected beneath the even surface. Distant mountains formed dark shapes separating the stars above from their reflection below. Against this faint light, a young woman sat in meditation on a rock surrounded by water. She lifted her head to watch a sudden brightness descend, growing bigger. The meteor exploded in white light at the lake's surface and sank into the depths, where it continued to glow.

Sliding from the rock into the water, she waded in to gather the light in her arms and lift the glowing orb out of the water.

Pressing the orb to her belly, she came to shore. A child took shape in the orb and by the time she reached shore, she was holding a child in her arms. Taking a few more steps, she set the toddler on the ground beside her. Holding his hand, they walked further ashore. The child ran ahead across a vast grassland. A white horse, its mane flowing in the wind, waited for the young man. Together, horse and rider leapt into the limitless sky, and flew over the immense expanse of the mountains and grasslands. Multi-coloured flowers rained from the sky around the young woman.

That familiar dream world, vividly more-than-real, faded while my attention turned to the soft rhythm of a drum and the words of a song. Wasn't this the young man singing from horseback in the sky?

'**Right where I am, transcending time and space, I am Gesar, King of Ling, wearing the dazzling armour of noonday sun, carrying the full moon banner of exultation, swirling the starlight sword of pure awareness, riding the miracle horse of universal life force, flying from moment to moment and shape to shape.**'

All too beautifully, two voices blended to describe the young man at home in a wilderness grasslands.

'**I am the indestructible warrior, free from time.**'

Only one voice now, and I opened my eyes knowing that voice was mine.

The drum was suddenly silent and, by the expression on Dechen's face, I knew one of the voices had been mine. But

363

I was more intrigued by the vision filling my open eyes — Dechen, my *Dakini*!

And, of course, the thought, 'if only she were my lover, too' did cross my groggy mind.

'Oh, Chodak-la!' Dechen exclaimed, weariness in her voice, 'you did it!'

Drawn by the excitement in Dechen's voice, Zema and Tashi rushed into the room, followed by Yangchen. They were extremely happy to see me awake. I was amused by their curious excitement.

'What did I do?' I asked, my voice weak.

Yangchen kneeled beside Dechen and took my hand.

'You're back with us! You were very ill,' she said, 'your wounds were badly infected. You're very lucky.'

'How long?'

'You were...' Dechen stopped as if there were too many people around to say what she wanted.

Yangchen turned to Tashi and said, 'Ask Jigme to go up the mountain and tell Rinpoche that our friend here is awake again, and it looks like he'll live to cause us more trouble.'

Yangchen looked at me again and giggled! She was happy and put her arm around Dechen to share a hug. Zema followed Tashi out of the room, and they returned with a kettle of tea and several bowls. Tashi set the bowls on the low table by my bed and Zema poured us all some tea. I was too weak to sit up. Dechen put an arm behind my back and helped me sit up while Yangchen arranged pillows for me to lean on.

Zema cautioned me to sip slowly. I felt weak and tired but a wide smile covered my face. I looked at each of these strong, wonderful women—Dechen, Yangchen, Zema. They'd cared for me, brought me back from the brink of death.

'What is it?' Dechen asked, prodding me to explain my silly grin.

'I was just thinking,' I responded immediately, 'how each of you are so wonderful! I'm so blessed to be in your tender care. I'm still alive because of you, I know.'

I closed my eyes. I was tired. Dechen's hand stroked my cheek, my forehead.

'You're warm. Sleep now. We'll leave you for a while.'

Yangchen took the pillows away and Dechen helped me lie down again.

'Was I singing?' I whispered when Dechen's face was close to mine. 'Were we singing together?'

'Yes!' she whispered in reply, 'I sang the Gesar story to you, and this morning, you sang with me.'

'Really?'

'Yes, you're a *babdrungpa* now.'

'Oh,' I closed my eyes. I was too tired to take in what this actually meant.

When I awoke next, it was morning. I looked out the open window. Dripping icicles hung from the eves. A mild breeze brought fresh air into my room. Managing to prop myself up to a sitting position, I realized I felt better, and looked around with a bit more awareness of my surroundings. I noticed another pillow and bedding next to mine. It looked like someone had slept next to me during the night. Zema must have heard me. She entered with a bowl of tea and some *tsampa*. She insisted on mixing it for me and made small amounts for me to eat.

'You haven't eaten much in days; go slowly. We managed to feed you tea with a little *tsampa* mixed in but not much else.'

'I'm starved.'

'You should be; you're as skinny as a twig. It will be a long time before you are strong again.'

Zema noticed me glancing now and then at the bedding beside mine.

'Dechen stayed with you day and night,' she responded to my unspoken question. She enjoyed my confusion, I think, and wasn't able to hide her amusement.

Later that morning, Dechen brought Rinpoche and Wangdu. It was good to see them again.

'Well, Chodak-la,' Rinpoche said after making sure I was as well as he'd been told, 'you gave us a scare. Good to see you are yourself again.'

'Myself again?' I looked at Dechen. 'Was I delirious? Did I behave badly? What did I say?'

'Don't worry. It was all in English!' Dechen joked.

I frowned. Knowing she'd been beside me throughout my illness, I began to hope I hadn't acted inappropriately or called her Jiachen. I couldn't remember anything, so perhaps I really was unconscious and very weak.

'Your behaviour was fine,' Dechen assured me, 'you were so sick we forced you to drink and take medicines. Besides, Rinchen-la mixed in some powerful stuff to keep you knocked out!'

'What was it?'

Rinpoche put a hand on my arm and said, 'Rinchen-la's potion helped you fully recover in another world.'

'She put me in a shamanic trance?'

Then I remembered what Dechen had said; that we sang together. We were together in another world. She is the *Dakini* of the lake!

Confronting the Warlord

It was several days before I could take a few wobbly steps across the room to the window. It had snowed again and, deep snow filled the courtyard.

Zema found me standing at the window and scolded me! I silently agreed I'd been foolish and let her help me back to bed. I was pushing my limits. My nurses were very strict, but I wanted to get on with life.

'How long?' I asked Zema when I was settled, 'how long have I been ill?'

'One month of winter has gone since those goons came to our village.'

I remember being here for two, perhaps three weeks. Her answer let me know I'd been unconscious or in a trance for a few days, maybe a whole week.

'I nearly gave up on you,' Zema continued, still not answering my question, 'but Little Tashi reminded me, time and again, that you are actually a "nice foreigner". I tried not to get too frustrated with you, but I'll admit I got rough sometimes when you gave me a hard time.'

I realized 'hard time' probably included managing incontinence and keeping me clean, besides dressing my wounds and giving me food and water! It must have been awful!

'How can I ever repay your kindness?' I asked Zema.

'Huh! Repay, he says!' she tried to sound irritated and indignant, but underneath I could tell she was grateful for my recognition of all she'd done. She was good through and through, despite the gruff exterior she frequently projected.

'It's over now and you'll be out of my hair soon enough. That's all the thanks I need!'

'You're too good to me, Zema-la!' I tried to take her hands in mine, but she managed to slip them out of reach and left the room. She soon returned with a bowl of *chang*.

'If you won't tell me how long I was unconscious, then tell me how long Dechen sang to me?' I asked.

'Such a lovely voice, that girl! And she never left your side. When she wasn't singing, she was asleep next to you.'

'Yes, you told me.'

The pillow and blanket were gone now.

'When she was awake, she sat in meditation until what they call "the trance" took over and she'd start to sing. Many people came to listen; her voice attracts people. It's because she sings as if she's right there telling us what's going on in Gesar's world! So many people came. We opened your window so more could listen from the courtyard. In whatever weather. Huddled around a big fire drinking tea or *chang*, they would listen to learn the story.'

'Did she finish the story?'

'They say it can never finish. But I had not heard so much of the story before.'

Samphel came in the room. His mood was pleasant but I could tell he had serious matters to discuss.

'Chuang, I mean, Chodak-la,' Samphel started with a trace of self-consciousness over my new name, 'we've run into some difficulties with the nomads. Lobsang is against the cooperative.'

'Don't trouble him with this now!' Zema scolded her husband, 'he's not well enough yet.'

'No! Please,' I insisted, 'I want to know what's going on.'

Exasperated, Zema walked out.

'Lobsang's determined to keep the tribes free of communist ideas and reforms no matter what we do in the villages and towns.'

'Have you invited him to come here?' I asked. 'We should talk to him!'

It stopped snowing and the air warmed up. All of next week was warmer. The river and streams were swollen. Thick morning mist filled the valley with a damp cold that penetrated to the bone. This cold was worse than the crisp freeze under cloudless skies. Fortunately, the mist burned off by late morning.

As soon as I felt able, I asked Zema if I might move to the more secluded room, upstairs on the roof.

'Dechen is using it, but I'll ask her.'

'Oh, never mind then.'

'Never mind what?' Dechen asked as she came into my room.

'I asked about moving to the upstairs room. Zema said you were using it.'

'I have been since you got better, but only for meditation. You can move there if you'll let me join you for meditations.'

'Certainly, I'd be honoured,' I replied quickly.

While I continued to recover, I stayed up there. Dechen joined me for regular morning and early evening meditation sessions, but otherwise left me to my writing. I continued to write my personal journal in English but I also wrote reports in Chinese, as if to Comrade Li. I had no intention of sending them; least of all to Commander Deng.

Lobsang showed up unexpectedly one day; he was gruff, hostile, wanting to have his say and depart as quickly as possible. Several nomad chieftains, the ones Samphel had encouraged to join the cooperative, were with Lobsang. They arrived with a determination to put an end to further discussions about the nomadic tribes joining Mola Cooperative. Rinpoche and Samphel managed to prevail on them to stay overnight by enticing to hear the beautiful *babdrungma*, Dechen-la, sing about King Gesar.

Lobsang, like so many Khampa warlords, imagined himself a reincarnation of the ancient king and could not refuse a chance to hear the Gesar story, especially from the beautiful singer he had heard so much about.

Lobsang and the other chieftains were entertained in Zema's kitchen while a large tent was pitched in one of the fields outside the village. Palden Rinpoche and Dechen quickly organized a special performance.

The surprise on Lobsang's face when I walked into the kitchen made me chuckle.

'You!' he said, 'the quick communist who put my man down? We thought you were dead! Everyone says that traitor Tenzin killed you!'

'Very nearly,' Samphel said, 'we brought him here after we rescued him, and kept his situation secret.'

'Thanks to the kindness of Zema-la,' I said indicating my gratitude with a bow toward her, 'and a few others, I was able to fight a fever and fully recover from several injuries.'

'You will also be interested,' Samphel added, 'that he has taken refuge in the Three Jewels and has become Palden Rinpoche's student.'

Lobsang regarded me with a silent, penetrating stare; searching, perhaps, for sincerity, or traces of superficiality. He was having trouble believing a Chinese communist could follow Buddha dharma.

'I'm still a communist,' I dared to say, 'because I believe people should be free of oppression, but my kind of communism is different from what those Party officials in faraway places are trying to enforce here.'

This got Lobsang's and the other chieftain's attention immediately. I had aroused their curiosity by openly defying the Communist Party.

I recognized Gyaltsen among the chieftains, and acknowledged him with a hand on his shoulder and a quick *'Tashi Delek'*. He smiled and returned my greeting.

I also recognized the man sitting next to Lobsang as the one who had challenged me at the tavern in Lithang.

'I believe we've met before but I've forgotten your name,' I said with a quick glance at Lobsang.

'Dorje,' the man replied with a grin. He seemed pleased that I'd remembered him.

I sat next to Dorje and began explaining my understanding of Buddha dharma to the whole group of nomad chieftains.

'It is true what the Buddha says; everyone wants to be happy, all of us deserve a good life without suffering. The way

371

to a good life for everyone is to regard all people, both friends and enemies, as equals. Instead of always separating ourselves as "us" and "them", we must see with the clear eyes of Buddha dharma that all people possess Buddha nature, whether they acknowledge it or not.' I smiled at Lobsang gently, and then continued, 'As followers of Buddha dharma we try to awaken all people to this truth by understanding their suffering, and showing them how to find happiness. This is the Middle Way, the way of non-violence, the way of Buddha dharma.'

Lobsang squirmed. He didn't like the implied criticism of his use of violence, or even that this behaviour was in opposition to the way of Buddha dharma. And it didn't help that the criticism came from a Chinese communist! Anticipating an explosive response, I quickly continued.

'I came to Kham as an idealistic communist. I truly wanted to help all of you live a better life and be happy, but I got discouraged when I found out how the Party goes about things here. I nearly gave up because they began to impose their ideas and reforms through the threat of violence. This only added to the suffering and oppression they assumed they were alleviating. Thanks to the people of Kham and all my friends here, I am learning how we can improve our daily lives while still devoting ourselves to discovering our Buddha nature.'

Lobsang was still listening.

'Now, let me explain why we want the free nomads to join our cooperative. We have less than one year to prove to the officials in Chengdu that we can make positive social and economic changes that will meet, and even surpass, the requirements of the Communist Party. We need to show them that all levels of Khampa society can live in harmony according to the highest communist ideals,' I explained, adding, 'we know we can produce much more than we use ourselves. Just look and see how rich we have made the landlords, nobles, and lamas! But with shared ownership of all produce, we can improve life for all of us, not just those who are already rich and powerful. We can provide all kinds of services that will benefit every member of the cooperative. By joining us, you will not lose your freedom. If you don't join us, you will be forced to settle in villages very much against your will.'

'They'll have to fight us first!' one of the chieftains butted in angrily.

'That will be a fight you will lose in the end,' I retorted. 'Do you know how many soldiers they'll bring up here next spring because of your attack in Lithang?'

I let that sink in. Lobsang remained silent. He was considering rather than dismissing what I'd said. A glance at Samphel was enough to know I'd said enough.

Tashi came up the stairs from the courtyard, leaned on my back and whispered in my ear.

'You must excuse me,' I apologized and stood up. With a bow, I added, 'Rinpoche-la has called me.'

Rinpoche wanted me to play the part of Gesar in the drama.

'Won't word get out that I'm playing the part of Gesar?'

'That deal was with Nawang and Tenzin. But they are gone now!'

I couldn't refuse. I found Dechen sitting in meditation inside the tent. Guests were gathering to watch us perform. Rinpoche told me to sit opposite Dechen. She smiled when I sat down and handed me a bowl. I took a drink, gave the bowl back and watched her take a drink, too, assuming it was one of

Rinchen-la's potions. We waited in deep, open-eyed meditation; her beautiful eyes on mine.

Rinpoche cleared his throat outside of the tent siding. It was the signal we were waiting for; all was ready.

'The *Dakini* Manene descends,' Rinpoche said to begin the performance, 'from the frozen starry sky into the palace bedroom where Gesar, King of Ling, sits in deep meditation. She takes his hands and, looking into his eyes, establishes her place in his heart.'

As Rinpoche began playing the small drum and occasionally blowing the horn, the side of the tent opened to reveal the two of us looking into each other's eyes. My hands were in Dechen's just as Rinpoche described. The audience's reaction was mixed; they were unfamiliar with Dechen's innovative style of drama yet they were intrigued and curious to find out what was going on.

Dechen began to sing and the audience was drawn in.

'Gesar, Great Warrior King of Ling, with the lightning sword of Wisdom and arrows of wind, riding Khyang Go Karkar, the miraculous horse, you radiate courageous confidence.'

Dechen rose to her feet and moved toward the audience, stopping directly before Lobsang.

'Even the bravest warrior may lose his way in a dense forest on a moonless night. He may be attacked by wolves, or childhood terrors. He may feel he is going mad. Wild with dread, he might fall from an unseen cliff.

Dechen turned back toward me.

'O brave Gesar, this world is just such a dark forest where love becomes brutal selfishness, wisdom becomes

374

cold calculation, prosperity, rabid greed, and justice, a means of oppression.'

Dechen turned her pleading gaze to include all the chieftains and the audience from the village. Each eye was transfixed on her radiant face, each ear waiting to hear her next word.

'Even now, this land is ruled by lustful and envious greed, it is a playground of cruelty and injustice. All are easy prey, all are pawns of demon lords lusting for death. From each of the four directions, great demon lords send evil emissaries to undermine Ling. Entering through the gates of selfishness, they enslave and delude, consuming and wasting the earth and all who dwell here.'

Lobsang and the other chieftains recognized how Dechen, as Manene, described current conditions in Kham. They stirred uneasily. But Dechen turned her back on them and returned to entreat me, as Gesar.

'To defeat them, you have entered their terrible domain. And you, Great Warrior King, must endure their madness. Your life here will be ceaseless warfare. But have courage! Again and again, rouse yourself, raise yourself up. Rely on your discipline, confirm your dignity. Uphold the all-victorious flag of unfailing inspiration.

'Your enemies, in the guise of demonic beings, are hatred and fear, greed and oppression, despair and ignorance. With your lightning sword and wind arrows, shatter their power over the hearts and minds of women and men.

'True warriorship relies only on the truth of your eternal kingdom. Be an unfailing, all-consuming torch, always ablaze to restore hope and dignity in the hearts of women and men.'

Rinpoche closed the side of the tent to conceal us from the audience. Still rattling the drum, he began playing his *drangyen* and provided a brief account of Gesar's conquest of Lutzen, while Zema-la, Tashi, and Rinchen-la scrambled to put an elaborate chuba on me. They did their best to make me look like Gesar, complete with armour, sword, bow, arrows, and flags protruding from the back of my helmet skyward.

'Gesar, Lion King of Ling,' Rinpoche concluded, 'having defeated the demon Lutzen by cutting off all 12 of his heads is about to return to Ling. The demon king's wife, however, pleads with Gesar to give her dead husband instructions that will liberate him. Gesar agrees, even though Lutzen is a demon, and not a mortal man like you and me.'

Rinpoche bowed and pulled the siding open again. When they saw me transformed, everyone gasped. Lobsang jumped to his feet and was about to protest angrily when I turned my eyes on him and began singing as if to him.

'**Lutzen, Demon Death Lord of the North, I am Gesar, Lion King of Ling, because of me you have known fear and have been vanquished!**'

I had absolutely no idea where these words of power were coming from.

'**Together, we have played out a certain drama where you were a demon and I, a king. Now, while I continue to play out my part in this world, you are unfettered. The dark, shifty realm of paranoia you ruled has dissolved. Your mind, once dense with rage and guile, filled with the desire to inflict suffering on others, now abides in pure naked awareness. The seeming opposition between life and death is cut through, and there is only the brilliance of limitless, empty space.**'

Lobsang took his seat again and listened carefully. He accepted that Gesar stood before him singing to the dead demon Lutzen.

'Vivid are the images arising in the great mirror of mind; do not grasp at these phantoms of existence, recognize that the mirror is both mind and beyond mind. Simply rest in wakefulness. Even now you can know the true nature of all beings, the hidden aim and end of all actions, the inner longing of all desires. All is resolved in dazzling measureless freedom. Allow love; do not hold back. Open your heart, Lutzen, be confident. Simply rest in peace and you will be free.'

When I concluded the song, Lobsang sat spellbound. The rest of the audience, too, remained quiet after Rinpoche stopped drumming and closed the tent siding to hide me.

As Dechen and Yangchen removed my costume, I heard Rinpoche and Lobsang in discussion.

'I've never seen a *lhamo* performed so well,' Lobsang admitted, 'nor have I heard that part of the story before. I have only heard songs of warriors telling about their battles.'

'We can only thank Dechen-la for this new vision,' Rinpoche acknowledged.

'How is it that the words spoken by Manene and Gesar so long ago describe what is happening to us right now?'

'You are really quite sharp, Lobsang-la!' Rinpoche said approvingly. 'We say this story is alive when its message directly relates to us today. This only happens when sung by a true *babdrung*. The same demonic powers that oppressed the people in the Kingdom of Ling a thousand years ago afflict us today. Whenever demonic forces appear, they must be opposed by windhorse warriors.'

377

'Windhorse warriors?' Lobsang asked, his curiosity somewhat roused.

'Yes, a warrior empowered to channel basic goodness into the world. A windhorse warrior engages evil forces but inflicts no harm on beings possessed by these forces. To do so, he must be wise and filled with compassion. This is the way of Buddha dharma.'

'Is this what you are teaching at your hermitage?'

'Yes,' Rinpoche replied. 'All the young women and men who go, there learn mindfulness and how to engage in non-violent confrontation.'

Inside the tent, my attention turned to Dechen. I could tell she was bursting to say something but could not speak without being overheard. Once our costumes were off and we'd put our winter *chuba*s back on, she thrust a whole pile of garments into my arms and pointed back to Zema's house. I followed her across the fields, through Zema's gate and into the storage room on the ground floor. As soon as I put down my armful, Dechen threw her arms around me and planted a kiss on my mouth.

'Oh, Chodak-la, that was spectacular!' she said. Then, blushing, she collected herself and added quickly, 'Rinpoche and Yangchen were convinced you could do it. It took me longer to be convinced. When you ran off in a huff and got yourself lost, I told Rinpoche it was a mistake to trust you. But Rinpoche and Wangdu wanted to give you a second chance. In the end, they were right and I'm so glad.'

I must have looked surprised and foolish because Dechen began to giggle like an excited girl, and I knew the kiss was more than enthusiasm about playing the role of Gesar. We kissed again, a little longer this time.

'So what happens now?' I was thinking about my role as Gesar as much as I was about the giddy feelings and long-suppressed desires I had for Dechen. She was now suddenly more than my meditation teacher.

'Ha! Ha! About the Gesar *lhamo* or something else?' She always read me like a book.

'Both,' I said. I was blushing, and tried to look away but her arms were still around me and her eyes, too captivating.

'We're both adults. I'm a modern woman, free to follow my heart. What about you?'

'Until... I mean, it was always only Jiachen before,' I stammered.

'Yes, my entangled sister!' she scoffed and threw a playful dart of pretended jealousy. 'It's not as if you and I are strangers.'

'You misunderstand me,' I said quickly. 'Since the moment we met, I have longed for this to happen, Dechen, I'm so happy!'

We kissed again. Like a dam overflowing, my heart flooded with fire; we shared the same divine fire of love. Recognizing the sacred bond between us, we looked deeply into one another through the gates of our souls, our eyes. How good and whole we felt! It was like being reunited after a long separation; like arriving home!

'We need to talk with Rinpoche,' Dechen eventually said. 'Yangchen, for one, anticipated this and will be delighted. Ama-la, and even Ba-la, will be too.'

We emerged from the storeroom to find Rinpoche and Lobsang making their way upstairs, followed by Samphel and the chieftain guests. Zema had invited the principle guests for the evening meal, with rounds of *chang* beforehand.

Rinpoche gave us a quizzical look, and then an approving wink as we watched him lead the guests past us.

In a state of unspeakable joy, we followed the last of the guests upstairs.

◆◆

The discussion in Zema's kitchen continued, with Rinpoche and Lobsang doing most of the talking, though Samphel, Dechen and I had our say, too. Lobsang and the chieftains listened to our arguments for joining the cooperative, and asked good questions. They saw the wisdom of pre-empting the Party's imposition of reforms but still resisted joining us.

There would be reforms, I explained, but our reforms would be an equitable redistribution of herds according to the ability of families to manage them on available grazing grounds. Produce such as butter, meat, hides, wool, and even dung for manure and fuel would need to be equitably distributed. The cooperative would see to it that every family had enough to eat and enough to trade for other provisions.

'Nomads are free!' one of the chieftains pointed out, 'we will keep ourselves free of the Chinese! And we know about the corrupt "sweet mouths" of Lhasa, and those who control the wealth in our towns and villages. We stay away from them.'

'True,' Rinpoche tentatively agreed, 'but you have your own means of control and oppression within your own society. Besides that, you bring hardship and suffering on caravans travelling through your grasslands.'

Resorting to banditry, Rinpoche pointed out, was not only against the law but against Buddha dharma. Lobsang and the chieftain who spoke scowled but did not counter Rinpoche's charge.

'You said earlier, Rinpoche-la,' Lobsang observed, 'that violent warfare against the Reds was also against Buddha dharma, and that we should be windhorse warriors. Can you explain to us what you mean by this?'

'Our great ancestor Gesar did not wage war out of selfish need, nationalistic pride, or racial hatred. As an enlightened being, he waged war on the evils that deluded his people. These evils were personified as demon kings of the four directions. Today our own people are enslaved by fear, greed, pride and hatred just as people were in Gesar's day. This enemy takes form not only as the so-called liberation forces of Chinese communism, but also the injustice, prejudice, and oppression within our own society.'

Lobsang frowned, as if he was somewhat unable to accept Rinpoche's statement equating the evils of Tibetan society with Chinese communism.

'In every part of society,' Rinpoche went on to explain, 'in the farming valleys and on the open grasslands, we are facing severe consequences for years of ignorance and disregard of the way of life King Gesar established for us a thousand years ago, based on Buddha dharma.'

'Buddha dharma is under threat,' Lobsang said returning to the question of warfare against the Reds. 'It is our duty to defend it.'

'Buddha dharma is not defended,' Rinpoche replied vehemently, 'by the slaughter of young farm boys who don't have the guidance or understanding to know what they are doing. But you are right, Buddha dharma is under threat. The way to protect it against truly powerful evil forces is to open our eyes and wake up to the way we should live. Buddha dharma is defended by practicing compassion.'

Lobsang was nodding his head but he looked down at the carpet.

'As I see it,' Rinpoche continued, 'there are three options before us. The first is to let the Reds come here to make us their slaves. If we let the Chinese Communist Party carry out reforms as they want to, we will suffer because they do not understand our way of life and how to live on our land. The second option is to resist their imposed reforms by taking up arms and defending our freedom. And if we drive the Reds out, it will be at great cost; there will be too much suffering— on both sides. In the end, this is never a victory; it is a loss, a moral loss.'

'How can you say that?' a chieftain objected proudly.

'Hear me out,' Rinpoche said calmly. 'The third choice, what you might call the Middle Way, is the way of Buddha dharma. This demands a shift in the way we normally think. In this world, we either run away from a threat or we stand to fight. Isn't that right? The first two choices I mentioned are these kinds of instinctive responses. If we choose the first response—fear of the enemy and submission—we are really running away from our responsibility to counter their control over us. We end up letting them control us. In choosing the second response, we must fight for our homes, our families, and our Buddha dharma. Fighting makes us blind with hatred and suffering. In our blindness, we won't see that we are killing human beings rather than fighting the evil forces that are the real problem. Both of these choices embrace violence; there is either violence against ourselves or used by both sides against each other.'

The chieftains squirmed and, like Lobsang, stared at the floor as if Rinpoche was chastising them.

'Our only real option is the Middle Way. This is the way of non-violence,' Rinpoche continued. 'This approach is about understanding the situation clearly enough to put an end to fear and aggression. Violence is not necessary. In fact, it is counter-productive.'

'We must resist,' I interjected, 'but resistance does not always mean the use of violent force.'

Lobsang turned to me with an angry expression. But Dechen spoke before he could respond.

'What Chodak-la said is absolutely right, Lobsang-la,' Dechen said supportively. 'Resistance does not always mean violence. Did you hear how we stopped Tenzin and Gan's troops when they came here to collect grain tax? Our warriors used no weapons.'

'I heard about it, yes,' Lobsang said disinterestedly.

Rinpoche shifted his position to change the mood and the direction of the conversation.

'Chodak-la is more than my student, Lobsang-la,' Rinpoche said, as he reached over and put his hand on my shoulder. 'I regard him as my younger brother. In Shanghai, he was the student of Master Tashi—the same man who taught me and Gyatotsang Akong in Mongolia. You remember Akong, Samphel's older brother?'

'I remember him.'

'This Chinese communist is more like one of us. No, he is more like we all should be. As a young man, he was educated to think like a modern man with no understanding about the real purpose of life. But he was fortunate to learn a few things from Master Tashi that helped him when he came here. He was ready to grasp Buddha dharma quickly, and has proven himself to be an excellent trainer of non-violent methods of defence.'

I was listening as carefully as Lobsang.

'My sister, Yangchen-la, lived in Shanghai,' Rinpoche continued. 'On my suggestion, she looked for and found Master Tashi because I knew he had gone to Shanghai from Mongolia. Together, they identified this man as a '*tulku*', an evolved being, when he was a child. Yangchen-la kept an eye on him, especially after he fell in love with my grandniece. It was actually because of my grandniece that he became a communist, and eventually came to Lithang.

'During his recent illness, he fell into a trance. Dechen-la recognized his condition and guided his spirit into the Kingdom of Ling. When this happens to someone, they become a *babdrung* and return to our world, able to recite the songs from personal experience. This evening, we witnessed that he is indeed a *babdrungpa*!

'It is because he is a *tulku* and a *babdrungpa* that I welcome Chodak-la among us. His communist background means he can help us find our way through the delusions spread among us. He is showing us how to resist them.'

I was surprised to learn that they considered me a *tulku*! It was true, Master Tashi had taught me more than I realized at the time. Now that I thought about it, I could see how he had done this. At every opportunity, Master Tashi insisted I pay attention to the present moment, to experience what was happening without judgement, without falling prey to negative thinking or emotions. If I missed a target, he would instruct me to accept it without dwelling on my shortcomings or blaming it on something. 'Just try again,' he would say, 'and focus on the right way to shoot the arrow again.' Master Tashi was teaching me mindfulness; he was teaching me how to live free from attachment to the contents of my mind, and to be the witness of my experiences rather than falling prey to self-conscious evaluations and attachments to the experiences themselves. He was implanting a non-dualistic, inclusive way of thinking.

Lobsang regarded me quietly.

'If you see him as your brother,' Lobsang suddenly said with a wide grin as he slapped my back, 'I will accept him, too.'

Though Lobsang said he accepted me, we could see he still held on to some reservations.

'I have one question for you, Rinpoche,' Lobsang said in a more serious tone. 'How the hell is non-violence supposed to work against soldiers with guns and flying machines in the sky that drop bombs?'

I found myself, like Lobsang, questioning how non-violent methods could be used to successfully halt PLA military might but Rinpoche suddenly stood up and interrupted my thoughts.

'Everyone, come outside to the fields,' he said. 'I think we need a little demonstration.'

We got up, went downstairs and out to the fields again. It was nearly sunset. Most of the nomads and villagers were gathered around campfires near Samphel's festival tent because Wangdu and several of the warriors from the hermitage were serving *chang* and refreshments. Rinpoche spoke briefly with Wangdu.

After Wangdu and several warriors cleared some space, several of Lobsang's warriors were invited to attack them, using their swords and knives. Shouting aggressively and swords drawn, Lobsang's men rushed toward Wangdu and his unarmed companions. There was some hesitance at first but when the first of Lobsang's men was disarmed and held on the ground, the others became more determined to make contact with their weapons. Very quickly, all of Lobsang's men were disarmed.

A warrior standing off to the side had a bow and arrow. Lobsang shouted an order and the archer pulled back the bow and shot an arrow. Wangdu plucked the arrow from the air with his hand. A gasp of surprise escaped many lips.

'That's all very good and interesting,' Lobsang admitted, 'but those are all ancient weapons. Can he dodge a bullet?'

Lobsang produced a pistol from his chuba and pointed it at Wangdu. Since I was standing beside him, I snatched the pistol from Lobsang's hand before he could fire.

'That, of course, is a valid point,' Rinpoche said to Lobsang, who was rubbing his wrist and glaring at me. 'Since it is nearly, yes nearly, impossible to dodge a bullet, it is best to never get in front of a loaded gun. We have to be smarter than the aggressor and find ways to avoid or stop them from using guns on us.'

Lobsang was annoyed and unconvinced.

'We will use our guns and our swords,' a chieftain shouted. 'We are thirsty for the blood of the *gyame*! This is our home and we will defend it!'

'This is our home,' Rinpoche agreed, 'but we can defend it without spilling the blood of innocent boys from the lowlands who are forced to follow orders. They build roads so they can bring in thousands, hundreds of thousands of soldiers and settlers. This is what must be stopped. We must block the roads, undermine their ability to move around and communicate, prevent them from feeding their troops. All this can be done without spilling human blood. We can destroy roads and property without killing people. This is the Middle Way, we must not commit violence against living beings.'

Lobsang listened. He nodded his head thoughtfully.

'Teach us this way,' he said, 'but we will keep our guns.'

'Of course, keep your guns,' Rinpoche said, 'there may come a time when guns are necessary. But we must avoid using them as much as possible. There are hundreds of options to try before guns are necessary. Let's explore them!'

Public Meeting

The new cooperative took shape quickly. Lobsang surprised us by becoming instrumental in persuading the local nomads to join the cooperative, and encouraged his warriors to attend our training program at the hermitage.

With Tenzin out of the way, Dechen and Yangchen made Gyawa their home base. Dawa and Thampa were very happy to have the family together. Pema and Thupten moved to Mola and worked closely with Zema and Samphel. Rinpoche, Wangdu, and I were busy with training at the hermitage or travelling to sort out details with various villages or clans.

Women took charge of organizing the distribution of grazing grounds for each clan's herds because they knew the grasslands and could make these decisions. The men, they said, could not settle disputes without shouting at each other, which too often resulted in the use of fists—sometimes knives and swords! They happily sent their men to the hermitage for training in non-violence and mindfulness. As a result, they began to see changes in their husbands' and sons' behaviour; showing more respect and willingness to share in the work of home and herd.

Dechen was everyone's spiritual advisor in Gyawa, Mola, and out on the grasslands. Everywhere she went women begged her to sing to them, and she used these opportunities to teach them mindfulness and the central importance of compassion.

Dechen and I were so busy with all these activities we seldom saw each other. I knew Dechen wasn't avoiding me; she was as eager to be with me as I with her, but we were both responding to the urgency of our mission. Whenever possible, if I knew she was nearby, I would make an unexpected visit to the nomadic camp or village where she was teaching. Our meetings were brief but fulfilling, even if they just gave us a chance to look into one another's eyes from a distance. Once in a while we had time for a short conversation, but the two of us never had time alone. Our yearning for each other only increased.

As in Gyawa, many residents in Mola township were indebted to money lenders in Lithang or to lamas at monasteries. Since the area was extensive and bringing the entire community together was difficult, each village sent representatives who met regularly. This body took the name 'Mola Representatives Committee', and took it upon itself to settle all debts. Resources were collected, mostly from wealthier members of the community as a levelling measure. It was now much easier to settle debts than it had been when we started in Gyawa. The looming prospect of enforced communist reforms encouraged many money lenders to accept repayments, or even to forgive debts outright because they feared being regarded negatively by the community and the new communist overlords.

To my surprise one day, Nima, the young monk assistant to the *khenpo* of Lithang Monastery, arrived in Mola with a message for Rinpoche. Nima asked to visit the hermitage and when he saw what was happening there, he asked if he could join us if he got permission from the *khenpo*. He returned a few days later with several other young monks, who asked to be trained in mindful non-violence. Nima also took great interest in how we organized the cooperative. He began to visit villages and nomad camps with Rinpoche or with me.

All of us were well on our way to meeting the required reforms by the end of the year. Our new cooperative clearly demonstrated that the people could voluntarily redistribute land and herds so that everyone enjoyed a healthy and happy life. Our success, I told everyone, obliged the Party to let us do communism our way, the Tibetan way!

It became somewhat embarrassing to me that everywhere I went, people began referring to me as Gesar! I assumed this was because of the *lhamo* performances but they insisted it was because I had shown them how to live according to Buddha dharma. Often, it was just a whisper to one another behind my back but once in a while an enthusiastic group of people gushed about Gesar directly to me, and asked me to put my hand on their heads in blessing. Samphel went along with all of this and insisted I comply with these requests. Even Nima encouraged the people to regard me as Gesar.

Winter turned to spring, and with it, the underlying threat that the PLA would return. Once snow on the high pass above Dartsendo melted, thousands of Red troops would arrive by the truck load and spread across the plateau.

To delay the arrival of PLA troops, Lobsang and Wangdu sent warriors to create landslides along the motor road. The more places we could make impassable, the longer it would take to repair. We concentrated on the branch of the road being built to Lithang. The more northerly main road that went to Chamdo, and on to Lhasa, was a secondary target as it didn't impact us directly.

Meanwhile, with the arrival of spring rains, fields were ploughed, fertilized, and planted. Calves, lambs, colts, and kids were born. Herds were moved to greening meadows higher in the mountains. In general, both cooperatives were off to a good start as spring turned to summer.

As our cooperatives took shape and expanded, we realized how much we needed Kunchen's support. As *khenpo* of the large Gelugpa, or Yellow Hat School of Tibetan Buddhism, Kunchen would be very influential if he agreed to support our cause. Once Nima and his fellow monks began helping us, I realized how much the monks and lamas were in contact with people all over the district.

With this in mind, Rinpoche—accompanied by Nima— made several visits to Lithang, and had long discussions with the *khenpo* and other leading lamas. The lamas often found it difficult to relate to our suggestions, and each idea was carefully measured against their traditional teachings. When the *khenpo* could join the discussions, he helped cut through most of the nit-picking. Rinpoche was grateful, but even so, he sensed Kunchen could not fully support our efforts.

'As you know,' Rinpoche said to me after returning from Lithang with Nima one day, 'our monasteries own vast tracts of land and large herds managed by local people. Monasteries have two, maybe three, options. One option involves joining cooperatives with the people so that monks and lamas work in the fields alongside everyone else in the community. The second option is to relinquish ownership of land and herds while continuing to live as before in the monasteries, and being totally dependent on the good will of the people for their survival.'

'I assume the monks and lamas prefer the second option,' I said, 'but that's problematic because the Party will see them as freeloaders.'

'Certainly the older, more conservative monks,' Nima observed, 'will resist any changes to their accustomed lifestyle.'

'That's right,' Rinpoche agreed, 'Kunchen suggested as much.'

'As I see it, a third option would allow monks and nuns to pursue their spiritual vocations,' Nima added, 'while also working to support ourselves.'

'But how much time,' Rinpoche asked, 'will monks and lamas be able to devote to spiritual practices and services to the people if they also work in the fields?'

'I think there's time enough for both,' Nima observed. 'Our monastic communities could do with some shaking up. I'm sure a daily routine could be organized to provide ample time for manual labour, study, performance of religious duties for the community, and spiritual practice.'

'The monastic life has its comforts and rewards,' Rinpoche noted. 'Too many settle into normal consciousness and finish life focused on daily needs and concerns like an ordinary person. Meditation and mindfulness are often not their highest priority.'

'And they should be!' Nima said, 'I've learned that here. Not at the monastery! From my own experience over the past few months, I've realized how few monks actually attend to their own spiritual growth. Instead, they use their time getting involved in things they shouldn't—like trade and money lending. Monastic communities should join local cooperatives. Monks should live and work like everyone else while contributing to the spiritual well-being of the community.'

'A spiritual revitalization?' Rinpoche asked.

'Exactly!' Nima agreed enthusiastically.

'Isn't it ironic,' I chimed in, 'that communist reforms could drive spiritual revitalization?'

'It's something that a few of our enlightened teachers have been striving to do for over a generation now,' Nima agreed.

'Like you, Rinpoche,' I said.

Nima nodded with a smile. His respect for Rinpoche was obvious.

'So where are the other enlightened teachers?' I asked Rinpoche. 'Shouldn't the monasteries be full of them? Isn't it time all monasteries become places where the local people come to learn to be compassionate, mindful and non-violent? The monks should be the ones leading the people in social and economic reforms. They should be serving the people as teachers and protectors and guardians of the peace, like Gesar's warriors!'

'Exactly!' Nima exclaimed again, he liked the expression. 'They should be the best windhorse warriors.'

'Slow down, both of you!' Rinpoche said responding to our enthusiasm.

'I completely agree with Chodak-la!' Nima said with a whole-hearted smile.

'That's what monks should be, of course,' Rinpoche agreed. 'And I've suggested to Kunchen that monks be trained like we are training our warriors. He's considering it, along with the suggestion to prioritize meditation.'

'Dechen has often expressed her interest in teaching nuns,' Nima reported.

'That is vitally important,' Rinpoche agreed.

About 10 days later, Rinpoche and Nima returned from another visit to Lithang with good news. Nima, with Rinpoche's support, made a good case for the monastery to initiate a cooperative venture with the townspeople of Lithang. Furthermore, the *khenpo* agreed to promote the idea of monasteries leading the initiative to form cooperatives throughout Lithang district.

Since Kunchen's influence was widespread, monasteries throughout Tibet heard about our idea of pre-empting communist reforms, and we began to get requests from far and wide for advice and training as many varieties of cooperatives prepared to form.

Meanwhile, a report came from Dartsendo saying Commander Deng was on his way back to Lithang. A huge convoy had made it that far but could not come over the pass because of a late, heavy snowfall. Lobsang's 'engineers' were preparing surprises for the convoy that would set back the completion of the road. He was determined to prevent the transportation of heavy weapons and supplies needed for a large army.

Though we did our best to delay him, Deng arrived without his convoy of trucks in early June. He had to abandon the convoy and, protected by a contingent of his best soldiers, arrived on horseback as he had the previous year. We were dismayed to learn that Nawang and Tenzin were also back in Lithang.

Deng had not forgotten the fury of the Khampa attack the previous year and, along with Nawang and Tenzin, stayed inside the heavily guarded military compound. Their attempts to negotiate with the various factions of the district failed unless Kunchen Khenpo was also involved. This greatly irritated Deng and, of course, Kunchen took pleasure in confusing and obstructing the commander's efforts. Kunchen informed Deng of the formation of 'hundreds of cooperatives' throughout Lithang district and beyond. This was a little over optimistic, perhaps, but it was true that more and more communities wanted to forestall Party reforms by voluntary redistribution of land and property, and forming a cooperative. We promoted the idea that this would give the Party no justifiable reason to introduce their own policies.

'What about Comrade Chuang?' Deng asked Kunchen, 'is it true he is dead?'

'I do not know,' Kunchen lied, 'but these cooperatives have formed because of his influence. He has been a great inspiration for us!'

Kunchen and Commander Deng, both shrewd politicians, enjoyed playing guessing games and manipulating each other. From his side, Deng played along with the idea that the cooperatives were a positive development, even though he had already shown us during the previous fall that he and the Party had other intentions. Kunchen guessed Deng was bluffing and would show his hand once the rest of his troops arrived.

In preparation for a drastic change in the balance of power, Kunchen called a public meeting at the monastery.

⊶⊷

Dressed like ancient warriors and carrying banners, a procession of Wangdu's and Lobsang's warriors, numbering over three hundred men and women, accompanied us to Lithang. Our group, also colourfully attired, included Samphel, Zema, Thampa, Dawa, Rinpoche, Yangchen, Dechen, Thupten, Pema, and several others. We were a sight right out of the legend of King Gesar, and created quite a stir as we approached Lithang from the ridge above to enter the monastery in grand style.

A feast had been prepared for the monks and our own group of travellers at the monastery. Following the feast, we presented a short preview of the *lhamo* we had planned. We hoped this would introduce the monastic community to the merits of the Gesar story. Though the Gesar story was popular among the lay people, the educated monastic community regarded it as fictitious, and a lesser teaching device.

The public meeting was the following day. In the morning, chairs for various VIPs were set up just outside the main temple doors at the top of the wide stairway. Dechen would stand between the VIPs and the audience of townspeople, villagers, nomads, monks, nuns, and warriors, who would sit or stand on the flagstones of the courtyard. Thus positioned, Dechen could sing directly to the leaders and to the people. Our plan, worked out with Kunchen, depended on the presence of representatives from every political faction of Lithang district, including the Communist Party. Important nomadic chieftains, head men from the larger villages and towns, and important lamas were the VIPs we had invited.

Since Commander Deng, along with Tenzin and Nawang, assumed that I was dead, I was to remain out of view. I made sure I could still see and hear what was going on in the courtyard below from a window on the second floor of a building overlooking the courtyard.

I watched as Deng arrived with Tenzin, Nawang, Major Gan, and two other PLA officers. They joined Kunchen, Samphel, Thampa, Lobsang, Gyaltsen, Sonam, and several other village and nomadic leaders, and they all took their seats in the triple row of chairs facing the audience in the shade of a white canopy.

As expected, a number of Deng's soldiers accompanied him to the monastery gates. The monks protested when the soldiers tried to enter with their guns but were unsuccessful. A few soldiers stood guard inside the gates but most moved close to the VIP seats, and made their presence obvious to the entire gathering.

Everyone grew quiet as soon as the small drum and horn could be heard. I knew Yangchen would be playing them behind the VIP area. When all was still, Dechen appeared dressed as Manene, Guru Rinpoche's messenger. She began to sing.

'**Within the Kingdom of Ling, there are those filled with lustful thoughts and envious greed. Selfishness deludes them and makes them easy pawns of demon lords.**'

I smiled sadly to myself. I could see that the message of the song was so easily lost on Deng; it was flying over the heads of his accomplices, too. And Tenzin, poor man, was practically drooling as he watched Dechen's every move! Filled with lust, he

397

was obviously not paying attention to the message, and clearly unresponsive to the irritated commander's many questions.

My attention was on the audience but when I returned it to Dechen's song, she was directing a message to the young Gesar. She was looking directly at me in my hiding place.

'**You must raise unfailing windhorse, the power of basic goodness, and follow the Middle Path across this roiling sea of confusion called the human realm.**'

Her words penetrated deeply.

'**These demon lords and their hordes are the perverted face of liberation. They delude minds by spreading the belief that freedom can be purchased with power and wealth. They undermine basic goodness in the hearts and minds of virtuous people and nations by destroying confidence in the goodness of egoless action.**'

Demon lords and their hordes were none other than the oppressive power of worldly systems gone terribly wrong. Power, and lust for power, had taken over the otherwise good, original intentions of the Party. The current leadership, and the hordes they controlled, were now bent on a perverse interpretation of liberation, limited to the external, objective world instead of the liberation of hearts and minds into joyful human fulfilment.

Against these demonic forces, I felt powerless, inadequate! How did Dechen and Rinpoche expect me to do anything significant to stop this poison?

Then, as if calling to me from the past, Jiachen's voice echoed in my heart, 'Awaken my people'.

I had it wrong. I, we, could not stop the poison. We could not defeat the demon lords and their hordes. All we could do

was awaken the people! It was up to all of us to wake up and
deny these demonic power over us.

'You must raise unfailing windhorse, the power of basic
goodness, and follow the Middle Path across this roiling sea
of confusion called the human realm.'

She repeated this as a directive with her gaze seemingly
to the sky but on me.

'O Great Dragon Lord, the time is now! You must
resist demonic forces. Otherwise, great evil will continue to
infect the earth. The Great Guru Rinpoche's will is your own
true nature. Your vow is to wakefulness. You must act, and
act now!'

Dechen paused while the drum and horn seemingly grew
very loud. She looked directly at each of the seated dignitaries,
lingering longest on Commander Deng. Turning around, she
looked to the great crowd of townspeople, villagers, nomads,
nuns, and monks who filled the courtyard. She looked at them,
making each of them feel they had made eye contact with her.
Having touched everyone's heart, she concluded her song with
the chorus.

'You must raise unfailing windhorse, the power of basic
goodness, and follow the Middle Path across this roiling sea
of confusion called the human realm.'

As if this was her signal, Yangchen's drum beat came to
a sudden end.

With a deep bow, Dechen finished her performance and
ran down the steps, and crossed the courtyard in front of the
crowd toward the building I was in. Rinpoche took the stage
and announced that a public meeting would be held shortly, for
which everyone was asked to stay.

I hurried downstairs to meet Dechen. We embraced and clung to each other for a few moments.

'You heard Manene's message?' she asked.

'Yes, it was very direct!' I replied. 'But it went right over the heads of Deng and his like!'

'That's fine, everyone else got it! That's what we want.'

Dechen and I made our way to the great hall so we could hear when to make my appearance. As soon as we got there we heard a commotion in the great hall, and peeked through curtains in a doorway. We had expected the general public to begin as soon as Dechen left the stage, so we were surprised by what we saw.

Deng had stepped across the high wooden threshold into the great hall of the temple with his shoes on, and walked directly toward the Buddha statues. Major Gan, two PLA officers, Nawang and Tenzin, followed close behind. Several monks hurried into the temple when they saw Deng's group entering. They shouted in horror to see Deng and his company desecrating the sacred space.

Deng stopped to light a cigarette with a butter lamp flame. Then he went to the great chair, sat down and, making himself comfortable, threw his feet up on the altar table, knocking over offering bowls in the process. He urged the others to sit on the desks that held sacred texts. To do so, the men stepped on the carpets and monks' cushions with their shoes.

'Where is that girl?' Deng demanded in Chinese when he saw the monks. Tenzin immediately translated. 'We want to see her. Bring her here!'

Kunchen, Rinpoche, Lobsang, and the other Khampa dignitaries, having taken the time to remove their shoes, entered the temple just then. Kunchen was outraged and stormed up to Commander Deng.

'How dare you desecrate this temple?' Kunchen shouted. 'Are you deliberately being discourteous? Please leave your shoes outside the door, do not smoke and do not sit where you are not invited to sit.'

Deng ignored the *khenpo* as his armed soldiers entered the temple. He ordered his soldiers to approach. They hurried to his side in a show of force. The soldiers, at least, showed more respect by running around the carpets and desks.

'Now, tell me,' Deng began arrogantly, 'what is this public meeting all about?'

'You will find out soon enough!' Kunchen declared, his anger not subsiding.

'Where's that girl?' Deng demanded again, 'Nawang tells me she is Tenzin's fiancé.'

Dechen turned immediately and started running back the way we'd come.

Thampa's Dream

It took a long time to persuade Commander Deng to return to the public meeting. Meanwhile, Wangdu and some of his warriors took the initiative and impressed the crowd by demonstrating martial arts skills using long sticks. Dechen and I watched from my hiding place above the courtyard. When Wangdu's warriors finished, a popular male folksinger named Loyang sang and played his *drangyen*. His songs were colourful, romantic, and often humorous. The crowd loved him.

During a particularly lovely song, Commander Deng stormed out of the temple. He rudely pushed Loyang out of the way, glared at the crowd and began screaming in Chinese. Tenzin hurried to his side to translate whenever Deng paused for breath. Once Tenzin began to speak, Deng paced back and forth impatiently, reminding me of my visits to his office.

'We have a message from the Communist Party,' Tenzin translated, proudly using the plural. 'This is the current situation. We have been doing our best to civilize you but you still act like animals! You don't dress like us, you don't speak like us, you don't think like us.'

The crowd reacted with angry shouts and plenty of derisive laughter.

'*Gyame*! You are the animals!' some shouted, 'go back to your pigsty, *gyame*!'

Not knowing Tibetan very well, Deng did not get what was being said. He ignored the people. His attention was on the entrances into the courtyard. Deng's confidence was bolstered when he saw more armed soldiers enter the courtyard: his reinforcements from Dartsendo had arrived.

'So we, the Communist Party of the People's Republic of China,' Tenzin translated and shouted Deng's words, 'have decided to give you a choice.'

I was growing more alarmed with each sentence Deng spouted. What was he up to? His attitude, his statements confirmed that the Party had lost all sense of reason. Demons had truly possessed the Communist Party! Deng, and presumably the Party, were determined to have their revenge for the way the PLA had been driven out last fall.

'This is your choice: the Red Road or the Black Road. Do you understand? There are only two roads—an easy choice—one or the other!'

Now the entire crowd was angry. No more laughter; just seething outrage. Rinpoche, Samphel, Thampa, and Lobsang began conferring with one another. Rinpoche glanced up in our direction as if pleading for us to join him.

'This is it, Chodak!' Dechen clung to my arm as we watched in horror, 'this is your time to act!'

I understood but I could not move.

'What should I say?'

Dechen shook her head as if to say 'no, don't worry about that!'. Instead, she took my hands in hers and looked deep in my eyes.

'Look at me!' she implored, 'you know what to do! Tell the people our vision and be fully confident they will understand! The time is right!'

I nodded. 'You stay here.'

I started to leave but turned back quickly. I gathered her in my arms and gave her a long kiss.

'Oh, Chodak-la,' she said with a pleased grin, 'don't you know by now? I'm your *Dakini*, I'm with you; always. Now go!'

When I got to the great hall of the temple, I found Yangchen near the door. She smiled and said, 'It's your time! Just go out there and be who you are! I'm going upstairs to be with Dechen.'

When she left, I stood where I could not be seen and listened to Deng's venomous spitting as he continued making outrageous demands.

'When the warlords of every tribe and the abbots of every monastery in Lithang surrender all arms and ammunition to the People's Liberation Army, when they turn over their fields and herds to the Collective, when every household in towns and villages and out on the grasslands willingly surrenders all their weapons and surplus property for redistribution, you will be walking the Red Road!'

This was clearly more than the people could tolerate. Many stood up and began shouting. 'Our cooperatives fulfil these demands! Honour our cooperatives! Honour our cooperatives!'

PLA troops responded by holding their rifles in ready position. Some troops moved into the crowd threateningly.

Deng continued to ignore the crowd's response.

'The Red Road!' Tenzin repeated louder. 'That is the only road to happiness, harmony, and prosperity. Only under the red flag of communism will you find liberation.'

Angry rumblings from the crowd grew more intense.

'If you all resist!' he glared threateningly, 'then that is the Black Road.'

Tenzin was thoroughly energized by the power he now seemed to possess, even though it was entirely vicarious! He raised his voice to demand a decision.

'You decide! ...Now!'

The crowd, however, became deathly silent in response. It was so obvious there was no choice.

Commander Deng, feeling pleased with himself and, therefore, slightly magnanimous, turned to Kunchen—inviting him to speak as if expecting the *khenpo* to express the people's unquestioningcompliance!

Kunchen eagerly stepped forward, his anger apparent to the entire assembly.

'Lithang-pa,' he began, 'as you can see the meeting we called has been diverted. As you can see, these enemies of Buddha dharma do not want to listen to us. They call us animals but they don't understand what they look like in a mirror! They don't dress like real Chinese, they don't speak like real Chinese, they don't think like real Chinese because they have sold themselves to demonic ideas and powers!'

Kunchen paused but not to give Tenzin a chance to translate for Deng. Deng was not his audience; he spoke to the people.

'Are these demonic powers going to decide the course of our future? They say we have a choice. Must we follow their Red Road of communism? If not, then we follow the Black Road. We know what that is, don't we?'

Voices rose in understanding from the assembly.

'We called this meeting,' Kunchen Khenpo said, and he changed his tone slightly. He turned to Tenzin as if expecting him to translate his words for Deng and his Chinese companions.

'Now they will listen to what we have to say. After all, whose country is this? Did they loan us our land, our animals, our homes so that one day we would give it back?'

'No!' shouted the crowd as if with one voice.

Then shouts of 'Black Road' suddenly erupted from different parts of the crowd as a way of voicing their outrage and rejection of the Red Road.

Asking for silence with raised arms, khenpo continued.

'During the past few years, we have seen that making changes in our society is a necessary objective. Many townships have formed cooperatives that include nomads inhabiting the surrounding grasslands. In other places, cooperatives are forming that include merchants, tradesmen, and even monks. We have described our progress to Commander Deng and his associates but they are not interested in what we have accomplished. Without regard for our progress and our wishes, they are making unreasonable demands. They behave just like they always do—as if they own us!'

The shouts of 'Black Road!' grew louder and more persistent. Soldiers bristled in response, and several soldiers on the platform behind Commander Deng moved toward the *khenpo*. Commander Deng motioned for them to stay back.

Palden Rinpoche glanced up at the window where I'd been before. He then turned and I caught his eye from the temple doorway. He nodded to indicate I should join him. Nervous and barefooted, I stepped over the threshold.

When I made my appearance, Deng, Nawang, and Tenzin reacted as if they'd seen a ghost! It amused me but I couldn't savour the moment because Kunchen urged me to speak immediately. I raised my arms asking for silence and attention.

'My Khampa brothers and sisters,' I said, declaring my solidarity with them, 'let me speak as one of you today!'

I was surprised how enthusiastically they accepted my presence. People from all over Lithang district were present, and I understood that nearly everyone knew me or had heard of me. I was their Chinese Khampa; I was Chodak-la, their Dharma brother. Many also knew me as a *babdrung* along with Dechen.

'Speak to us as Gesar!' Someone in the crowd shouted in confirmation.

'Gesar! Gesar! Gesar!' the crowd re-joined.

I had to raise my arms again. I took a deep breath, and realized I could speak as both Chodak and Gesar; I distinctly felt myself to be living in two worlds simultaneously. One foot was firmly in this world with the people of Kham facing their oppressors, and the other foot was in the parallel world of my visions.

'Let us not speak again of the Black Road. Nor will we travel this Red Road under the conditions presented to us.'

The crowd started going wild with approval. I waited for silence again.

'Can we abandon Buddha dharma and follow their way of materialism and separation? Their Red Road will separate us from Buddha dharma! For us, that is the Black Road.'

I paused, and the crowd remained silent. They understood the importance of my words.

'As followers of Buddha dharma, we can speak only of the Middle Way, a third option.'

Again, I paused to let the people consider what a middle way might be.

'Not a compromise! There is a way forward that includes the best that true communism has to offer without straying from Buddha dharma. It is a road that honours goodness. We can call it the Golden Way. That is the way we choose!'

The crowd began to murmur. Many were curious and apprehensive to hear more about this new option. Soon, someone shouted 'Golden Way' and others took up the call.

A chant began: 'Golden Way! Golden Way! Golden Way!'

Outraged, Commander Deng turned accusingly to Palden. Behind me, I heard Deng shout at Rinpoche over the roar of the crowd in his broken Tibetan.

'What you try to do?'

Palden Rinpoche shouted back in fluent Chinese.

'Listen to me, Deng! We don't want communism imposed on us here anymore than the Mongolians wanted what the Russians imposed on them. You are insanely repeating the same mistake.'

'What's this Golden Way?' Deng shouted back. 'Some kind of Buddhist communism? Impossible! Beijing will never accept it. The only option is to accept communism as dictated by the Party or fight a battle we are sure to win. Numbers, old man, numbers. We can mobilize millions if necessary!'

'Yes, millions of ignorant, manipulated, under-fed farm boys, homesick for their rice paddies back home. Countless lives will be wasted in your madness.'

'What of it! Our people breed too fast as it is.'

Rinpoche must have turned away from Commander Deng in disgust. The heated exchange was over but the crowd was still demanding the Golden Way.

Now, Kunchen raised his arms asking for the crowd's undivided attention.

'We must not surrender our property or our way of life,' he said. I was not sure right away if he was agreeing with me

or not. 'We must not give up Buddha dharma. The Red Road
is wrong for us! What Chodak-la says is right. Buddha dharma
calls us to walk the Golden Way of wisdom and compassion.'

The crowd quieted. They wanted to hear more about the
Golden Way.

'Why not walk the Golden Way together?' I said to them
again. 'Let Khampa and Han, let all Tibetans and all people
of this world walk the Golden Way! Why not choose to be
fully human?'

I paused and there was complete silence. My proposal
was all-inclusive, universal in scope. They could see that and, in
their hearts, I knew they agreed.

'The Golden Way alone leads to a better world; a world
of goodness for everyone. Let us start a new story that puts
to rest the tired old patterns of power and control based on
fear. Let us base life on equality, inclusion, love, and wisdom,'
I urged, adding, 'what we need is a story that allows each of us
to live our true potential, that allows each community to make
its own decisions about what they will produce, how they will
live and how they choose to benefit communities nearby. This
is what we call an enlightened society. This is true civilization.
It is based on understanding that a life well-lived is founded on
basic goodness and love.'

Once again the crowd voiced its choice.

'Golden Way!

'Golden Way!

'Golden Way!'

'The Golden Way alone will lead us to an enlightened
society like King Gesar created in the Kingdom of Ling! It
will give us goodness in the form of prosperity for all, and

encourage each of us to live according to our true potential as fully awakened human beings. We will be better communists than the example presented to us by the Chinese or the Russians because we will live as bodhisattvas, always concerned about the happiness of others.'

'Golden Way! Golden Way! Golden Way!' the people exploded again.

Kunchen, I could tell, wanted to address Commander Deng and his officers. When the crowd was quiet again, he spoke confidently in Chinese, and then in Tibetan for the crowd's benefit.

'Your Red Road is the way of endless suffering. We are people, not animals! We will not live as slaves in your heartless pursuit of material happiness. We know there are injustices in our society that need reform. We have already started to correct them but you show no interest in our progress. We will only accept reforms that follow Buddha dharma. The Golden Way is the only road for us. It is the only road leading to true liberation!'

Commander Deng's outrage reached its peak. He pointed at all of us Tibetans on the platform, and gave his soldiers an order.

'Arrest them! All of these counter-revolutionaries!'

The soldiers moved toward us, and I could see Tenzin reach into his chuba for his pistol.

Wangdu's warriors reacted quickly. Tenzin, Commander Deng, every soldier, and their officers were quickly restrained and disarmed. Soldiers standing among the crowd and at the gates were likewise disarmed and restrained by Lobsang's warriors, who had spread themselves throughout the crowd to be near every soldier. The crowd roared with approval.

The meeting was over. The people had a new purpose!

Palden Rinpoche and I calmly led Kunchen through the crowd to his residence building, next to the temple. As we passed through the crowd, many reached out to touch me in recognition of my inspired suggestion and leadership.

'Gesar! He is surely Gesar!' someone shouted. Others in the crowd joined in.

'Chodak-la's Golden Way! We will follow Chodak-la's Golden Way!'

Wangdu's warriors escorted Deng and his soldiers back to their camp with the promise that their weapons would be returned later. And, of course, as promised, weapons were returned but only after each was made irreparably inoperable.

Lobsang had not given up on the option to use armed force against the PLA. Though he was upset about the waste of usable weapons, Wangdu convinced him that the return of the useless weapons underscored our message of non-violence. Meanwhile, Kunchen placated Lobsang by showing him the huge collection of arms and ammunition stored at the monastery. Like Lobsang, Kunchen was not convinced we could defeat the PLA using only non-violent methods.

Reluctantly, Rinpoche agreed the monastery could keep their weapons as a back-up. I was of the opinion that we should destroy all weapons but I kept my mouth shut.

We stayed at the monastery a few more days as *khenpo's* guests. Those from Mola were housed in a large building just outside the back wall of the monastery while Dechen, her parents, and guests from Gyawa were housed in a smaller house next door. We all shared the meeting room in our building.

After I settled in the small room given to me, I went to find Dechen and, mutually drawn, we met between the two

411

buildings. Alone, we embraced and found a quiet place to talk and watch the late afternoon sun go down over the mountains, across the vast Lithang grasslands.

'That was exactly the right thing to say, Chodak-la!' she sounded thrilled. 'The Golden Way; perfect. The Golden Way of Buddha dharma is the road to Shambhala.'

'Any ideas how we go about implementing it?'

'That will come to you, to us, too!' She sounded confident. 'The main thing is that the idea, the vision has been given to the people. It is up to everyone, not just us, to make it happen!'

'I hope so,' I said, my mind already racing to work out details.

'I was watching Tenzin when you came out of the temple,' Dechen said, and started to laugh. 'He looked like he was about to mess his pants! Then it was all he could do to keep from shooting you on the spot! I saw his hand fondling the gun in his *chuba*.'

'Yes,' I agreed. 'I saw him out of the corner of my eye. Rinpoche was watching him, too. If he tried anything, it wouldn't have gone that far.'

'Why Commander Deng brought that vile pair back here, I have no idea!'

'Nawang and Tenzin?' I asked.

'Yes, they've got Deng on their side about the marriage arrangement. I must talk with Father and make sure he understands my position once and for all. Again!'

'Surely, Dechen-la, your father understands. Don't be hard on him, please. He'll find a way out.'

'You don't understand. These agreements have deep cultural roots. If we don't watch out, the wedding will be on and I won't be able to get out of it.'

'There's always a way,' I said with confidence.

Dechen took my hand, drew close and looked in my eyes.

'It's you I want to marry, Wei Ming.'

'Dechen,' I was thrilled and pulled her into my arms. Then, because I'd seen Western romantic movies, I got down on one knee, took her hand and looking up into her beautiful eyes, said, 'Dechen, will you marry me?'

'Yes, of course, I will, Wei Ming,' she said quickly, then with a frown, added,   'but it's not so simple!'

She pulled her hand away to wipe tears from her eyes. I stood up and offered her comfort with an embrace. Smiling again, she looked up and gently said, 'I would like to be called *Khandro* Dechen!'

'*Khandro?* What does that mean?'

'Calling a woman *Khandro,* or *Khandrolma,* is a way of recognizing a woman as the enlightened spiritual wife of an enlightened teacher, as his *Dakini.*'

'Well, you definitely qualify, but I'm not an enlightened teacher, you know.'

'Oh, but you are, and what you did today qualifies you!'

'Really?'

'Of course. Yangchen said so.'

We laughed, and then embraced and kissed again; allowing a glowing warmth to spill from our hearts in joy.

'Let's talk to Yangchen and Rinpoche,' I suggested.

'First, I have something to say to Father!'

Decisively, she broke my embrace and hurried away.

'Dechen?' I tried to call her back, but she kept going.

413

The next morning while I was meditating with Rinpoche and Yangchen, Dechen came to the door.

'Can I come in?' she asked with a sense of urgency in her voice.

'Come,' Rinpoche answered.

Thinking she wanted to talk with Yangchen and Rinpoche about getting married, I smiled with excitement. But it soon became clear she was distressed.

'What is it Dechen-la?' Rinpoche asked.

Dechen put her hand lightly on my shoulder, and sat down beside me.

'What is it?' I asked.

'A dream,' she said. She looked at Rinpoche and Yangchen pleading for their support. 'Father had a dream. He woke up in the night and tried to sleep again, but he was so distressed he had to wake Ama-la and me to keep him company.'

'Well, my dear,' Rinpoche said, 'tell us.'

'That's the problem! He wouldn't tell us! All he said was he had to see Commander Deng as soon as possible.'

'Commander Deng?' I blurted in surprise.

'When we pressed him repeatedly, all he would say was "it's about a horse race".'

'A horse race!' Rinpoche's response was an exclamation, not a question. He clapped his hands in immediate understanding.

'What did he mean?' Dechen pressed.

'Oh, I think it is not such a bad thing,' Rinpoche replied, and like Thampa, would not elaborate. 'We must trust Thampa-la to negotiate with Commander Deng as his dream dictates.'

I looked from Rinpoche to Dechen. I could see that Dechen suddenly made a connection, too, and then looked even more worried.

I remained in the dark.

I didn't know what Dechen had said to her father about us but it must have been significant enough to interrupt his sleep and dream up some crazy plan to see Commander Deng!

Thampa had left early that morning. An atmosphere of anticipation hung over our every activity. All we could do was wait for his return to see what he had to say about his visit to the commander.

I was thankful for the monks chanting in the great hall. The deep resonance of their voices was a grounding force. The world continued as it should!

Around noon, Thampa was seen climbing up the hill toward the monastery. He was a heavy man, so his progress was painfully slow. We waited.

When he arrived at last, we ushered him into the meeting room, served him tea with *tsampa*, followed by *thukpa* and *chang*, before he was ready to speak. He clearly enjoyed keeping us in suspense. Eventually, he began a painful, moment-by-moment account of what had transpired with the commander.

'The commander sat in a chair that turned easily this way and that, however he wished it to turn. His desk was shiny with a glass top.'

From Thampa's description, I realized Deng had new furniture in his office.

'He offered me a cigarette, so I took one. He lit it for me but I must say, I coughed because the smoke went into my lungs when I tried to breathe it in like he did. Nasty things! I thought he would see me as an equal in our conversation if I accepted his friendly offer of the cigarette.'

Thampa frowned, looked around the room and continued. He had all of us waiting to hear every word.

'I was quite pleased that he welcomed my visit and acknowledged me as the ex-governor of the district.'

He looked at each of us to make sure we were all there; Dawa and Dechen, of course, and Rinpoche, Yangchen, Wangdu, Samphel, Zema, and even Kunchen, Lobsang, Nima, and I were all gathered to hear him.

'I began by telling him about the young Gesar returning from exile in the wilderness. When he arrived in Ling, he heard about a horse race taking place. The outcome of this horse race was crucial to his own future because the winner would not only become King of Ling but also marry the beautiful Secheng Dugmo, who would reign with him as Queen.

'As you know, my Chinese is better than Commander Deng's Tibetan, so we spoke in Chinese. It was hard to tell the story in Chinese, but I made myself understood. After I finished, the commander said, "Yes, I've heard of this before. It's a good story but why are you telling it to me?".'

I looked around the room, hoping for a clue to understand Thampa's reasoning myself.

'I told Commander Deng about the big horse racing festival we hold in honour of King Gesar on the Lithang grassland on the full moon of the fifth month. It will be in three weeks' time this year.'

Thampa stopped, and looked at Dechen and at Dawa with a flicker of anxiety.

'I am to give my daughter in marriage to a man who wins a horse race?' Dawa exploded when she suddenly understood Thampa's plan.

Several people in the room gasped, me included. I was mortified. Any hope of marrying Dechen was dashed.

'Commander Deng,' Thampa continued, 'was so excited he leapt from his chair. "To the winner?" he shouted. "The winner marries your daughter?".'

Thampa chuckled and looked around the room. It suddenly dawned on him that some of us might not be too pleased with his decision to negotiate an arrangement without our knowledge. He looked at Dechen apologetically and held up his hands for forbearance.

'Just a minute,' he begged. 'There's more. Let me finish before you get angry. I know I've been rash, but I had to obey the dream. You'll see why.'

We kept quiet a little longer, hoping for a better outcome than the one I imagined.

'As I said, Commander Deng was very pleased and began to chuckle. But I said there were some conditions. I told him about my agreement with the Tserings. I told him that when both my daughter, Dechen, and Nawang's son, Tenzin, were little, we had exchanged friendly comments about the two of them getting married. There was never a formal agreement but once Tenzin saw Dechen again as a young woman, he began to insist on the marriage.'

'I let Commander Deng jump to the conclusion that I wanted Tenzin to win the race. He said he could arrange the details of the race. I was not to worry. I also let him think I was worried because Comrade Chuang was a rival and was a very able horseman. This surprised the Commander. "Comrade Chuang? The Golden Way man?", he exclaimed. He sounded angry at first but suddenly smiled and said, "Leave it to me. I see no problem!" Then he got out of his swinging chair and came around the table to put his arm around my shoulder as

417

I stood up. He guided me to the door slowly, as if we were best of friends.'

Thampa paused again. I was still perplexed. The situation was getting worse, not better. What had Thampa done? Deng would find a way to arrest me, send me away, or kill me to make sure Tenzin wins. Deng would fix the race in Tenzin's favour, one way or another.

'As we got to the door, I stopped and asked if I could say one more thing. He said, "Yes, of course." So I said that I will only agree to give my daughter in marriage to the winner if you allow the winner of the race to decide which road our people will follow— the Red Road or the Golden Way. This, I think, is only fair and in keeping with the legend of the man we honour as our great ancestor King.

This surprised all of us, Rinpoche included.

'I could immediately tell that Commander Deng was far from pleased with this condition. He released my hand and stood back, thinking. It put him in an awkward position. But soon he said, "Hmm... Very interesting idea. I will need to consider very carefully." But I could see he swiftly came to a decision and said, "No! There is no need to consider. I will organize everything!". With a huge grin, Deng slapped me on the back and opened the door for me.'

When Thampa was finished, we were stunned to silence. Thampa had created a situation in which anyone could win the race and marry Dechen! Though Deng would try to fix it in Tenzin's favour, someone else could win and make the choice between Deng's Red Road and our Golden Way. Unless, I won. I had to win for two reasons!

'Between now and the time of the festival,' Lobsang was saying when I turned my attention back to the general discussion, 'more soldiers are sure to arrive. There will be a massive search for our friend Chodak-la to prevent him from taking part in the race. Deng will set a high price for his arrest, no doubt. But my warriors will hide Chodak-la in Chengtreng until the time of the race. Meanwhile, we will do our best to prevent more soldiers from arriving in the area. Deng must be kept as weak as possible for as long as possible.'

'My warriors will be here in Lithang,' Wangdu said, 'we will do everything we can to prevent Deng from making arrests and interfering in other ways as we make preparations for the festival. We will try to find out how he intends to fix the race.'

'The conditions of the race are exactly the same as in the Gesar legend!' Rinpoche observed. 'Thampa-la, your dream is prophetic. Thank you for taking the initiative. And, Chodak-la, you will enter the race the same way young Gesar entered Todong's horse race to win the Kingdom of Ling and Sechen Dugmo's hand.'

'Wait a minute,' I objected. I was thinking of every possible obstruction. 'You sound so confident, Rinpoche-la. The odds are very much against anyone, most of all me, winning the race for the Golden Way.'

'True, it is hard to believe you will win, Chodak-la,' Rinpoche retorted. 'But you must go beyond belief. You must know you will win.'

Into Chengtreng and Back

Rinpoche suggested an evening walk to change our perspective, following the stressful events of the day. Rinpoche and I started up the path toward the ridge behind the monastery. Before we'd climbed very far, Yangchen called out to us. We turned to wait, and my heart skipped a beat when I saw Dechen with her.

Dechen and I walked together while Yangchen and Rinpoche lagged behind. It was evident, we were being given time together. A little further uphill, we found a place to sit and enjoy the brilliant starry sky. Dechen and I held hands, talked, and laughed. It was a joy to know that Rinpoche and Yangchen acknowledged our love.

Too soon, Rinpoche called to us and we returned to his room. The room was warm, and the soft glow of butter lamps was comforting. Yangchen suggested we sit facing each other, as we often did in meditation. I wondered what was going on but when Dechen fixed her eyes on mine, I stopped thinking about anything else.

'Dechen-la,' Rinpoche began, 'you have known, and Chodak-la, in your heart you have known, too, that you two are connected.'

Dechen and I smiled at the same time. My heart felt as if it would burst with this truth.

'Thampa-la forced our hand sooner than expected,' Rinpoche said, and took a deep breath as if to get in touch with his deepest being.

'As you've probably guessed, Chodak-la, there is a special quality about this bond between you and Dechen.'

Rinpoche paused again, and looked at each of us.

'You are more than ordinary lovers,' he openly declared, 'you have a relationship that transcends life in physical form. You are both bodhisattvas who have incarnated together, again and again. Do you understand me?'

I had never been convinced of the actuality of reincarnation. How could we know?

'I see,' Rinpoche said as he watched my face betray my scepticism, 'you don't accept reincarnation. Just listen a moment.'

Rinpoche chose not to explain the details of reincarnation and continued his train of thought.

'You have vowed to incarnate again and again to hasten the spiritual transformation of all beings into spirit-matter. In each incarnation, your situation is different; you each may have been the opposite sex in another life or even the same sex, but you always found each other—even if you were born in very different and faraway places. Like this time. Wei Ming, you were born in a wealthy, Westernized family while Dechen's soul split into twin girls who were separated at birth. One went to Shanghai and found you while the other travelled the world to educate herself.'

This information was over the top! How could Rinpoche know this? But, really, did it matter? Though my rational mind reeled with questions, qualifications, and objections, in my heart none of this mattered. Dechen and I had been brought together somehow, and all I wanted was to be with her.

'Rinpoche and I,' Yangchen suddenly added, 'are also connected in a similar way. In this incarnation, we happen to be brother and sister. Our task has been to find you both, to bring you together so we all can fulfil our purpose.'

Now Yangchen, too!

'We know this,' Rinpoche, said responding to my unspoken alarm, 'the same way Thampa-la knows you will win the horse race in three weeks. He had a dream that told him what he must do. He bravely did it. Yangchen and I have also had dreams that have led us to where we are today. Dechen has had similar dreams. As have you, I'm sure.'

I nodded because I had to admit my recurring dreams about the woman in the lake and her child, boy, young man in the wilderness, could qualify as a significant dream that had brought me to this place and moment, too.

'As bodhisattvas,' Rinpoche continued, 'our role is to present a vision of goodness and truth to the people. If we do not present a clear vision, we fail in this lifetime's mission. If we present it but it is not followed, or something prevents the people from following it, we have done the best we could do.'

This part I understood.

'Chodak, yesterday you presented a very clear vision to the people,' Rinpoche acknowledged.

'But there is still more to do. Sometimes we have to enact the vision to prove its beauty, its truth and its goodness. Winning the horse race,' Rinpoche said, 'is the way we will show the people that the Golden Way is indeed the way we must go.'

I understood how proclaiming the Golden Way had deeply inspired the people. And I knew how winning the horse race and proclaiming the Golden Way would seal the hearts of the people, but I was focused on whether or not Dechen and I could continue to be lovers in this lifetime. I knew right then and there how deeply I loved her, and probably, as Rinpoche was saying, always had loved her.

'An official public wedding ceremony,' Rinpoche was saying as he looked from one to the other of us, 'will be held after the horse race. But let this night be your real wedding; you may consummate your love and renew the vows you have spoken to each other for countless lifetimes.'

'Yes, Rinpoche-la,' Dechen said, and eagerly squeezed my hand; she had a broad, confident and loving smile.

I was too overcome with joy and anticipation to speak; my stomach lurched. What if I didn't win the horse race and someone else claimed Dechen as his wife? How would we deal with that? Would we just say, 'Sorry, she's already married?' It was deceitful to offer her hand in marriage if it wasn't possible! Would everyone take Rinpoche's word for it that we have been lovers across lifetimes? It would never hold up in a court of law! We were asking for trouble.

'Tomorrow, Chodak, you will ride away into exile in the wilderness. You will return as a vagabond horseman,' Rinpoche said, and I could tell he was enjoying the mythic scale of our plan. 'Over the next three weeks, both of you will be in retreat. You will focus on strengthening and energizing your connection with each other in every way. The race will begin and you will win because the bond between the two of you is unbreakable! Do you understand?'

'Of course,' Dechen said. Her resolve, unshakeable.

'Everything depends on the strength of your love,' Yangchen said, as if she'd heard my unspoken doubts. 'You will use this unbreakable bond between you to overcome all obstacles placed in your way. You will reach the finish line first and stand with Dechen. Have no doubts.'

Rinpoche and Yangchen conducted a short wedding ceremony in which they both gave us khata, and recited a short blessing as Dechen and I touched our foreheads together. The ceremony over, Rinpoche and Yangchen stood up and, closing the door behind them, left us alone in the room.

My guide into Chengtreng was Dorje, the man who challenged me outside the tavern that first summer in Lithang. Dorje's band of warriors and I, disguised as nomads, set out in cold pre-dawn stillness. We climbed the ridge behind the monastery and slipped away from Lithang toward the wilderness of Chengtreng, southwest of Gyawa and Mola townships.

We got reacquainted that day, Dorje and I. We had several good laughs about our first meeting; some at his expense and some at mine. He enjoyed initiating me into his rugged way of life; we never set up a tent, hunted for our food, and kept moving from place to place.

After a few days of wandering, we came to a place with piles of stones, *mani* stones inscribed with 'Om Mani Padme Hum'. They were around the entrance to a cave. Going inside, I had an odd feeling of being at home.

She was here! Dechen, my beloved was here waiting for me!

The cave had many paintings on the walls but three drew my attention because one was a beautiful Tara *Dakini* that looked just like Dechen. Another was the ever-youthful Manjushri, holding the blazing sword of wisdom and lotus blossom of compassion. Between them was a sky-blue Kuntuzangpo in an embrace with his consort, representing primordial and natural goodness of mind. It reminded me of our wedding night.

In this cave, deep inside a mountain in the middle of Chengtreng wilderness, I marvelled how close I felt to Dechen. I remained love-sustained, intoxicated throughout my brief retreat. In deep meditation, I soared with Dechen as entwined spirit-matter beings spanning the beginning and end of time and space. A river of light poured forth from my heart and spanned the distance between us.

Dechen had whispered a mantra she wanted me to say constantly, 'Om tare tuttare ture soha'. It would remind me of her constant *Dakini* protection, from external and internal delusions while we remained apart. I decided to give her a mantra, too. It was 'I am my beloved's and my beloved is mine'. We agreed to recite both of these.

On our wedding night, the night before my exile, Dechen and I had experienced time standing still. Our active minds stilled, our eyes focused in the depth of one another's soul, and our bodies joined in physical bliss, we participated in the eternal cosmic dance of spiritual lovers. Every last feeling of separation was overcome; we were one in body, mind, and spirit. Together, we embodied wisdom upheld by compassion. Our separateness cleared away, we were as we'd always been— one mind, one heart, one soul ablaze with love.

Whole.

Inseparable.

'Khandro Dechen,' I had whispered.

'Chodak Rinpoche,' she had replied.

Dorje interrupted my meditation one morning to say it was time to return.

'I've lost track of time,' I said to Dorje, 'will we get back in time for the race?'

Dorje laughed.

'The horse race is on the day following the next full moon,' Dorje explained. 'Relax, we have several days left. We'll get you there in time.'

He wanted to sound confident but I could see that he was quite worried. It was his responsibility to protect me from Deng's soldiers.

'What is he going to wear?' a warrior asked Dorje when I reappeared among them.

'In the legend, Gesar shows up disguised as a beggar,' Dorje explained. 'I've been considering the kind of disguise Chodak-la will need so no one can recognize him.'

'Any ideas?' I asked.

Dorje began to laugh. 'How about a Naxi? If they recall the story, they'll be looking for a scruffy nomad, but we can fool them if you look like a Naxi trader! You've got a non-Tibetan look that might pass for Naxi!'

'Where will we get a Naxi costume from?' one of the warriors asked.

'No worries. Some of Wangdu's warriors are Naxi. I'm sure we can borrow a complete outfit, shoes and all.'

I had to admit the idea of using a Naxi costume was ingenious. Naxi, Yi, and Lolo traders often came as far as Lithang with the tea caravans from the South. Seeing one of them, especially at a large summer festival, would not be unusual. I'd seen them myself and had an idea how they behaved. I thought I could do a reasonably good job pretending to be one.

It was a relief to know that details were more or less taken care of, but I was still apprehensive. If the race was fixed in Tenzin's favour, how could I win? It was a worry that loomed larger as the day approached.

We rode out of Chengtreng wilderness to Rinpoche's hermitage. The next morning, I made my trek to Lithang, looking like the grubby helper of a legitimate Naxi trader. One of Wangdu's Naxi warriors was my 'master' for this journey. We bypassed Gyawa and took the direct trail from Mola to Lithang. It took two days of walking with our small caravan of yaks, loaded with bricks of tea and sacks of rice. On the afternoon of the second day, I entered town with my Naxi master's small caravan.

Lithang was crowded with people from every direction. They came for the festival but mostly because so much was at stake. They were eager to find out if the winner would choose the Red Road or the Golden Way.

It was easy enough to blend into the crowd. When we saw other Naxi traders, we stayed clear. Instead of trying to sell our goods, we continued through town to a secluded stream north of town, where I set up a simple camp. Wangdu's Naxi warrior left me there with the assurance that he and others would be nearby, keeping guard. The great race would start when the sun rose over the eastern ridge above the monastery. I could

427

see the starting line not far away in the middle of the Lithang grassland, to the west of my camp.

As I settled in for the night, my thoughts were scattered and anxious. Instead of stilling my mind by repeating our mantras, I worried about the outcome of the race. Was the Golden Way so vitally important that I was willing to risk everything—my love, my life—in a crazy horse race? Could I watch as Dechen was given to another man? Could I let someone like Tenzin, whom Dechen had rejected, declare that the people would follow the Red Road and submit to the dictates of the Chinese Communist Party?

It didn't help that the night began with a thunderstorm. Huddled under a Naxi rain covering made of bamboo and leaves, I tried to still my shivering body. The flashes of lightning and raging thunder in the sky above underscored my state of mind. Close to midnight, the storm ceased but not the darkness, nor my apprehension.

A staccato sound of horses' hooves alerted me to someone approaching. All ears and eyes, I scanned for danger and waited in trepidation. I hoped my stillness would keep me from being discovered. If the intruder stumbled upon me, I had to trust my disguise would conceal my true identity.

'Dechen and Yangchen were worried about you,' said a voice I recognized as Nima's, before I could see him clearly. 'I brought you some food, a dry blanket, and a horse.'

'Nima! My dear friend!' I said with great relief. 'You have no idea how wonderful it is you've come!'

He, too, was dressed as a Naxi. Assuming we were alone, we spoke as Chodak and Nima rather than pretending to be Naxi traders.

I did not immediately recognize the horse with Nima, but when he nuzzled me and made a familiar noise, I knew it was Little White disguised like myself.

'Tell me, Nima, how's Dechen?' I craved to know how she was doing.

'She's fine but anxious about you.' Nima went on to tell me that Dechen had spent most of the past three weeks in retreat at the nunnery. She had joined Yangchen at the little house near the monastery just that day.

'I saw her briefly this evening before I came here. She gave me these things to raise your spirits.'

Though I knew in my heart she was doing well, it was comforting to hear about her from another person.

'I can stay on guard while you rest,' Nima offered. 'Or, if you can't rest, I'll keep you company!'

'Thank you. I'm not exactly in the mood to sleep. I'm cold and troubled. Your company is most welcome!'

We ate the still-warm *momos* and drank some *chang*. The thought that this meal came from Dechen warmed me more than the food itself. It was ambrosia from my lover! After eating, Nima and I settled into an easy conversation.

With his encouragement, I recounted my personal journey from a childhood of privilege in Shanghai to becoming an idealistic communist who helped save the city from destruction in the wake of the nationalists' withdrawal. I talked about Jiachen's martyrdom, and my decision to take the Revolution to Tibet.

'The rest you know,' I concluded.

'True, I know about your time here, but this is the first time I've heard about your life before you came here, Chodak-la,' Nima observed, 'what an amazing life you've had!'

To deflect attention from myself, I encouraged him to tell me his story.

'There is nothing much to say,' he began shyly. 'My parents were poor and served a rich aristocrat in Batang. When the aristocrats moved to Chengdu, they took my family with them. I was the second son, so I was educated with the idea that I would become a monk. I learned to read quickly and when a lama from Lithang visited us in Chengdu one time, he must have thought I was intelligent. He persuaded my parents to send me to the Lithang monastery. I came here when I was 10, and have been here ever since, except for visits with my family in Chengdu each year. The rest you know.'

'You are so modest,' I responded, appreciating his strength of character and remembering his insightful contributions to our movement. 'Rinpoche told me you are a *tulku*, the reincarnation of a learned master of his own tradition.'

'Did he?' Nima questioned quietly, 'I don't like to rely on things like that.'

He had a way of deflecting attention from himself, and turned the spotlight back on me.

'You have opened my eyes,' Nima said, 'you came here deeply committed to seeking justice and equality. Your methods emphasized group participation and consensus. These were new concepts that are shaking up our rigid society.'

'You exaggerate,' I said self-consciously.

'No, it's true. You came with a much more mature and refreshing attitude to life than we generally see here.'

'But what about Rinpoche, Yangchen, and Dechen?' I asked. 'They want reforms, too. I regard them as truly advanced human beings; as enlightened ones who know what's best for us as individuals and as a society.'

'That's true, but you have grown since I first met you, and now I include you in the same category as Rinpoche, Yangchen, and Dechen. But they, too, have grown as a result of your insights. Without you, I doubt we would have found the solution of the Golden Way. We would not have been able to organize the cooperatives and still keep our way of life and Buddha dharma.'

'You think too highly of me, I'm afraid,' I said in an effort to curb any sense of pride.

'You are a true bodhisattva,' Nima continued, 'I'm not the only one who says this. This evening, whenever Dechen mentioned your name, she said "Chodak Rinpoche". In her eyes, and in everyone else's, you are so dearly loved and respected. Besides that, they know you have sacrificed the life you could have enjoyed in Shanghai for a life of hardship here in Kham.'

'No, no, Nima!' I emphatically responded, 'it has not been a sacrifice in any way. On the contrary, I've gained so much here.'

Remembering Dechen's plight, I added, 'No. If anyone is self-sacrificial, it is Dechen. Look what she'd doing. It puts me to shame. She is willing to chance her happiness to the outcome of this horse race!'

'True,' Nima agreed, 'but then, so are you. Don't you think you'll be just as devastated if someone else claims Dechen?'

I sadly nodded in agreement, and then we both drifted into our own thoughts. Eventually, I changed the subject by returning to the previous thread of our conversation.

'It's sad, isn't it, that society prevents rather than help people reach full maturity. Too many people get stuck at a developmental level dictated by pressures from their social groups. Let's hope our revolution liberates people economically, socially, and spiritually—so more people can grow to full maturity as awakened ones.'

'I couldn't agree with you more!' Nima said excitedly.

'Here's something you might also give some thought to,' I said, after a moment. 'Since I came here, I've been watching what is happening in China from a distance. It seems the Chinese Communist Party has become increasingly tyrannical. They are inflexible in their objectives, and are trying to lock down or shut out any fresh ideas. I'm reminded of something the great Taoist master Lao-tzu said:

"Men are born soft and supple; dead, they are stiff and hard. Plants are born tender and pliant; dead, they are brittle and dry. Thus, whoever is stiff and inflexible is a disciple of death. Whoever is soft and yielding is a disciple of life".'

Nima was smiling and nodding his head vigorously. He understood the Chinese.

'This tyranny of the CCP comes from a fear of losing control,' I said. 'They tell themselves that the Party exercises the will of the masses but in actual fact, this has been reversed; there is no possibility of the people being able to exercise self-determination.'

'That's right,' Nima agreed, 'we have absolutely no voice in decisions. It assumes the masses are not as progressive or, as they would say, enlightened as they are when, in fact, they are only as socially and emotionally developed as a five-year-old.'

'Haha,' I laughed in agreement. 'Yes, and as Lao-tzu points out, controlling people creates disharmony. People don't like to be told what to do, where to go, what to eat, how to dress. Especially by people who are narrow-minded and fearful.

The Party speaks endlessly about the virtues of social harmony while sowing separation and disharmony. In the long run, they create their own destruction. It may be many, many years from now, but their destruction is assured and self-inflicted.'

'In sharp contrast,' Nima said excitedly, 'our revolution needs to be soft and supple! We must be willing to change and bend with the needs and desires of the people. We need to listen, come to mutual agreement, and move forward at a pace we can all adjust to.'

'That's how true communism works,' I said. 'Change comes about as a result of two opposing points of view struggling until something new emerges. In our situation, the two opposing forces are the traditional values of Tibetan culture and the imposition of communism from the outside Neither option is good for the people...'

'Yes!' Nima jumped in before I could complete my thought. 'What you have proposed is the third way, the Golden Way. It is something new, something that transcends both communism and our traditional culture. A new enlightened society can only come to be if our revolution transcends Chinese communism and traditional Tibetan culture. And this can only happen if our revolution is also a spiritual revival.'

'Nima, I'm proud to call you my friend. You truly understand the Golden Way,' I said happily, and added in a more sombre tone as the magnitude of the task before us weighed on me, 'should anything happen to me, I want you to have my journals. They are in English, but even so, you must keep them out of the hands of Party officials. I've told Dechen, Rinpoche, and Yangchen that you should have them.'

433

'I'm honoured, but nothing can happen to you,' Nima said, refusing to entertain the possibility of things going wrong. 'We must not talk of such things.'

Then changing the subject, he added with concern, 'I'm sorry. I'm keeping you up. You need to rest, Chodak-la!'

'Yes, I guess I should try to sleep. But first, I want to meditate.'

I straightened by back and rested my hands in my lap. Immediately, from the very first breath, I entered that deepest of rests in my *Dakini*'s loving embrace—surrendering to the continuously transforming present moment, to the now. After, I don't know how long, I emerged from my meditation, to see Nima meditating, too. Tired, I lay down to sleep. The clouds had disappeared and the world was bathed in brilliant moonlight.

I would ride on Little White in the morning with Dechen as the magnet drawing us, despite obstacles, to her side.

We would fly to her side!

I dreamed of the beautiful young woman by the lake. This time, after lifting the shining orb of light from the depths and taking the child to the shore, the dream continued beyond the point when the young man got on the white horse and leaped into the sky.

A young man, flying overhead on a white horse, sees the shining goddess by the shore of the lake. Landing on the vast expanse of grassland, he races toward her. Dismounting before her, he pledges himself to her on bended knee. She takes his hands, raises him up and they embrace as lovers.

The Big Horse Race

At first light, I was already up and seated in meditation. I opened my eyes to see Nima waking up nearby. My pack animals slept on their feet. Little White, a dirty brown colour, neighed softly when he saw me watching him. I got up and stroked his muzzle with an arm round his neck.

'Everything is arranged,' Nima said abruptly as he woke. 'Just get to the starting line. Behave like an idiot who doesn't know what's going on. That should be easy enough!'

Nima chuckled.

'No problem,' I replied, appreciating the joke. 'I'll be the drunken guy on a crazy horse, or is it the crazy guy on a drunken horse!'

'Ha! Ha! You get the picture!'

We both laughed. It helped us cope with the anxiety we both felt about the outcome of the race.

'*Tashi Delek*!' Nima said as he led the pack animals back to town. I would need good luck for sure.

I left the campsite immediately, too. Dirty Little White and I proceeded to our fate! The fate of Lithang! Perhaps the fate of Kham and the rest of Tibet.

But I tried not to think of that; I thought only that the race will take us to Dechen!

Dirty Little White and I made our way to the middle of the vast grasslands. Horsemen were beginning to gather at the starting line.

As daylight increased, I looked for the finish line of the race. I'd seen it from the ridge as I approached Lithang, and estimated it was 10 kilometres or more from the starting point. I could just make out the large tent with hundreds of colourful banners and flags waving in the early morning breeze.

I imagined Dechen there. Was she waiting in anguish for the race to begin and end? Was she hiding deep inside a tent with Yangchen and other women? Were women distracting her by fussing over her costume, her elaborate jewellery, her make-up? Or was she confident of the outcome and sitting in full view?

I chose to imagine her seated regally on a stage, drawing me and Little White to her like the most powerful magnet, the most beautiful goddess you can imagine.

Oh, how I wanted all of this to be over.

I reminded myself to empty my heart and mind, to submit, to allow Dechen to attract us.

I tied my mind to my breath. In, out. Be here, be in this eternal moment; and in this one. I admonished myself, above all, to feel the activity of love, the cosmic uniting force drawing me to my beloved.

I repeated, 'I am my beloved's and my beloved is mine! *Om tare tuttare ture soha!*'

A large number of horsemen had gathered. So many young men wanted to win Dechen's lovely hand in marriage! It was daunting to realize the staggering competition I faced. There were many Khampa riders, of course, but I was startled to see so many Chinese soldiers and officers on horseback, too. They were obviously there to bend the odds in favour of Deng's Red Road.

News of the event had travelled far enough; I recognized Golog and U Tsang riders by their dress. Even some of the Naxi, Li, and Yolo traders I'd seen in town were represented. Men from far and wide were hopeful of marriage to Dechen.

It was enough to make me collapse and crawl away, but that would mean conceding to defeat. Again, I reminded myself to empty my mind and heart of these distractions.

The horsemen lined up. The sun was about to crest the ridge.

Someone shouted at me even though I had not tried to join the line-up.

'Get out of here, you stinking foreigner! This is no place for a mama's boy!'

I got it; the Naxi were a matriarchal society. All Naxi men were mama's boys. I didn't laugh, of course, but I didn't take offense either.

'What's going on?' I asked innocently in what I hoped was a Naxi accent. 'Some sort of race? What's the prize?'

'Go on! Get out of here!'

I led Little White slowly to another spot behind the spectators.

The sun peaked over the ridge! A banner was raised and the horses took off!

Spectators at the starting line burst into shouts of:

'*Ki Ki So So Lha Gyalo!*

'*Ki Ki So So Lha Gyalo!*

'*Ki Ki So So Lha Gyalo!*'

437

This was my moment.

Leading Little White into the dust left by the departed horsemen, I pretended to be too drunk to get on him.

I heard the man who had insulted me shout out, 'I told that Naxi tea trader's slave to get lost. What does he think he's doing?'

Little White pranced around me in circles while I made a few failed attempts to get on.

Then I suddenly got on and leaned close to Little White's ear and whispered, 'Let's go to Dechen!'

Little White bolted after the other horses.

Though I was last, the race was on!

Ten kilometres is a long way, so I was sure Little White would be able to catch up.

Through the dust left by the horses ahead of me, I could still see the pavilion where Dechen waited. I imagined Commander Deng sitting in the front row of chairs set up for VIPs. He would be gloating over his forgone conclusion of the race. No doubt he would have Thampa and Dawa seated next to Nawang and his wife. He would be the first to congratulate them on their good fortune. I imagined Dawa on the brink of tears. And poor Thampa, I was sure, was straining under the burden placed on him by his agreement with Commander Deng. I knew Dawa well enough to know how angry she must be with Thampa right now.

I was distracted again.

Re-focus.

Submit.

Empty mind.

Fill heart with love.

'I am my beloved's and my beloved is mine. *Om tare tuttare ture soha!*'

I rode.

Little White ran faster than ever; faster than any horse I'd ever ridden. We were catching up. Was he flying? Was he the reincarnation of Khyang Go Karkar, Gesar's magical horse?

The more I focused on our goal and synchronized with the rhythm of his strides and his breathing, the faster Little White flew. Together, we had one thought—get to Dechen!

Soon, we were passing other horses; Khampa riders, Chinese riders, riders from all over Tibet and the southern tribes. Only a small tight group of riders was ahead of us. Among them, I recognized Tenzin. Little White and I made our way steadily forward until we were alongside Tenzin. Keeping pace with Tenzin, I removed my Naxi headdress. Tenzin was startled when he suddenly recognized me.

'Chuang?' he exploded.

'I heard there was a wedding today.' I said coolly, 'are you headed that way?'

The audacity of my presence and my remark completely enraged him. He tried to whip me. Little White and I anticipated his move and easily jumped out of reach.

Just then, a noisy object raced toward us from the side-lines. In a well-rehearsed manoeuvre, Tenzin traded his horse for the back seat of the motorcycle. He waved victoriously and left all of us horsemen behind.

The finish line was out of sight, of course. Deng thought Tenzin could play this trick and get away with it.

Little White and I continued. We would not give up, we would not despair. We were ahead of all the rest and did our best to keep up with the motorcycle while focused on our goal: Dechen.

Unfortunately for Tenzin, the ground became more and more uneven. The motorcycle was having difficulties maintaining speed.

'Can't this thing go faster?' I heard Tenzin shout in growing desperation as he looked over his shoulder and saw me coming.

Crossing a stream, the engine sputtered and stalled. The driver struggled to get it going again. Several horsemen, with me in the lead, caught up with the motorcycle just as the driver got it going again. It sped over smoother ground toward a waiting black horse identical to Tenzin's first one. Tenzin made a quick transfer but we were not far behind. He galloped ahead into full view of the finish line, confident his fresh horse would easily outrun us.

I could see Commander Deng standing; he was already applauding Tenzin's victory. Thampa and Dawa were too sick at heart to stand. Dawa's hands covered her face. I could see Dechen standing in front of the VIPs just as I'd imagined her earlier. She was being strong and had not given up hope; our magnificent magnet!

There was a collective thrill of excitement rippling through the crowd when they saw a rider gaining on Tenzin. The race was not over! Hope seemed to flare up among them but no one had recognized me yet.

Then I saw Thampa involuntarily leap to his feet. He was the first to recognize me. He seemed to be saying, 'Dawa! Dawa! Look, it's Chodak! He's right behind Tenzin! He's catching up!'

I saw that Commander Deng recognized me too! I imagined him shouting.

'Stop him!'

But no one paid any attention to the commander. Everyone was standing now and cheering because it would be a very close race.

Some shouted, 'Gesar!'

Others, 'Tenzin!'

I continued to gain on Tenzin so that when I caught up with him, he was taken by surprise. His fury returned and, as before, he lashed at Little White's face with a whip. Little White and I were just far enough out of reach that the whip missed and Tenzin's violent movement threw his black horse off balance. Together, they stumbled into the dirt short of the finish line.

I sailed across the line on magical Little White!

Poor Tenzin tried to get on his horse again, but riders behind me deliberately knocked him down again for his foul play with the motorcycle.

I trotted tired Little White triumphantly toward Dechen. I dismounted and stroked Little White's muzzle gratefully.

'Well done, Khyang Go Karkar!' I whispered. How could I doubt now that this little white stallion was a manifestation of Gesar's magical horse? He neighed softly while tossing his head up and down looking at Dechen.

A young warrior took Little White's reins from me as Palden Rinpoche greeted me joyfully. He ushered me, still in my Naxi costume, up the steps to the platform where Dechen waited to greet me with joyful relief.

As in my dream, I went down on bended knee in front of Dechen. She clasped my hands tightly as if never wanting to release them again, and raised me to my feet. As we were gazing at each other, sweet memories of our last hours together filled my heart; we were truly one being. Now we would be together all the time.

After this brief private moment, we turned our radiant smiles to all the spectators and riders who were filling the space before the platform. Turning to look behind us at the VIPs, I saw Thampa and Dawa embraced in a tight, happy hug. Samphel and Zema were also there. So was Kunchen Khenpo with a couple of other high lamas. Obviously, Deng had some of his officers there, too. There were some prominent merchants and nomadic leaders among the VIPs, too. In all, I guessed there were 18 dignitaries in the seats behind the platform where Dechen and I would address the people. I couldn't help notice Commander Deng's angry scowl as he leaned toward one of the officers and whispered in his ear.

Dechen and I took our seats on a single, wide throne. Holding hands, we sat meditatively while Palden Rinpoche placed a golden *khata* over both our shoulders as a sign of union. A colourful *chuba* covered my Naxi costume. Next, he presented me with a sword, symbolic of the blazing sword of wisdom, and a flower symbolizing the sacred lotus and the Heart Sutra.

All smiles, Rinpoche turned to the growing crowd.

'The miracle has taken place today just as it did one thousand years ago. An outcast has secured the place of highest honour and claimed the hand of the most beautiful woman in the land. But unlike Gesar in the Kingdom of Ling, today's winner will not become our king. Nevertheless, we await what the winner has to say to us. You all know him as Chodak-la, who has been among us long enough to know us, to love our way of life and to follow Buddha dharma. Though he is Chinese and came here as a member of the Communist Party, he is now a follower of Buddha dharma and a *babdrung* of the Gesar legend.'

He continued, 'I invite you to imagine that you are in the time of Gesar, witnessing that day one thousand years ago when Gesar was crowned King of Ling. Let's listen to our *babdrungpa*, Chodak-la, as he brings us Gesar's words, and ask yourself if they have meaning for us today!'

Our planned re-enactment of Gesar's victory began when Dechen and I stood to address the crowd together. The drum and horn used to inducing a shamanic trance was no longer necessary; our bliss already opened the gateway so we could stand together in both the worlds. I held the sword across my up-turned hands in front of me, and spoke loud and clear as both Chodak and Gesar.

'You know in your hearts that I am Gesar, King of Ling, and at my side is our Queen, Sechen Dugmo. We pledge to bring you dignity, justice, and the liberation of an enlightened society.'

Taking the sword in my right hand, I raised it high over my head so that it flashed the mid-morning sunlight over the crowd. I turned to Dechen beside me and, taking her right hand in my left, held it close to my heart. The position of my right and left hands imitated exactly the hand positions of Manjushri, who raises the sword of wisdom and cherishes the lotus blossom supporting the sacred sutra extolling compassion.

In this way, I was simultaneously Manjushri, Gesar, and Chodak; I was simultaneously in the Kingdom of Ling, in the present, and in the world of Shambhala that transcends time and space.

The sword in my hand blazed with divine fire; a fire that represented the love flowing through us as we stood side by side before the people. To our delight, the sword's divine fire was lighting up the faces and hearts of the people gathered around us. By its light it was easy to see that every person, whether Khampa or Han Chinese, was here to honour their ancient Warrior King and his Queen—and beyond them, to encounter Manjushri and his *Khandrolma*.

'**I hold the sword of Wisdom in one hand and the hand of my beloved in the other. Together, we will walk the path of wisdom and compassion. It is our honour today, here in Lithang of our world, to invite you all to walk with us along the Golden Way to Shambhala.**'

The crowd, the Khampas, and even some of the Chinese soldiers, caught up in the drama of the day, roared with jubilance.

'Golden Way!

'Golden Way!

'Golden Way!'

I lowered the sword and, still holding Dechen's hand, looked at my beloved with heart-felt adoration.

'**Today I proclaim my devotion to you, Khandro Dechen. You are the jewel of my heart. Know that when I look at you, my joy has no limits. You are inspiration and guide as we all walk the Golden Way.**'

It was Dechen's turn to speak.

'**Today I proclaim my devotion to you, Chodak Rinpoche. You are the sword of Truth. Know that when I look at you, my joy has no limits. You are inspiration and guide as we all walk the Golden Way.**'

444

We turned to invite the people to join us. Dechen and I spoke in unison now: **'Whether you believe us or not, it is true: united, all of us can prosper and be happy. United, we can bring this world to its full beauty and live in it as fully awakened human beings. Come with us on the Golden Way! Let us fearlessly establish an enlightened society by opening our hearts and allowing love.'**

The people interrupted us with shouts of 'Golden Way!'

'All who love these rivers and mountains, come with us. Come with us, all who honour every woman as mother or sister or daughter or wife, and honour every man as father or brother or son or husband. Together, we can defeat demonic forces that separate us from joy and bind us in ignorance through fear, power-lust, and greed. Together, we will live from heart-wisdom and join earth with heaven.'

Dechen and I watched as Tibetan and Chinese people mingled together. They were whole-heartedly chanting 'Golden Way! Golden Way! Golden Way!', and it filled us with joy.

I had a vision of a time when both Tibetan and Han would live together in communities where each person is honoured; a society of those who make the happiness of others their highest value. There would come a time when seeking the common good was as natural as breathing. By following the Golden Way, we would become a society of bodhisattvas!

Thampa and Dawa got up from their seats to join us. Tears of joy streamed down their cheeks. Samphel and Zema were close behind. Rinpoche also came forward with Yangchen. Thampa and Dawa proudly stood next to Dechen while Samphel and Zema came to be with me. I was moved to realize they wanted to be family for me. All these people were now my immediate family and, with Dechen by my side, I felt happier and more blessed than any time in my life.

But my joy and my euphoric vision of the future was short-lived. Other emotions, in sharp contrast, intruded like a stab of pain when I saw the hatred and threat of violence in Deng's eyes. Red with rage, he glared at me and, as if possessed by a demon, he gesticulated with his disfigured, webbed hands and shouted incoherent orders.

I understood at once; his plan for Tenzin to win had failed and I was to blame. He raged because it was unthinkable that the people would unanimously choose to follow the Golden Way.

'Arrest him!' Deng shouted more coherent suddenly, 'arrest them all!'

Major Gan scrambled to obey while other officers, and many soldiers, reacted with a look that said 'you can't be serious!'.

Deng's shouting made the people uneasy. They began looking around at the soldiers next to them with suspicion, when only moments earlier everyone had been enthusiastically chanting for the Golden Way.

'This is a plot!' Commander Deng shouted while pointing at us. 'I want those traitors arrested!'

Several soldiers moved to obey Deng's command. Holding pistols they were not supposed to have, they forced their way toward the stage. The armed soldiers' progress through the crowd, however, was effectively blocked; the people understood the intent of the soldiers' movement, and did their best to keep them from getting to us on the stage.

Deng saw what the crowd was doing and shouted a general order to his soldiers in the crowd: 'I order you to surround this whole area. Don't let anyone get away!'

Reluctantly, it seemed to me, other soldiers moved out to the edges of the crowd. They began forming a ring, linking arms and make a solid barrier. The Khampa women and men, seeing their freedom challenged, began forcing their way through the barricade. Aggressive behaviour and shouting escalated.

Wangdu and his warriors had mingled with the crowd. When the soldiers moved to encircle the audience, Wangdu's warriors quickly followed and, at Wangdu's command, overpowered the smaller lowland soldiers. Then Lobsang and a few of his warriors apprehended Commander Deng, Major Gan, his body guards, and several other officers.

The mood had changed. Even though Deng and his soldiers were under guard, the people were distressed and angry.

'How can we trust these *gyame*s?' someone shouted.

'Will the *gyame*s really let us walk the Golden Way?' another asked.

'They can't keep their word for a single day, how can we ever trust them?' someone shouted from another direction.

Someone close to the stage shouted at me, 'Why have you promised us the Golden Way when we all know the *gyame* will never allow it?'

I really wanted to address that question but Kunchen Khenpo was already on his feet, standing face-to-face with Commander Deng.

'Commander Deng!' the *khenpo* shouted so that everyone could hear him. 'You agreed to the terms of the horse race! Did

447

you, or did you not agree that the winner would choose the road forward for our people?'

Commander Deng, with his arms securely held behind his back by a strong Khampa warrior, did not offer a reply.

'Yes, you agreed!' the *khenpo* shouted again. 'You agreed because you believed you could fix the race to make sure your man would win. Shall I tell the people how you cheated?'

'How did the *gyame* cheat?' someone shouted.

'In the middle of the race, in the part that cannot be seen from here, the commander's chosen winner traded his horse for a motorcycle, and later switched to a fresh horse.'

'Cheating *gyame*!' another voice responded from the crowd.

'Even so,' the *khenpo* continued, 'Chodak-la won the race. To join the race, he had to disguise himself as a Naxi trader because he would have been arrested if recognized. The commander had to keep Chodak-la out of the race because he knew he represented the desires of the people!'

'We will only follow the Golden Way!' another voice shouted. This was followed by another round of shouts from every Tibetan present.

'Golden Way!

'Golden Way!

'Golden Way!'

'Commander Deng,' the *khenpo* said again in a loud voice after the people were quiet, 'is it not clear to you? The people want the way of cooperation, equality, justice, dignity, and goodness. Can you guarantee that the Communist Party will give this to us? The Party is supposed to represent the will of the people. Do you not hear their will?'

'We want to live according to Buddha dharma. We will not be *gyames*!' a young monk shouted out this time.

'If the Chinese Communist Party listens to the people, please explain why you ordered your soldiers to arrest the good people on this platform, and why you ordered your soldiers to detain everyone?'

Commander Deng still refused to speak. Not knowing Tibetan very well, he didn't pay attention to what Kunchen was saying. But the *khenpo* was speaking more to the crowd than to Deng.

Defying Commander Deng's hateful glare, Palden Rinpoche summarized Kunchen's speech for him in Chinese.

Still, Commander Deng refused to speak.

'Will you please answer?' Rinpoche asked Deng, 'the people want an explanation and an apology.'

'Comrade Chuang,' Deng finally turned to me and exploded bitterly, 'you are a traitor! You have led these people into rebellion. You're a counter-revolutionary!'

'No,' I replied calmly, 'I have listened to the people. I have taught them the highest ideals of the communist way. They sincerely want to integrate communist principles with their way of life. It would be in the best interests of the Chinese Communist Party to recognize Tibet as an ancient and honourable civilization. Accepting the choice these people have made will extend goodwill toward them as brothers and sisters of the greater worldwide communist revolution.'

The people were still angry and restless. Something needed to be done to reassure them.

'Chodak-la!' Dechen tugged at my sleeve and whispered in my ear, 'let me sing!'

449

She raised her arms for attention and began to sing beautifully. She slipped easily back into her *babdrungma* trance.

'**Now is the time for resolution. Aggression, depression, fear, and doubt must end! All that is good is yours already. You have the power to live as fully awakened human beings.**'

Everyone, Khampa and Han Chinese alike, stopped where they were to hear Dechen sing. Her enchanting, authoritative voice began to dispel critical thoughts and negative emotions. A more positive mood took root again. Though the Chinese could not understand her words, they responded to her voice and the positive energy around them.

'**Authentic presence is always yours! Even in times of darkness. This is the teaching of Buddha dharma, the blessing of basic goodness. Claiming this is the way of truth and beauty.**'

Dechen had everyone's attention. Now, instead of singing, she spoke earnestly to the people just as I had done in Lithang when I called for the Golden Way.

'We all know what we risked today. I think you might agree that I risked more than anyone else by offering to marry the winner of the race. But the outcome of the race, though left up chance, was sure from the beginning! No, not because we rigged it in Chodak-la's favour but because our collective will ordained it. It is our collective desire to walk the Golden Way!

'This is the power of collective will. The outcome of the race confirms it. It is our desire to cast off the sticky net of illusion thrown over us by two opposing forces. We have been dealing with one of these forces for hundreds of years; it is the Black Road of our own Tibetan society in its determination to resist change through suppression, and keeping things as they are.' Dechen paused for a few moments. Assured no one was offended by her subtle cultural criticism, she continued, 'The other force is equally oppressive. It is the Red Road forced on us from outside our borders, outside our society. Though it was potentially a good system, it has become corrupted by the demons of fear and greed that seek to ensnare us in perversions of truth. These two forces, from within and without, are in conflict. There is no happy outcome in a conflict between these two because the bloody stain of violence and hatred will always remain no matter who wins.'

'The Golden Way introduces a third force; it liberates us from both sources of oppression. It invites us to awaken and see the illusion around us for what it is. If we walk the Golden Way, we will live in freedom and equality; freedom from fear, freedom from oppression, freedom from hunger and unrewarding labour, freedom to love and be loved, freedom to thrive and be happy, and freedom to learn and become the best person one can possibly be.'

Looking all around the hall, she said, 'Dear friends, the Golden Way is the higher way of our Buddha nature. By following the Golden Way, we will be connected individually and communally with a higher, spiritual reality. Within each of us is a ceaseless fire of love. Let us live in this love so the wisdom of innate goodness can guide us. Let's live with dignity and put love for one another at the centre of our life together.'

She continued with passion, 'My dear friends, we have been destroying our world by our separation from one another. The world is harmed by choosing to stubbornly cling to our imagined isolation from each other. It is healed when we

451

choose unity. Hard inner work is necessary; we must learn to still our minds, shatter the fixations of our egos, and open our hearts. It is within our power to awaken to the truth and beauty of unity in our common Buddha nature. It is also in our power to recreate the world by taking the bodhisattva vow of assuring the happiness of others before our own.'

Dechen paused. Her audience was moved to reflection.

'This way is golden because it is the way of goodness for all of us, Han Chinese and Khampa alike,' Dechen concluded. 'My deepest wish is that we will all follow the Golden Way!'

Enthralled by Dechen's words and the people's reaction, I didn't notice Tenzin pushing his way to the front of the crowd. I turned to see him raise a pistol.

It was pointed at me.

He fired!

Transcendence

Dechen was thrown backwards onto me! Her elaborate headdress spun through the air. Blood covered me as we fell, her body cradled in my arms.

All I could think was 'Not again, Jiachen! Oh, not you too! Dechen, my beloved Dechen!'

I held her, clutching her more tightly than I'd held Jiachen so many years earlier. Tears welled in my eyes, sobs escaped my throat; while I held onto the hope that she would recover, I knew the bullet wound in her chest was fatal. I could not let her go. What would I do without her? She had become my reason for living. My longing for her had just been fulfilled. We were to be together for the rest of our lives.

Why did she step in the way? Why hadn't I been shot instead? Why Dechen and not me? Filled with the wildest extremes of emotion, I rocked this way and that with Dechen cradled in my arms. Jewel of my heart, my inspiration, and guide! My Dechen, my *Dakini*, my Golden Way!

Dechen's eyes were locked on mine. Her hand, trembling with emotion, was gentle on my face. She understood my fears and tried to reassure me.

'Do not mourn for me,' she whispered when she pulled my face closer to her lips. 'I'm with you. Remember, as your *Dakini*, I'm never far from you. Don't give up on our mission!'

Her hand relaxed. She couldn't talk anymore. I looked in her eyes again. There was such love, such a deep, eternal connection between us. Her love lingered like a fragrance while the light in her eyes faded.

And just like Jiachen had done, Dechen lifted me with her up above the ground, above the heads of the crowd where we could see-feel into everyone's heart.

We experienced the people's great confusion. Looking further away—across the land and the future—we watched darkness approach. An evil force was sweeping in to establish a stronghold. Even so, there remained a glimmer of hope that a force of goodness could remain unextinguished, until kindled into a blazing light again. The ember would be kept alive.

Dechen gently returned my awareness back to my physical body, and I was still clutching her lifeless body on the platform. And just as Jiachen had done, Dechen spoke inside me in a perfectly distinct voice. 'Tell the people to hold the blazing sword of wisdom high and treasure the gift of compassion close to their hearts. They must not give up!'

My private grief more under control, I looked around at several faces watching me in disbelief that Dechen had been killed. I knew I needed to be strong for them; I needed to let them know what Dechen had just told me. But still craving Dechen's body close to me, I could not get up. I looked at her beautiful face but there was no life in it any more, no spark of love and joy.

One wailing voice suddenly rent the silence of the perplexed crowd. It was Tenzin. He had collapsed in grief not unlike my own.

'Why?' Tenzin wailed, 'why did she step in the way! I shot at Chuang!'

It was clear to all what had happened; with one short step, Dechen had put my life before her own. Ever my *Dakini*, ever my protectress! She had enacted the bodhisattva vow for all to see. Giving her life to save mine. No greater act of love!

Tenzin turned the gun to his own head but Wangdu was there in time to grab it before he pulled the trigger. Several warriors helped Wangdu subdue and hold the crazed assassin. To everyone's surprise, a Chinese soldier hit Tenzin hard in the gut, and would have continued if he'd not been stopped by a warrior.

As waves of raw emotion swept through the crowd, I lifted Dechen's lifeless body in my arms, determined not to let the beauty of our vision, of the Golden Way, be destroyed by Dechen's murder.

She hung in my arms like a sleeping child. I looked at all my dear friends, my Khampa sisters and brothers all around me, the people of Kham who had accepted me, who had transformed me, who called me Chodak! Nearly sobbing, I raised my voice and barely managed to keep it steady, loud, and clear. I spoke to them from my heart, a heart that now included Dechen's. Knowing that our hearts were one and stronger this way than either of us alone, I could speak truth to the people.

'Even though *Khandro* Dechen's physical body is ruined, she is still with us. She is not far from us; not far from me nor from you. In her new, radiant form she is even stronger. She energizes us with hope!'

I switched to Chinese for the benefit of my Han brothers. Then after each statement, I gave a Tibetan translation so my Kham brothers and sisters would hear what I said in Chinese.

'To my Han brothers I say: let the Red Road be blessed by the brilliant light of Buddha dharma. Let Han and Tibetan walk the Golden Way of goodness together!'

The people were attentive; my words, magnified by the strength Dechen poured into my heart, spoke directly to their hearts.

'Over the past few months, the people of Lithang have accomplished great things. Farmers, nomads, merchants and monks have come together and agreed to treat each other as equals, and assure each other's welfare. We have exceeded the requirements of the Communist Party's planned reforms; wealthy landowners have given their property to the community, and everyone works together to share the bounty of our harvests and herds.' Still feeling Dechen's strength, I continued, 'We have promised each other that no one will be left out, none will go hungry, and none will lack a warm place to sleep or adequate clothing. We will care for the sick and the impaired. No one will be alienated. And most of all, we will follow and teach Buddha dharma. We will live as awakened beings in an enlightened society.'

With Dechen speaking through me, I knew, without a doubt, that love is stronger than death because we now shared one soul and spirit.

'This is the way forward!' I said deliberately, turning to address my words to Commander Deng, who seemed horrified by the body in my arms. 'This is the revolution the people of Lithang are asking for. We wish to travel the Golden Way and we invite everyone in Lithang district, all over Kham, all over Tibet, all over China and the rest of the world to do likewise.

'How can we accept the Red Road when it is offered by power hungry men in distant cities? We want the Golden

Way, a truly revolutionary change willingly created by the local people. The people want to share life's goodness in common, and to honour the best of our local traditions, our history, our civilization, and our language as we practice Buddha dharma. We want to follow the Golden Way!'

The people heartily agreed and chanted together.

'Golden Way!

'Golden Way!

'Golden Way!'

'The last thing Dechen said to me as she died was to tell you that there is still hope. We must hold the blazing sword of wisdom high and treasure the gift of compassion close to our hearts. It is up to us to make the Golden Way a reality. We must not give up!'

I turned and looked out toward the distant mountains, aware that Dechen's broken body continued to bleed in my arms. Though all of us were numb, I knew my words had been heard.

The mid-morning sun was shining. A gentle, warm breeze blew in from the South. Dechen's body—still warm in my arms—suddenly felt heavy, though I felt the touch of her spirit-body around me like a hug and a lingering kiss. It filled me with joy. The fragrance of her presence spread over the people, and I was convinced many caught it.

Dawa's weeping for her daughter brought me back to the present. She was clutching Dechen's hand, stroking her face. Her body was taken from me gently by Thampa and Dawa. They laid her on the carpet-covered platform. Yangchen, Thampa, Samphel, Zema, and Rinpoche came to bid their beloved Dechen goodbye, and to comfort me. Samphel and Zema each embraced me before turning to embrace Thampa and Dawa. Yangchen clutched me and wept bitterly.

'She said we have not completed our task,' I told Yangchen with tears in my eyes. 'We must continue to inspire the people.'

Yangchen nodded in agreement, though a sob racked her body and tears flowed even more.

With deep empathy for us, the people were quiet and attentive until, out of the silence, an angry voice reminded us that we still faced powerful divisive forces.

Darkness found its way back into our presence.

'This race,' Deng suddenly shouted out in Chinese as if seizing the moment when everyone would be distracted by grief. Incoherently, he attempted to refute the *khenpo*'s accusation of cheating, 'this performance has been a plot conceived by the charlatan, Palden, and the traitor, Chuang!'

Deng drew energy from the crowd's shocked attention. He continued his tirade.

'All this talk about Golden Way is a fantasy. It is religious insanity! Face the facts! We live in the real world! The Red Road alone can take us where we want to go.

'No Golden Way!' Deng shouted in Tibetan, 'only Red Road!'

People countered Deng with loud shouts of:

'Golden Way!

'Golden Way!

'Golden Way!'

Wangdu realized it would be better not to let Deng address the crowd, and gave an order to remove him from the platform.

'No Golden Way!' Deng shouted again in Tibetan as he was being removed. 'Since you have rejected the Red Road, you have forced us to tread the Black Road! Do you understand?'

I nodded at Rinpoche to suggest he speak to the people.

Rinpoche raised his arms for attention.

'You know in your hearts what is true,' Rinpoche declared, 'there is a more beautiful world! Listen to your hearts. The Golden Way is the way of love! It is up to us to create it.'

Our victory was short-lived. Commander Deng was good to his word. Reinforcements, thousands of them, began arriving in Lithang over the next few days. Out of fear, most people dispersed to their villages and camps. Others took refuge in the monastery, where Lobsang's warriors and many of the monks prepared to engage the Red Army.

Commander Deng was under pressure to ensure that Party dictates were implemented in Lithang district. Even if he had ever understood the significance of the Golden Way, he was in no position to let us implement it. How would he explain the genius of the Golden Way? Would the Party ever grasp the simplicity of people loving one another and sharing the good things of life in common? The CCP was based on power and control. Their ethos was the antithesis of 'love your neighbour as yourself', which we held as the bedrock of our trust in the Golden Way.

Deng managed to regain control of Lithang by awakening fear in peoples' minds; he terrorized the people into immediate, unhappy compliance with the ways of the Red Road and turned it, as he promised, into the Black Road if anyone dared to resist it.

In the aftermath of Dechen's death, we took time to tend to the matter of a funeral. Thampa and Dawa took Dechen's body to Gyawa, and those closest to Dechen followed. We built a funeral pyre on a ridge outside the village, the very place I'd heard my *Dakini* singing to me about Shambhala on that day when I left in anger and got lost in the wilderness; the very place where smoke from her altar fire of juniper branches rose into the air to briefly take the shape of a horse.

Dechen's body, sitting in meditation posture, burned as we—her immediate community—watched and mourned. Surprising myself, I watched dispassionately. What I assumed would be a heart-wrenching event turned into a moment of joy when Palden Rinpoche and Yangchen gave me *lungta* to toss into the rising column of smoke and heat. Rinpoche held a handful of red ones, Yangchen had a handful of white, and I clenched some golden ones. As we tossed them together into the column of smoke above the flames, the red, white, and gold mingled in the uprising heat to twinkle like stars in the deep blue depth of the void above. And there, once the last trace of her physical body was consumed, the unmistakable radiant body of my beloved arose out of the flames like a phoenix, and swirled upward with the *lungta*.

'Look!' Yangchen exclaimed, 'it's both of my darlings together in one rainbow body again.'

I felt both Rinpoche and Yangchen put an arm around me as tears streamed from our eyes; not tears of sorrow, but of joy. Only the three of us could see the rainbow body as she rose higher and higher into the sky. The rest of the family seemed not to notice.

Completely absorbed in this vision of my beloved, I was not surprised when suddenly, like an eagle's piercing cry, she began to sing with exuberant brilliance from high above. It was the same song she sang to me at this very place many months ago.

'When you realize where you come from, and who you are, you become tolerant, kind-hearted, and joyful. That place that is no place is your true home, that place where love comes from is the pure land of goodness called Shambhala.'

When the last note of the song blew away with the wind, her rainbow body dissolved into a white cloud that descended to enshroud us in mist. Her presence, I realized, would be everywhere—as far as the world extends.

And again, she spoke in my inner ear, 'We have not failed. The field looks empty but it has been ploughed and seeded. At the right time, the entire field will be filled with goodness.'

Character List

The story is told from the point of view of **Chuang Wei Ming**, later given the name **Chodak**, meaning 'the dharma spreader'.

MAIN CHARACTERS

Jiachen: The beautiful love interest of Chuang in his university student days in Shanghai.

Dechen: The beautiful singer of the King Gesar legend and daughter of Andrutsang Thampa and Dawa; Jiachen's twin sister. Meaning: good health and great happiness.

Thupten: Instrumental in Chuang's plan to set up the first cooperative.

Tsering Tenzin: Initially Chuang's assistant in his first cooperative, later his opponent and rival. Meaning of Tenzin: protector of dharma.

Palden Rinpoche: Dechen's highly respected spiritual teacher, organizer of King Gesar drama performances.

Andrutsang Thampa: Governor of Lithang when Chuang arrives. Later agrees to give his land holdings to Chuang's first cooperative.

Dawa: Andrutsang Thampa's wife, Dechen's mother, Yangchen's daughter.

Commander Deng: People's Liberation Army officer responsible for implementing Communist Party directives in Kham, newly annexed as part of Sichuan Province.

Gyatotsang Wangdu: Samphel's nephew and leader of Palden Rinpoche's non-violent warriors.

OTHER CHARACTERS

Yangchen: Jiachen's and Dechen's grandmother, Tibetan. Meaning: sacred one.

Master Tashi: Chuang's kung-fu, riding and archery teacher. Meaning of Tashi: prosperous one.

Master Fan: Jiachen's father.

Nuying: Jiachen's mother.

Huizhong: Jiachen's family maid servant.

Comrade Li: Chuang's superior, based in Chengdu, Sichuan.

Phuntso Wangyal: A Tibetan revolutionary who inspired Chuang to work for a truly Tibetan communist revolution.

Tsering Nawang: Tenzin's father, district manager of Lithang, civil authority appointed by the Chinese Communist Party to replace Thampa. Meaning: the possessive one.

Pema: Thupten's wife and labour organizer in the cooperative. Meaning: a lotus.

Gyatotsang Samphel: Headman of Mola Township, Chuang's second cooperative.

Zema: Samphel's wife and farm labour organizer.

Lobsang: Chieftain and warlord of several nomadic tribes in the wilderness of Changtreng. Meaning: kind-hearted one.

Major Gan: People's Liberation Army officer assigned to help Tenzin manage the first cooperative.

Kunchen Khenpo: Abbot of Lithang monastery.

Loyang: A popular folksinger.

Nima: A monk at Lithang monastery, who becomes Chuang's friend. Meaning: sun

Sonam: Nomadic chieftain of a tribe forced by Commander Deng to settle in the first cooperative. Meaning: fortunate one.

Sonam (little boy): Thupten and Pema's 7-year-old son.

463

Karma: Nomadic woman who befriends Chuang. Meaning: a star, fate or destiny.

Jigme: Karma's husband who captures Chuang and beats him.

Gyaltsen: Chieftain of Karma and Jigme's tribe.

Dorje: One of Lobsang's warriors who, on challenging Chuang at a tavern, is humiliated but later becomes Chuang's friend. Meaning: thunderbolt.

Rinchen: A woman shaman who gathers medicinal herbs and treats Chuang when he is injured. Meaning: holder of intelligence.

Tashi: Samphel and Zema's young daughter. (Not to be confused with Master Tashi).

Rabten: Lithang tavern keeper, Thupten and Chuang's friend.

Jampa: (Deceased) Yangchen's and Palden's older brother; father of Akong and Samphel.

Note:

The suffix **la** following any of the names above is an affectionate honorific.

The suffix **pa** following words such as babdrung, babdrungpa indicates a male bard or singer; following words such as Kham, Khampa is 'man from Kham'.

The suffix **ma** following words such babdrung, babdrungma indicates a female bard or singer.

Tibetan Words

Babdrung: Shamanic bard of the Tibetan oral tradition. Babdrungma: female; babdrungpa: male.

Bodhisattva: Someone who has aroused the compassionate wish to attain enlightenment for the benefit of all beings, and also wishes to bring them to that state. (From Sanskrit)

Buddha dharma: The teachings of the Buddha, also refers to the spiritual path or spirituality in general. (From Sanskrit)

Chang: Beer made from barley, rice, or millet, served hot or cold.

Chuba: The wrap-around robe with long sleeves, worn by Tibetan men and women. Nomads make chuba out of sheepskin and wear the fleece next to their skin for maximum warmth. Often made with woollen cloth or cotton, chuba for women can be stylishly made with fine embroidered silk.

Dakini: A female embodiment of enlightened energy, one who traverses the 'sky' of the expanse of wisdom, also spiritual wife of an enlightened master.

Drangyen: Six-string musical instrument, more like a lute than a guitar.

Gyame: Outsider, enemy of Buddha dharma, often a derogatory term referring to the Chinese.

Khandro, Khandrolma: Honorary name or title of an enlightened woman who is recognized, too, as a Dakini.

Khata: A ceremonial scarf, usually of white silk, but can be golden, too.

Lhamo: Opera, either secular or religious themes.

Lungta: Windhorse, the 'energy of basic goodness' and carrier of enlightenment; lung - wind, ta - horse. Also refers to small squares of paper imprinted with an image of a horse carrying three jewels representing the Buddha, the Dharma, and the Sanga on its back. These papers are tossed into an updraft on a mountain pass to be carried high into the sky to rise until they disappear above. (Windhorse warriors are enlightened warriors or bodhisattvas.)

Mani: From the mani mantra, Om Mani Padme Hum, mani means lotus; stones are often inscribed with this mantra, and piles of these stone are found all over the Tibetan plateau.

Thanka: A painting on cotton or silk of a Buddhist deity or mandala.

Thukpa: Soup, with meat and vegetables, often with homemade noodles.

Tsampa: Barley flour, the staple food of Tibetan people.

Tulku: An incarnation, usually refers to a reincarnated Buddhist master.

The Legend of King Gesar

The legend of Gesar of Ling is as important to the people of Central Asia as the legend of King Arthur or the Iliad of Homer is to people of the West. And like the story of Arthur, the legend may or may not be based on a historical king, and may be greatly embellished. Supernatural powers, spiritual insights, and divine origins are all part of the story. Variations of the story are found in different parts of Tibet, Mongolia, Tuva, Buryatia, and other parts of Central Asia where the Tibetan form of Buddhism has influence.

Until the 20th Century, the legend was kept alive through a rich oral tradition by bards, or 'babdrungma' and 'babdrungpa', who were said to receive their insight into the story through personal experience. These women and men—Gesar singers—initially may have endured serious illnesses but when restored to health, with the help of a shaman, often reported having entered the Kingdom of Ling to witness Gesar's reign. Because of these 'eye witness' accounts, the story is said to have legitimately grown over the centuries.

Though a few bards still carry the story forward, the legend of King Gesar has been transcribed from the oral tradition. The reader can find several brilliantly retold accounts in the books listed below.

The Superhuman Life of Gesar of Ling, Alexandra David-Neel & Lama Yongden, Shambhala, 1981

The Warrior Song of King Gesar, Douglas J. Penick, Wisdom Publications, 1996

Gessar Khan, A Legend of Tibet, Ida Zeitlin, Pilgrims Publishing, Varanasi, 2004 (first published in 1927 from the Mongolian version)

The Epic of Gesar of Ling, translated by Robin Kornman, PhD, Sangye Khandro, Lama Chonam, Shambhala, 2015

There is perhaps no greater authority on Gesar than the writings of Chogyam Trungpa, who claims descent from Gesar's lineage. His brilliant book **Shambhala, The Sacred Path of the Warrior**, Shambhala, 1984, is a training manual for the Shambhala warrior, or, if you will, a 'Windhorse warrior.' About Gesar, Trungpa has written:

> Other legends say that the kingdom of Shambhala disappeared from the earth many centuries ago. At a certain point, the entire society had become enlightened, and the kingdom vanished into another more celestial realm. According to these stories, the Rigden kings of Shambhala continue to watch over human affairs, and will one day return to earth to save humanity from destruction. Many Tibetans believe that the great Tibetan warrior king Gesar of Ling was inspired and guided by the Rigdens and the Shambhala wisdom. This reflects the belief in the celestial existence of the kingdom. Gesar is thought not to have travelled to Shambhala, so his link to the kingdom was a spiritual one. He lived in approximately the eleventh century and ruled the provincial kingdom of Ling, which is located in the province of Kham, Eastern Tibet. Following Gesar's reign, stories about his accomplishments as a warrior and ruler sprang up throughout Tibet, eventually becoming the greatest epic of Tibetan literature. Some legends say that Gesar will reappear from Shambhala, leading an army to conquer the forces of darkness in the world.